Personal Construct Psychology

Personal Construct Psychology

New Ideas

Peter Caputi, Heather Foster and Linda L. Viney
University of Wollongong, Australia

John Wiley & Sons, Ltd

Other Wiley Editorial Offices

John Wiley & Sons Inc., 111 River Street, Hoboken, NJ 07030, USA

Jossey-Bass, 989 Market Street, San Francisco, CA 94103-1741, USA

Wiley-VCH Verlag GmbH, Boschstr. 12, D-69469 Weinheim, Germany

John Wiley & Sons Australia Ltd, 42 McDougall Street, Milton, Queensland 4064, Australia

John Wiley & Sons (Asia) Pte Ltd, 2 Clementi Loop #02-01, Jin Xing Distripark, Singapore 129809

John Wiley & Sons Canada Ltd, 22 Worcester Road, Etobicoke, Ontario, Canada M9W 1L1

Wiley also publishes its books in a variety of electronic formats. Some content that appears in print may
not be available in electronic books.

Library of Congress Cataloging-in-Publication Data

Personal construct psychology: new ideas/Peter Caputi, Heather Foster and Linda L. Viney.
    p. cm.
    Includes bibliographical references and index.
    ISBN-13: 978-0-470-01943-6 (pbk.: alk. paper)
    ISBN-10: 0-470-01943-3 (pbk.: alk. paper)
    1. Personal construct theory.   I. Foster, Heather.   II. Viney, Linda L.   III. Title.
    BF698.9.P47C37 2006
    150.19′8–dc22

                                                                                2006019151

British Library Cataloguing in Publication Data

A catalogue record for this book is available from the British Library

ISBN-13 978-0-470-01943-6
ISBN-10 0-470-01943-3

Typeset in 11/13pt Times by SNP Best-set Typesetter Ltd, Hong Kong.
Printed and bound in Great Britain by TJ International Ltd, Padstow, Cornwall.
This book is printed on acid-free paper responsibly manufactured from sustainable forestry
in which at least two trees are planted for each one used for paper production.

Contents

SECTION II   ASSESSMENT AND UNDERSTANDING

SECTION III   PROBLEMS OF LIVING

SECTION IV   EVIDENCE-BASED INTERVENTIONS

SECTION V   OTHER INTERVENTIONS, CLINICAL AND EDUCATIONAL

About the Editors

Peter Caputi is a senior lecturer in the School of Psychology at the University of Wollongong. He has published over 30 journal articles in the areas of Personal Construct Psychology, information systems and measurement issues in psychology, as well as co-authoring a textbook in research methods. He has reviewed for the *International Journal of Personal Construct Psychology*, now the *Journal of Constructivist Psychology* and *Personal Construct Theory and Practice*. He has also edited conference abstracts for the *Australian Journal of Psychology*.

Linda L. Viney is Professor in Clinical Psychology at the University of Wollongong. She was instrumental in introducing Personal Construct Psychology in Australia and published extensively in the area as well as generally in clinical, counselling and health psychology. She has been Consulting Editor and Editor of the *Australian Psychologist*, and official journal of the APS. Linda has also been Foundation Member of the Editorial Board of the *International Journal of Personal Construct Psychology*, now the *Journal of Constructivist Psychology (1988–)*, and Guest Editor of the issue based on the Fourth Australasian Conference on Personal Construct Psychology, which she co-ordinated, in Volume 3 (1990). Special Editor 1999, *Community Mental Health Journal*, for the American Association of Community Psychiatrists.

Heather Foster PhD, Dip Ed (Tech.), is a registered psychologist who has applied personal construct psychology in clinical, academic and research areas of psychology. Her research interest is in changes in mid-life, particularly menopause. She draws on a wide background in psychology and vocational education and training and worked for many years in the NSW vocational and education training system. Her work included counselling, teaching, curriculum, policy and management roles, and involved writing, editing and managing the production of educational publications.

List of Contributors

Richard C. Bell   University of Melbourne, Australia

Mike Bender   Private practice, UK

Nina Bruni   RMIT University, Melbourne, Australia

Vivien Burr   University of Huddersfield, UK

Trevor Butt   University of Huddersfield, UK

Carole Carter   University of Wollongong, Australia

Sabrina Cipolletta   Universities of Padua and Bozen, Italy

Julie Ellis   La Trobe University, Australia

Paula Eustace   Deakin University, Australia

Heather Foster   University of Wollongong, Australia

Nicholas Gilbert   Barnet, Enfield and Haringey Mental Health NHS Trust, UK

Bob Green   Community Forensic Mental Health Service, Australia

Alessandra Iantaffi   Private Practice, UK

Lisbeth G. Lane   University of Wollongong, Australia

Larry M. Leitner   Miami University, USA

Pamela Leung   Hong Kong Institute of Education, Hong Kong

David M. Mills   The Performance School, Seattle, USA

Derek C. Oliver   United States Army, USA

Janina Radó   Tübingen University, Germany

Prasuna Reddy   University of Melbourne, Australia

Sally Robbins   Coventry Teaching Primary Care Trust, UK

Nicole G. Rossotti   Private practice, South Australia

Mark W. Schlutsmeyer   Sutter-Yuba Mental Health Services, California, USA

Harold Seelig   Institut für Sport und Sportwissenschaft, Universität Freiburg, Germany

Deborah Truneckova   University of Wollongong, Australia

Finn Tschudi   University of Oslo, Norway

Linda L. Viney   University of Wollongong, Australia

Bill Warren   University of Newcastle, Australia

Mary H. Watts   City University, UK

David A. Winter   University of Hertfordshire & Barnet, Enfield and Haringey Mental Health NHS Trust, UK

Preface

In 1955, George Kelly published his seminal work, *The Psychology of Personal Constructs*. This two-volume work was theoretically challenging and provocative! It provided a statement about how people make sense of their worlds, as well as an approach to clinical practice, based on an original theoretical framework. In presenting his theory, Kelly abandoned traditional concepts in the psychological literature, concepts such as motivation (Monte, 1987). Instead, Kelly proposed that individuals engaged in "scientific" activities similar to his own endeavours. Kelly saw people as "personal scientists" seeking to understand their lives by devising and testing hypotheses about their worlds and the people that share them (Monte, 1987).

The central concept in Kelly's theory is *construction* or *construing*. People construe or make sense of their worlds, the events in them, and of themselves. This process of construing (and re-construing) results in a system of constructs that provides a unique framework for understanding and anticipating events in one's world. The underlying philosophical assumption in personal construct theory is that "all of our present interpretations of the universe are subject to revision or replacement" (Kelly, 1955, p. 15). This postion is referred to as a philosophy of *constructive alternativism* (Winter, 1992, p. 4). This position posits that an individual is not "limited to" a particular interpretation of their world. People can re-interpret their worldview and make way for alternative, more meaningful interpretations of their universe (Winter, 1992). However, the philosophy of constructive alternativism is not a solipsistic position. Kelly does not deny the existence of an objective reality. Rather, he argues that we cannot experience the real world directly. We construe that world; we give meaning to it and anticipate future events (Winter, 1992, pp. 4–5).

People construe their worlds in various ways. People's experiences of the world are diverse. Although having its origins in clinical psychology, Kelly intended his theory to have a wide range of applicability. The literature associated with Personal Construct Theory (PCT) demonstrates that Kelly's ideas have been applied to areas as architecture and death studies (Neimeyer, 1985). The central focus of the theory, however, is still with psychothera-peutic applications, although the theory is underused in clinical practice, and few clinical programs in universities cover the theory in detail (Winter, 1992).

The chapters in this book represent current applications of PCT to a diverse range of topics. In addition, they represent the internationalization of Personal Construct Psychology research, with contributions from authors from the United Kingdom, the United States, Europe and Australasia. There are five main sections to this book. The contributors to *Section I: Theory and History* provide a snapshot of some of the current theoretical and methodo-logical issues in PCT. Linda Viney discusses PCT-based models and the role that such models may play in assisting psychotherapists' work with people. Trevor Butt's Chapter demonstrates how Kelly's theoretical roots are grounded in pragmatism. The relationship between "the artistic outlook" and the psychology of personal constructs is explored in Bill Warren's Chapter. In Chapter 4, Paula Eustace shows how Kelly's work is consistent with a post structural interpretation of social processes, and she suggests the pos-sibility of including discursive practices within a constructivist position. Prasuna Reddy and Richard Bell and Harald Seelig and Radó address methodological and analytic issues in Chapters 5 and 6. *Section I* concludes with a very personal account of the history of PCT in Australia, and ways in which isolated research communities can cope with the tyranny of distance.

Section II: Assessment and Understanding begins with Larry Leitner's chapter on therapeutic artistry, the role of therapeutic creativity and the ther-apist as artist. Derek Oliver and Mark Schlutsmeyer present a PCT perspec-tive on mutliculturalism in psychotherapy in Chapter 9. Sally Robbins and Mike Bender provide an interesting account of understanding dementia using PCT. In Chapter 11 David Winter and his colleagues present the findings of a study supporting the link between psychotherapists' theoretical orientations and their core construing. In the final chapter in this section Julie Ellis pre-sents a personal construct perspective of nurses' professional identity.

The third section of the book, titled *Problems of Living*, begins with a chapter by Nicole Rossotti and her colleagues dealing with role of trust and dependency in people's lives. Bob Green provides a PCT account of factors contributing to cannabis use. In Chapter 15, Carole Carter and Linda Viney explore the application of PCT to our understanding of the effect of clients disclosing after sexual assault. In Chapter 16 Lis Lane and Linda Viney present their work on using personal construct theory, in particular role relationships, to make sense of women's experiences of breast cancer. Alessandra Iantaffi's Chapter on researching the personal experiences of disabled people, especially women in higher education concludes *Section III*.

Good evidenced-based research is important in any domain of psychological inquiry. In *Section IV: Evidence-based Interventions*, personal construct theory forms the basis for three varied areas of empirical research. These studies test and provide evidence for the effectiveness of personal construct approaches taken. In Chapter 18, Heather Foster and Linda Viney present a study dealing with women's changing constructions at the time of menopause. Lis Lane and Linda Viney write of a study investigating the benefits of group psychotherapy with survivors of breast cancer. The third chapter in this section is by Deborah Truneckova and Linda Viney and reports on group work with troubled adolescents.

The five chapters that make up *Section V: Other interventions, clinical and educational* demonstrate the wide applicability of personal construct theory. In Chapter 21, Pam Leung reports on pre-service teachers' perception of successful language teachers. Sabrina Cipoletta, in Chapter 22, explores movement in personal change, a personal construct approach to dance therapy. Following this, in Chapter 23, David Mills investigates the relationship between George Kelly's personal construct theory and Alexander technique. Finally, in Chapter 24, Viv Burr applies a personal construct perspective to a discussion of the art of writing in relation to embodiment and pre-verbal construing.

REFERENCES

Monte, C. F. (1987). *Beneath the mask: An introduction to theories of personality*. New York: Holt, Rinehart and Winston.

Neimeyer, R. A. (1985). The development of personal construct psychology. Lincoln: University of Nebraska Press.

Winter, D. A. (1992). *Personal contruct psychology in clinical practice: Theory, research and applications*. London: Routledge.

Acknowledgements

We thank the contributors to this volume for their excellent and interestingly varied chapters, which provide evidence of the flexibility and international scope of personal construct theory. We are grateful to the following members of the Wollongong Personal Construct Group who contributed to reviewing individual chapters: Nadia Crittenden, Jocelyn Harper, Lis Lane, Gillian Malins, Deborah Truneckova and Beverly Walker. We are grateful also to Marie Johnson for her skill in formatting the chapters for the book. Finally, we thank Colin Whurr and our publishers, John Wiley & Sons, for their support for this contribution to personal construct literature.

SECTION I
Theory and History

1

Applying Personal Construct Models to Work with People[1]

LINDA L. VINEY

There is considerable pressure on practitioners who work with people to provide manuals or blueprints for approaching their tasks. However, personal construct practitioners believe that people are creative agents with free will, rather than robots or machines (Fransella, 2003; Kelly, 1955/1991; Raskin & Bridges, 2002; Rychlak, 2000), so that they resist providing such manuals. However, they do provide models that enable generalisation from one client to another or from one community to another. Models consist of a set of conceptual propositions. These propositions have consequences to be deduced (Hesse, 1967). Models and theories have similar structures (Hesse, 1967). Models are based on an underlying theory and inform both the planning of practice and interpretation of its outcomes. The scope of a model, then, is narrower than a theory. Each theory can have many models, but each model has only one theory. Theories need to be true, but models may not be. Models apply the ideas of a better known domain to a lesser known one (Harre, 1961). Models can also aid in understanding, generate new hypotheses, provide more information about the rules of inference about the phenomena, enable the expression and extension of psychological knowledge, help to evaluate the theories from which they spring and aid in the learning of skills by practitioners (Braithwaite, 1962; Harre & Secord, 1972). The propositions of models can also therefore be extended to aid us practitioners into strategies that we can follow.

---

[1] Based on an Invited Plenary Address for the 14th International Personal Construct Psychology Congress, Wollongong, NSW, July, 2001.

Personal Construct Psychology: New Ideas. Edited by Peter Caputi, Heather Foster and Linda L. Viney. Copyright © 2006 John Wiley & Sons, Ltd.

This chapter is about the use of models in personal construct practice. Some standards by which they can be judged are provided, as well as the functions that models can achieve. Two examples of models are then described: one for a client and the other for a community. The paper owes much to Dr Lindsay Oades, with whom I first explored the implications of models, but for personal construct research (Viney & Oades, 1998). Both he and the Wollongong Personal Construct Research Group have been very helpful in honing this chapter.

SOME STANDARDS FOR PERSONAL CONSTRUCT MODELS

Models must be *firmly based in the theory* from which they emerge (Howard, 1998). A model that is only loosely related to its parent theory may be confusing and misleading to the practitioners who attempt to use it. In the case of personal construct models, their propositions must be firmly based in the theory on at least four different levels. Most fundamentally, they need to be consistent with the assumptions about epistemology, approaches to the truth and other metapsychological assumptions of personal construct theory that have been identified (Chiari & Nuzzo, 1995; Neimeyer & Raskin, 2000). The propositions of the model also need be consistent with the most crucial philosophical assumption of personal construct psychology, constructive alternativism, or that there are as many views of the world as there are people to have those views (Kelly, 1955/1991). Then the model propositions need to be consistent with the concepts of Kelly's theory, as well as with the concepts of the more recent extensions of the theory, if practitioners choose to use them.

Models also need to be *clearly and concisely described*. A model that is presented in a manner that is hard to understand is not going to attract practitioners. A two-fold standard is being suggested here. The first of these standards implies that a good model is one that is easy to comprehend and so to use effectively to generate practice (Paxton, 1976). The meaning of the messages in the propositions of a model should be unambiguous, and so open to only one interpretation. The second of these standards suggests that a good model is also one that is expressed using as few concepts as possible, but also as few words as possible, as briefly as it can be. Conciseness in a model, then, implies both simplicity of ideas and of the words used to express them.

Models must be *internally consistent* (Radford & Burton, 1974). A model that is based on concepts and assumptions that are in conflict is not going to help practitioners; in fact, it is going to confuse them. One way to ensure that a personal construct model is internally consistent is to show that none of its propositions are in conflict with the concepts of personal construct theory. The model needs then to fit simultaneously with its assumptions at a metapsychological level, with the assumption of constructive alternativism and with the concepts of the theory. If these checks are carried out, and any failing proposition rejected, then the propositions of the model are likely to fit well with each other, as they should.

Models also need to be *parsimonious* or frugal. A model that is presented in a manner that is not as simple as it can be, taking into account the complexity of the phenomena considered, is going to irritate practitioners. The goal of the model builder should be to account for the maximum information with the minimum of propositions (Paxton, 1976). Where models with different numbers of propositions attempt to account for the same phenomena, those with fewer propositions are to be preferred. This principle of parsimony was formulated by William of Occam in the twelfth century, and is used today across a wide range of domains of thought, including the physical and social sciences.

Models need to *deal adequately with the psychological events* on which they focus. An otherwise elegant and appealing model is of no use to personal construct practitioners if it does not deal adequately with the phenomena which are at the centre of their practice. So while it is the case that models need to be consistent with the assumptions, theories, concepts and methodologies on which they are based, they also need to deal adequately with events. The propositions of a model should deal adequately with whatever physical, psychological, historical and contextual events the practitioners have in mind.

Models must also meet yet a final pair of criteria of being both *comprehensive and specific* (Marx, 1976). These criteria are somewhat in conflict because one aims for wide scope while the other aims for precision. Models, then, need to be sufficiently broadly-based to be able to include all relevant events, yet precise enough to make prediction possible. A model that consists of propositions that are limited and vague is not going to help them, as practitioners, and it is going to frustrate them. Models need then to be made up of propositions that provide both a sufficiently broad understanding of events, but also propositions that are sufficiently specific to make predictions that lead to assessments and interventions that are useful.

SOME FUNCTIONS OF MODELS

Models *prevent practitioners from being overwhelmed by the complexity* of personal construct theory and of the events with which they deal. In its simplest form, it is a theory with 1 basic postulate and a set of no less than 11 corollaries. However, all those who have worked with the postulate and corollaries have found each one to be of considerable subtlety and complexity. So even deciding which part of the theory to apply to the psychological phenomena of interest can be difficult. Using a model, with a finite set of propositions, in personal construct practice, therefore, helps to focus on the parts of the theory that are relevant. Each one of those propositions uses only some parts of the theory, and so releases practitioners from responsibility for the other parts of the theory. Also, the physical, psychological, historical and contextual (familial, organisational and cultural) events with which practitioners deal also provide a very high degree of complexity, which can make it difficult for us to focus on some events rather than others. Using a model, with a limited set of propositions about a limited set of events, helps to focus on the events that are relevant and ignore those that are not.

Models make *accountable* and available to a greater extent, the theory that excites personal construct practitioners. This theory, as I have noted earlier, is an extremely complex and extensive one. Use of models based on it helps to make available and accessible parts of the theory that can become lost in or, at the least, overshadowed by other parts of it. The accountability of models, then, is one of their important functions.

Models also can provide *new ideas* for practitioners. This important heuristic function they share with theories (Hesse, 1967). This quality of both theories and models has been described as "fertility" (Lakatos, 1970). The production of new ideas results mostly from the juxtaposition of concepts and events in each of the propositions of the model. When the concepts and events come together, practitioners often find themselves generating new ideas about the events in which they are so interested, but about which their ideas may have been somewhat limited.

Models give practitioners, too, *better definitions* of, firstly, the concepts, and, secondly, the research variables, so that they can conduct much better assessments and interventions. The generation of clear definitions of the concepts in the propositions of the models ensures that such concepts are readily available and so can be carefully evaluated. These definitions also provide a degree of specificity which is helpful to better practice. Both of these characteristics of clarity and specificity lead to better definition and understanding of the variables that represent, in practice, the concepts at the theoretical level. Articulating the propositions of the models can also make it easier to check that there is an isometric relationship between concepts and variables.

Models give practitioners better tools for *checking that their collections of information are appropriate to the theory* they are using. As practitioners spell out the propositions of their models, they can check on the assumptions that they make about people which could determine how they should understand and work. For example, personal construct theory assumes that the person is an active chooser and creator of meanings in a social context (Chiari & Nuzzo, 1995; Fransella & Dalton, 1991). It therefore may follow that the assessments and interventions should allow both parties to be treated as active creators of meaning in a social context (Viney, 1987). Another example of how the propositions of models constrain the practitioners who use them follows. If the model propositions assume that the meanings created by people on the basis of their individual and often different life experiences may be unique (Kelly, 1955/1991) then much information about their clients, and their assessment and intervention, should make sure it includes any unique aspects.

Models enable practitioners to *make predictions* about their practice. Kelly (1955/1991) saw a good construct system as a "useful" system, and to him "useful" meant being able to employ the meanings involved to anticipate and control one's own behaviour and those of other people. When he applied these ideas to practice, Kelly may well have maintained that good practice involves the testing of predictions about the events of interest. The ability of practitioners to use the propositions of a conceptual model to generate hypotheses that can be tested is extremely important to them. That the propositions of the model have been clearly articulated also make it easier for practitioners to devise hypotheses that are both directly relevant to the events to be assessed and worked with and more immediately testable, than when no model is available.

SOME PERSONAL CONSTRUCT MODELS

Seven models from the Wollongong PCP group have been published. The earliest of these was Viney's (1990) on psychological reactions to illness and injury, and crisis intervention counselling (Viney, 1995) and the model of Marilyn Rudd's of the reactions of caregivers of demented spouses (Rudd, Viney & Preston, 1999). The most recently published of our models are those of Lis Lane for group work with women with breast cancer (Lane & Viney, 2002; 2005) and that of Heather Foster on workshops for reactions to menopause (Foster & Viney, 2002; 2005). There is also the model of group work with adolescent offenders and non-offenders (Viney & Henry, 2002). Deborah Truneckova has developed another model for distressed school-based adolescents (Truneckova & Viney, 2005). Four of my other graduated doctoral students also have developed such models which they have tested:

Carole Carter, Jeannie Higgens, Lindsay Oades and Patricia Weekes. These were models that made work with survivors of sexual assault, police, AIDS prevention in adolescents and parents of developmentally disabled children possible.

Two examples of personal construct models will now be shared briefly. They are both new. The first deals with individual clients, and both the propositions and the strategies following on from them are provided. The second model deals with the community.

THE CLIENT MODEL

The first of the propositions of the model of working with a client to be introduced is of constructs as the *meanings that everyone creates from their experiences*. These meanings involve interpretations, but also predictions.

Table 1.1   Personal construct model propositions and related strategies for clients (following Kelly, 1955/1991; and Viney, 2000)

Propositions	Strategies
1. Constructs are unique meanings developed through experience	1. Focus on clients' meanings, on which *they* are the experts
2. Meanings are bipolar, providing choices between alternatives	2. Recognise that clients' choices of meanings provide their choice of action
3. Meanings are linked into systems, with some more influential than others	3. "Ladder" to identify clients' most influential meanings about self, and protect them
4. All people have meanings that are preverbal	4. Be open to clients' preverbal meanings
5. People experiment with their meanings	5. If they feel safe, clients experiment with their problematic meanings in therapy
6. There are many different ways to make sense of events	6. Clients can re-interpret events in therapy
7. Negative emotions signal need to change meanings, e.g. anxiety and anger	7. Negative emotions need to be expressed, identified and accepted in therapy
8. Positive emotions signal confirmation of reinterpretations of meanings	8. Positive emotions should be more common later in therapy
9. Confirmation of people's meanings is often provided by other people	9. Confirmation by therapists of clients' meanings is important early in therapy; later clients need confirmation provided by others

They are *unique*, because each person has had somewhat different experiences over the different course of their interactions with others, and the world, from their earliest years. These attributes of meanings require that, when personal construct therapists interact with their client, they need to listen very carefully for the meanings of that client. This form of listening, called "credulous listening" involves containing, to some extent, the meanings of the therapists and acknowledging the role of the client as an expert on his or her own meanings is a helpful strategy.

These meanings are also *bi-polar*, so that every one of people's interpretations of themselves and events involve choice between alternatives. The client then has choices about the interpretations he or she makes of himself or herself and his or her worlds, and so choices about his or her actions. Many clients, who have difficulty trusting their therapists, do not have such a belief. Aiding clients to become aware of these choices can be helpful to them. Some clients, however, are still not in touch with some poles of the meanings they once used to use; for example, some people who are severely depressed cannot retain access to any poles of their meanings other than those that are totally pessimistic and sad.

People's meanings are linked into *systems of meanings, of which some are more influential and useful than others*. It is important, then, for therapists to protect the most influential and useful meanings of their client, especially those about himself or herself and the world. The procedure of "laddering" can be used to identify the most influential meanings about self that are both useful and also disruptive for the client (Fransella & Dalton, 1991). This is an extremely helpful strategy.

In this personal construct model of working with the client, another proposition is that many of people's meanings are unconscious. These types of *meanings are described as preverbal*, to indicate that they either may have been developed by a client at a time before he or she was using words, or cannot be expressed in words because of the strong and distressing emotions linked with them. Therapists, then, need to attend carefully to signs of unverbalised meanings in their client. This acknowledgement of preverbal construing in clients does not detract from seeing clients as experts. However, it does mean that therapists have access to some meanings and feelings to which clients do not have. Then therapists work with clients to make clear some meanings and help them to test their own and these additional meanings. In this process, the client reconstrues.

The next three sets of propositions and related strategies have to do with people as testers of meanings and the emotions that follow from this testing process. People function like scientists, testing their hypotheses about the world; but it is their interpretations and predictions that they test. In therapy, then, it is a natural and ongoing process of *meaning-testing that occurs for a client* in therapy. A client needs to feel safe enough to experiment with their problematic meanings in therapy. This is one way in which the therapeutic relationship is central to therapy.

People have many different ways to make sense of themselves and events. Reality may exist, but people have only indirect access to it by *exploring a range of alternatives*. This concept is a liberating one for the client, because it means that in therapy he or she can re-interpret the events of his or her life.

When people *test their meanings, and they are not confirmed, it is then that they experience distressing feelings*. Using this approach, when a client feels *anxious*, it is when he or she recognises that the events he or she experiences are beyond the range of his or her interpretations and predictions. When he or she feels *guilt*, it is because his or her actions do not fit with his or her expectations for his or her interactions with others. When he or she feels *angry*, it is because he or she is refusing to give up the interpretations and predictions she or he has been making. Expression of these emotions is an important strategy of this model of therapy, but what is added is understanding of those emotions in personal construct terms.

When people *reinterpret their meanings, test them and they are confirmed, they experience positive and enjoyable feelings*, like happiness, contentment and pride. Positive feelings should therefore be more commonly expressed by the client in this model of therapy in later sessions.

The last proposition and strategy to be dealt with here involve the role of confirmation of meanings. When people test their meanings, confirmation of some of those meanings, especially the most powerful of these meanings, is important to them. Such *confirmation is often provided by other people*. To have people around who provide a range of different sources of confirmation can be helpful, because people are then no longer dependent on one source which may fail them. Early in therapy, therapists provide much confirmation for the influential and useful meanings of their client about himself or herself. This is another of the ways in which the therapeutic relationship is central to a model of therapy with a single client. However, later in therapy the client is encouraged to become aware of other sources of confirmation of his or her influential meanings, and to develop a range of such sources.

The *model of the client is evaluated* now, using the standards provided. Its propositions seem firmly based in personal construct theory, and they are clearly and concisely described. They should be internally consistent, in the sense of being based on the assumptions and concepts of the theory. The model appears to be parsimonious, in that it has the minimum number of propositions. It deals with events that are relevant to practitioners, and it is probably both comprehensive in breadth and specific enough in focus. In terms of the functions fulfilled, this model aids in preventing practitioners from being overwhelmed by the complexities that clients can pose, and provides them with new ideas and strategies for working with clients. It has helpful definitions of aspects of clients, so as to lead to better assessments and interventions, and aids in making predictions about their practice with clients that they can then test.

THE COMMUNITY MODEL

The first proposition of the model of working with a community agrees with Kelly (1955/1991) that, with people acting like scientists, behaviour can be seen as the independent rather than the dependent variable. People are

Table 1.2   Personal construct model propositions and related strategies for communities (following Balnaves & Caputi, 1993; Kelly, 1955/1991 & Walker, 1996)

Propositions	Strategies
1. People are continually trying to make sense of their worlds by developing meanings	1. Focus on communities' meanings, on which *they* are the experts
2. Meanings can be shared by people	2. Some shared meanings are community-wide meanings
3. Shared meanings, like individual meanings are responsive to change	3. Community-wide meanings are also responsive to change
4. People representative of a community share constructs with that community	4. Community-wide meanings can be accessed by exploring the meanings of its representatives
5. Shared meanings may be changed across the entire or part of the community	5. When community representatives undertake public changes in their meanings, role modelling allows other community members to change those meanings
6. Acceptance of change in, until then shared meanings, will depend on the relationship between the community member and the group changing	6. Acceptance of the change in meanings in a public group will be affected by the extent to which the community member identifies with that group

continually attempting to *make sense of their worlds by developing hypotheses and testing them.* The strategy that grows from this proposition is the focus on the meanings that make up the hypotheses of the community, on which the community members are expert.

The second is that *people share meanings.* Some constructs from those individual systems can then be shared by groups of people. The strategy flowing from this is recognition that shared meanings can be community-wide meanings.

The third proposition is based on the work of Balnaves and Caputi (1993) who have proposed the concept of corporate constructs, which are processes that depend on language and a public sense. Forms of writing and number systems are corporate constructs, since they have a public and shared meaning. These *shared meanings like individual meanings' are responsive to change.* A community can undertake therapeutic change in shared or corporate constructs in a manner similar to individuals.

If individuals, in a representative group of a target community, share their construing and then define any constructs that are common across the group members, these shared constructs are likely to be shared across the whole target community (Walker, 1996). The fourth proposition follows. *Individuals representative of the community share constructs with that community.* Knowing that meanings shared by communities can be accessed by exploring the meanings of representatives from these communities is the useful strategy here.

The fifth proposition deals with the role modelling of the change processes. *Shared meanings can be changed across the entire or part of that community.* Kelly (1955/1991) viewed culture as a shared system of meanings, providing an array of pre-existing discriminations that a particular language symbolises. The expectancies of the group thus serve as the validators against which people test the predictive efficiency of their construct systems (Walker, 1996). When individuals make predictions about the world, they can have these predictions validated through the experience of others, within the same community. It follows that when representatives from a community undertake a public reconstruction process, this role modelling enables other community members to undertake a similar change process.

The last proposition deals with social identity and persuasion. Van Knippenberg (1999) found considerable support for social categorisation of the source of a message playing a major role in the likelihood of this message to be accepted. *Acceptance of change in, until then shared meanings, will depend on the relationship between the community member and the group changing.* It follows strategically that acceptance of the public group messages will be mediated by the extent to which the community members identify with the said group.

The *model of communities evaluated now.* Its propositions, too, are firmly based in personal construct theory and clearly and concisely described. These propositions also are internally consistent and parsimonious, and have the minimum number of propositions. The model deals with events that are relevant and both comprehensive and specific. In terms of the functions fulfilled, this model also aids in preventing practitioners from being overwhelmed by the even greater complexities that communities pose, and provides then with new ideas and strategies for working with them. It has definitions of a range of aspects of communities that are useful, so as to lead to better assessments and interventions in this difficult area. This second model also aids in making predictions about their practice with communities that practitioners can then test.

ARE MODELS APPROPRIATE AND USEFUL TO PERSONAL CONSTRUCT PRACTITIONERS?

Models are appropriate and useful to the personal construct practitioners for these reasons. Firstly, the application of models made up of propositions is appropriate because it is a logical extension of Kelly's well-known metaphor of the person as scientist, a theory- or model- employing scientist. Secondly, it is useful, and especially more useful than manuals, because it is generalisable, from one client and community to the next. Finally, while formulating models is intellectually very demanding, once the propositions, and possibly some strategies are in place, it frees practitioners to work effectively and productively with clients and communities.

REFERENCES

Bergmann, G. (1957). *Philosophy of science*. Madison: University of Wisconsin Press.

Braithwaite, R. B. (1962). Models in the empirical sciences. In E. Nagel, P. Suppes & A. Tarski (Eds), *Logic, methodology and philosophy of science*. Stanford: Stanford University Press.

Balnaves, M. & Caputi, P. (1993). Corporate constructs: Are constructs personal? *International Journal of Personal Construct Psychology*, 6, 119–138.

Chiari, G. & Nuzzo, M. L. (1995). Personal construct theory within psychological constructivism: Precurser or avant-garde? In B. M. Walker, J. Costigan, L. L. Viney & B. Warren (Eds), *Personal construct theory: A psychology of the future*. Melbourne: The Australian Psychological Society.

Foster, H. & Viney, L. L. (2002). Meanings of menopause: Development of a personal construct model. In J. Fisher & N. Cornelius (Eds), *Challenging the boundaries: Perspectives for the new millennium.* Milan: EPCA.

Foster, H. & Viney, L. L. (2005). Personal construct workshops for women experiencing menopause: In D. Winter & L. L. Viney (Eds), *Personal construct psychotherapy: Advances in theory, practice and research.* London: Whurr.

Fransella, F. (2003). *International Handbook of Personal Construct Psychology.* Chichester: John Wiley & Sons, Ltd.

Fransella, F. & Dalton, P. (1991). *Personal construct counselling in action.* London: Sage.

Harre, R. (1961). *Theories and things.* London: Blackwell.

Harre, R. & Secord, P. F. (1972). *The explanation of social behaviour.* London: Blackwell.

Hesse, M. (1967). Models and analogy in science. In P. Edwards (Ed.), *The Encyclopaedia of philosophy.* Vol. 5 pp. 349–359. New York: Macmillan.

Kelly, G. A. (1955/1991). *The psychology of personal constructs.* New York: Norton.

Lane, L. & Viney, L. L. (2002). The meanings of a diagnosis of breast cancer: A personal construct model. In J. Fisher & N. Cornelius (Eds), *Challenging the boundaries: perspectives for the new millennium.* Milan: EPCA.

Lane, L. & Viney, L. L. (2005). Personal construct group work with women with breast cancer: Role relationships and support. In D. Winter & L. L. Viney (Eds), *Personal construct psychotherapy: Advances in theory, practice and research.* London: Whurr.

Lane, L. G. & Viney, L. L. (2005). The effects of personal construct group therapy on breast cancer survivors. *Journal of Consulting and Clinical Psychology, 73(2),* 284–292.

Lakatos, I. (1970). Falsifications and the methodology of scientific research programs. In I. Lakatos & A. Musgrave (Eds), *Criticism and the growth of knowledge.* Cambridge, England: Cambridge University Press.

Marx, M. H. (1976). Formal theory. In M. H. Marx & F. E. Goodson (Eds), *Theories in contemporary psychology.* New York: Macmillan.

Neimeyer, R. A. & Raskin, J. (2000). *Constructions of disorder.* Washington, DC: American Psychological Association.

Paxton, R. P. (1976). Some criteria for choosing between explanations in psychology. *Bulletin of the British Psychological Society, 29,* 396–399.

Raskin, J. & Bridges, S. K. (2002). *Studies in Meaning: Exploring constructivist psychology,* New York: Pace.

Rudd, M., Viney, L. L. & Preston, C. (1999). The grief experienced by spousal care givers of dementia patients: The role of place of care of patient and gender of care giver. *International Journal of Aging and Development, 48,* 217–240.

Rychlak, J. (2000). A psychotherapist's lessons from the philosophy of science. *American Psychologist, 55,* 1126–1132.

Truneckova, D. & Viney, L. L. (2005). Personal construct group work with troubled adolescents: Helpful and unhelpful processes. In D. Winter & L. L. Viney (Eds), *Personal construct psychotherapy: Advances in theory, practice and research.* London: Whurr.

Van Kippenberg, D. (1999). Social identity and persuasion. In D. Abrams & M. A. Hogg (Eds), *Social Identity and Social Cognition.* Blackwell: Oxford.

Viney, L. L. (1991). Towards a personal construct model of psychological reactions to physical illness and injury. In G. J. Neimeyer & R. A. Neimeyer (Eds), *Advances in personal construct psychology,* Vol. 1. New York: JAI Press.

Viney, L. L. (1995). A personal construct model of crisis intervention counselling for adult clients. *Journal of Constructivist Psychology, 9,* 109–126.

Viney, L. L. & Henry, R. M. (2002). Evaluating personal construct and psychodynamic group work with adolescent offenders and non-offenders. In G. J. Neimeyer & R. A. Neimeyer (Eds), *Advances in personal construct psychology*, Vol. 4, New York: JAI Press.

Viney, L. L. & Oades, L. (1998). *The use of conceptual models in personal construct research.* Eighth Australasian Personal Construct Conference, Brisbane, Queensland, July.

Walker, B. M. (1996). A psychology for adventurers. In D. Kalekin-Fishman & B. M. Walker (Eds), *The construction of group realities*. Krieger: Malabar: FL.

2

Personal Construct Therapy and Its History in Pragmatism

TREVOR BUTT

Kelly insisted that he was puzzled that Personal Construct Theory (PCT) could be considered to be subsumed by other psychologies of his day (1969a, p. 216). However, he mentioned William James approvingly on the first page of his 1955 book, and acknowledged the pragmatism of Dewey, "whose philosophy and psychology can be read between many of the lines of the psychology of personal constructs" (1955, p. 154). In this chapter, I want to dwell on this pragmatic foundation of PCT. Warren (1998) has already done an excellent job of spelling out PCT's links with and roots in philosophy. So, here I see myself as elaborating some of his arguments. However I think this is both necessary and useful, because construct theorists can still believe that Kelly developed his theory *de novo*. This was not Kelly's position, of course. Citing Dewey as an example of a leader in his field, he says:

> The leader simply adds a large increment to an already massive structure in order to complete an invention, whether it be social or physical. The main structure is supplied by the average and mediocre people, each of whom brings his little contribution and throws it onto the pile. (Kelly, 1979, p. 16).

Everyone stands on the shoulders of others when it comes to theory making. In this chapter, we will examine the work of the pragmatists on whose shoulders Kelly stood: William James, John Dewey and George Herbert Mead.

Personal Construct Psychology: New Ideas. Edited by Peter Caputi, Heather Foster and Linda L. Viney. Copyright © 2006 John Wiley & Sons, Ltd.

PRAGMATISM

Pragmatism was a philosophical movement that developed in the late nineteenth and early twentieth century in the United States, only to be displaced by the rise in logical positivism in mid century (Thayer, 1982). Charles Peirce is generally recognised as the founder of the movement, although it was William James who successfully elaborated and advocated it to a wider audience (Mounce, 1997). James was professor of psychology at Harvard, and produced his *Principles of Psychology* in 1890. This wide-ranging work was widely read, including in Europe, where it resonated with the nascent existentialist movement and clearly influenced the growth of phenomenology. But in the USA, it was soon to be eclipsed by Watsonian behaviourism, and consigned to philosophical history. In 1904, Dewey, who had been at the University of Chicago, moved to New York, leaving his friend and colleague George Mead there. Although their focus of convenience was different (Dewey's in education, and Mead's in social psychology), we can certainly see the thought of one reflected in the other. Dewey is recorded as saying "I dislike to think what my own thinking might have been were it not for the seminal ideas I derived from him" (Thayer, 1982, p. 338). But the department of philosophy then split, with John Watson, their junior colleague, joining the group that founded a separate department of experimental psychology at Chicago. The pragmatism of Mead and Dewey was subsequently defined as at the contrast pole to the new psychology. So we can only fully appreciate the marginal position of pragmatism in mainstream psychology by understanding its history.

Kelly rejected the dominant psychology of his day – S-R behaviourism – and drew on the alternative pragmatist vision of psychology. In the Preface to *The Psychology of Personal Constructs*, he tells the reader how the theory owed nothing to the orthodox psychology of its day. It arose instead in clinical practice, and the book began life as a clinical manual, only later transformed into a theory of personality. Immediately we see his pragmatic approach; theory comes from action and must always have what James (1995, p. 77) termed a "cash value" in practice. Let us now consider how key features in the psychology of personal constructs reflected the work of James, Dewey and Mead.

THE PERSON AS A FORM OF MOTION

At the end of the nineteenth century, philosophers were divided into two camps: empiricists and the idealists. Empiricism held that our knowledge of the world came from our senses, while idealism emphasised the role of the mind in structuring the known world. So empiricism conceptualised a passive person that responds to stimuli, and we can see clearly that this view was later championed by the behaviourists. Idealism, on the other hand, gave the person's intellect rather too much agency. This view came down from Descartes' dualism which saw the mind as a sort of pilot in the mechanical body. The problem then, was not only how the person is connected to the world, but also how minds are related to bodies. It was these dualisms that the pragmatists (see Farr, 1996), as well as the existential phenomenologists (for example, Merleau-Ponty, 1962) wanted to overcome. For Dewey, such dualisms were particularly problematic:

> The question of integration of the mind/body in action is the most practical of all questions we can ask in our civilization. Until this integration is effected in the only place where it can be carried out, in action itself, we shall continue to live in a society in which a soulless and heartless materialism is compensated for by a soulful but futile idealism and spiritualism. (Dewey, 1931)

"Action" here refers to something that is different from mere behaviour; it is behaviour infused with intentionality and meaning. We are reminded of Kelly's emphasis on action – his extensive use of enactment and fixed role therapy. Like Dewey, he rejected the simple S-R behaviourism of his day. Behaviour was for him the independent variable (Kelly, 1977). It was not caused by anything, but "channelized" by anticipation. The person is "a form of motion" (Kelly, 1955, p. 48), always engaged on some project or other. This echoes Dewey's (1982) paper (originally published in 1896) on the folly of taking the reflex arc as a model of human action. He argued that terms like "stimulus" and "response" were abstractions from the flow of action in which the person was always engaged.

Kelly refused to divide the person up into faculties of behaviour, emotion and cognition. In his Fundamental Postulate, he talked instead of the "person's processes". Whereas orthodox psychology routinely thinks in these tripartite terms. Kelly followed the pragmatists in focusing on the whole person. Too often, there is an implicit Cartesian dualism at work here. Cognition is seen as the property of the mind, and behaviour that of the mechanical body. Emotion is seen as a rather strange link, with a foot in both camps. Different theorists still speculate as to whether it is cognitively inspired or originates in the brain. The way in which it is discussed in most introductory texts testifies to this confusion. James' theory of emotion is often misunderstood as a contribution to reducing the cognition to the bodily: we are scared because we run. But James was arguing here against dualism. For him, it was not that the cognition is caused by the behaviour. He was asserting that emotion consists of the whole action. Emotion is about something; it is intentional (Mounce, 1997). Without our embodiment, the very concept of feeling would be meaningless. It relates to the whole person's connection with the world. Kelly (1955) had a similar view. His conception of emotion is anti-reductionist, and speculates about the different types of transitions in construing that constitute different emotions.

CONSTRUCTIVE ALTERNATIVISM

James rejected the generally accepted view of the mind as a mirror of nature. The function of the mind was not to represent any outside reality. Instead, the mind had evolved because it had a job to do. And that job was to make something of circumstances. This conception was adopted by pragmatism. Menand puts this nicely:

> They [the pragmatists] all believed that ideas are not "out there", waiting to be discovered, but are tools – like forks and knives and microchips – that people devise to cope with the world in which they find themselves. They believed that ideas are not produced by individuals, but by groups of individuals – that ideas are social. They believed that ideas do not develop according to some inner logic of their own, but are entirely dependent, like germs, on their human carriers and the environment. And they believed that since ideas are provisional responses to particular and unreproducible circumstances, their survival depends not on their immutability, but on their adaptability (2002, p. xi–xii).

Here we see the separation of construction and event, a conception at the centre of personal construct theory. The notion of discovered truth is replaced by constructions that are to be judged not in terms of their truth, but their usefulness. This refusal to deal in the currency of truth based on a more or less accurate representation of the world, is derided by some as relativism. But Dewey underlined the dangers of "truth" being used to reinforce the adoption of some constructions at the expense of others:

> When a man is not satisfied, in ordinary intercourse, with saying that two and two make four, but finds it necessary to honour this formulation with the title of truth, we have, as a rule, good grounds for believing that the man is not speaking as a business man, or as a mathematician, but as a preacher, or at least an educator. And when we hear not that the assassination of Caesar by Brutus was an historic event, but that it is an historic truth, we may safely prepare for the enforcement of a moral, not for the noting of an incident (1993a, p. 11).

So Dewey distinguished between events in the world and the construction of these events. One might construe the death of Caesar as either a murder or an execution, and a claim of truth privileges one construction over another. Dewey was unhappy with philosophy's search for a truth and reality that was in some sense "feudally superior" to everyday occurrences (Dewey, 1993b, p. 2). He saw this as an essentialist Greek legacy reinforced by the Christianity of the Middle Ages.

We have here the seeds of Kelly's philosophical position – constructive alternativism. Everything depends on the adoption of different perspectives. As Rorty (1982), the current standard bearer of pragmatism constantly reminds us, there is very little that is not fundamentally changed through re-describing it. Looking at people as if they were each a scientist changes our understanding of the difficulties they get into. No longer can we maintain the idea that a person is a simple victim of circumstances, struck down by neurosis. If they are the victim of anything, it is their theory, or as James put it, their philosophy of life. In the opening of a series of lectures he gave in 1906, he quoted G. K. Chesterton approvingly:

> There are some people – and I am one of them – who think that the most practical and important thing about a man is his view of the universe. We think for a landlady considering a lodger, it is important to know his income, but it is still more important to know his philosophy. We think that for a general about to fight an enemy, it is important to know the enemy's numbers, but still more important to know the enemy's philosophy. We think the question is not whether the theory of the cosmos affects matters, but whether, in the long run, anything else affects them. (James, 1995, p. 1).

THE PERSON AS SCIENTIST

One gets the strong feeling in reading Dewey, as one does reading Kelly, that people should not just accept as truth the folk wisdoms that surround them. We should question assumptions, look closely at evidence, come to our own conclusions. We might be encouraged to believe that our culture's values are natural, or that they convey God's law. But no one has God's perspective; we are all of us grounded in the world, and its "truths" are equally available to us all through our alternative construing. When Kelly introduced the person as scientist metaphor (1955, p. 4), he likened it to the Protestant Reformation. Here, the acceptance of the wisdom of an hierarchical order of priests was replaced by the idea that each person should become their own priest. In the same way, he suggested, people should be thought of as their own scientists.

Dewey strongly advocated a liberal democratic position in both politics and philosophy. Abduction (as opposed to induction or deduction), or hypothesis-testing is our guarantee of achieving viable constructions, and experiment the ideal way of proceeding in this quest:

> Even with his best thought, a man's proposed course of action may be defeated. But in as far as his act is truly a manifestation of intelligent choice, he learns something: – as in a scientific experiment, an inquirer may learn through his experimentation, his intelligently directed action, quite as much, or even more, from a failure, than from a success. (Dewey, 1993c, pp. 133–134)

The pragmatists looked to the scientist as a moral hero. Science challenged dogma, and was responsible for the progress visible at the start of the twentieth century. Scientific investigation particularly via experimentation provided the paradigm for inquiry. Its disinterested stance and careful observation give us the best chance of overcoming our prejudices and loaded questions. Cromwell (2003) remembers how Kelly favoured clear questions and brittle hypotheses as essential tools in psychological inquiry. Again following Dewey (see above), his approach underlined how we stand to learn most from these. Mental processes have evolved in order to give us a better grip on the world of events through the development of a viable construct system.

We see this attitude in James' elaboration of Dewey's conception of truth. This is not to be evaluated by some imaginary fit with "reality". It only makes sense in terms of the impact it has on our lives; "True ideas are those that we can assimilate, validate, corroborate and verify. False ideas are those that we cannot" (1995, p. 77). In a statement which we can see echoed in Kelly's notion of the invitational mood (Kelly, 1969b), James says:

> Pragmatism . . . asks its usual question. "Grant an idea or belief to be true" it says, "what concrete difference will its being true make to anyone's actual life? How will the truth be realised? What experiences will be different from those that would obtain if the belief were false? What, in short, is the truth's cash value in experiential terms?

Hypotheses are to be entertained on an "as if" basis and tested for their validity.

SOCIALITY

The social world is the site for our most important experimentation, and both Dewey and Mead stressed the social nature of our construction. But it was

Mead who developed pragmatism as a social psychology. One of his main purposes was to show that mind could be rooted in the organism without recourse to reductionism or dualism. Darwin was one of the strongest influences on the pragmatists generally, but particularly on Mead (Farr, 1996; Joas, 1985). His argument was that humankind had evolved as it had because of its elaborated capacity for co-operation. In humans, a conversation of gestures has evolved to the point where shared symbols can be used to communicate messages of extraordinary complexity. Essential to this process of co-operation is the ability to take the position of the other and assess a situation through their eyes. This, of course, is what Kelly described as taking a role with respect to the other; the definition of sociality.

Mead argued that it was not that individuals came together and jointly forged society. Instead, individuals were the product of society. The individual is a social construction, but once constructed is a centre for choice and agency. This position is accepted by pragmatists from Dewey to Rorty (1982), but was first elaborated by Mead (1982a, 1982b). His philosophy of the social act focuses on how the acts of one member of a species are guided by its anticipated effects on others. In everyday social life, we inevitably find ourselves acting with others in mind. We might be trying to persuade, impress or cajole them. But in each case our action cannot be adequately described in S-R terms. In Kelly's terms, the other is not merely a behaving mannequin. Once again, as in all pragmatic accounts, sociality is grounded in action:

> We awaken to the hostility of our neighbour's attitude by the arising tendency to attack or assume an attitude of defense. We become aware of the direction of another's line of march by our tendencies to step to one side or the other. (Mead, p. 348)

Consciousness arises from our ability to reflect on our social action. In Mead's terminology (following Darwin), it is an "emergent property", and emerges, or has evolved, because of its pragmatic value:

> We are conscious of our attitudes because they are responsible for the changes in the conduct of other individuals. A man's reaction towards weather conditions has no influence upon the weather itself. It is important for the success of his conduct that he should be conscious not of his own attitudes, of his own habits of response, but of the signs of rain or fair weather. Successful social conduct brings one into a field within which a consciousness of one's own attitudes helps toward the control of the conduct of others. (1910/1982, p. 348)

We can see here how Mead argued that sociality evolved. Kelly of course, was not concerned with its evolution, but primarily with its implications, especially for the therapeutic relationship (Kelly, 1955). But Hinkle claimed that in informal discussions with Kelly, he found that the sociality corollary was in many ways central to the project of PCT. He said Kelly dreamed of a society in which the understanding and appreciation of human experience provided the foundation for human relationship and moral reasoning. He quotes Kelly as saying "Yes, I guess I do think of PCT as an implicit ethical system: just imagine a world in which we understood one another as people!" (Hinkle, 1970, p. 107).

THE IMPORTANCE OF HISTORY

We can see then, that PCT is firmly rooted in the philosophy and psychology of pragmatism. This gives it a solid base and also helps us understand its congruence with other products of pragmatism that now flourish in social psychology. Although Mead's work was ignored within orthodox psychology, it formed the foundations of the Chicago school of micro-sociology that came to be called symbolic interactionism (Blumer, 1969). This tradition has recently produced a rich seam of narrative work in which the person is conceptualised as an author or autobiographer rather than a personal scientist (Plummer, 2004). It is interesting that the transformation of PCT into constructivism, primarily in North America, has increasingly involved drawing on narrative methods of research (Raskin & Bridges, 2002). In fact, constructivism seems to me like an interesting and fruitful blend of pragmatism and existential phenomenology (Butt, 2004). It is a pity though, that this ancestry is not always fully acknowledged (Butt, 2006).

In the natural sciences, it may be the case that reading a text written a century ago is of historical interest only. But this is not the case in psychology. The writings of James, Dewey and Mead still have much to teach the psychologist of today. Their understanding of the relationship between mind and body and the way individuals are embedded in society is still useful.

REFERENCES

Blumer, H. (1969). *Symbolic interactionism*. Englewood Cliffs, NJ: Prentice Hall.
Butt, T. W. (2004). *Understanding people*. Basingstoke: Palgrave.
Butt, T. W. (2006). Re-construing constructivism [Review of the book, *Studies in meaning 2: Bridging the personal and social in constructivist psychology*]. *Journal of Constructivist Psychology*, *19(1)*, 91–96.

Cromwell, R. (2003). Kelly's influence on research and career. In F. Fransella (Ed.), *International Handbook of personal construct psychology*, (pp. 415–423). Chichester: John Wiley & Sons, Ltd.

Dewey, J. (1931). *Philosophy and civilization.* New York: Minton, Balch & Co.

Dewey, J. (1993a). The problem of truth. In D. Morris & I. Shapiro (Eds), *John Dewey: The political writings.* (pp. 10–19). Indianapolis/Cambridge: Hackett.

Dewey, J. (1993b). The need for a recovery of philosophy. In D. Morris & I. Shapiro (Eds), *John Dewey: The political writings* (pp. 1–9). Indianapolis/Cambridge: Hackett.

Dewey, J. (1993c). Philosophies of freedom. In D. Morris & I. Shapiro (Eds), *John Dewey: The political writings* (pp. 133–141). Indianapolis/Cambridge: Hackett.

Farr, R. (1996). *The roots of modern social psychology.* Oxford: Blackwell.

Hinkle, D. (1970). The game of personal constructs. In D. Bannister (Ed.), *Perspectives in personal construct theory.* London: Academic Press.

James, W. (1995). *Pragmatism.* New York: Dover Publications.

Joas, H. (1985). *G. H. Mead: A Contemporary re-examination of his thought.* Cambridge, MA: MIT Press.

Kelly, G. A. (1955). *The psychology of personal constructs.* New York: Norton.

Kelly, G. A. (1969). The psychotherapeutic relationship. In B. Maher (Ed.), *Clinical psychology and personality: The selected papers of George Kelly* (pp. 216–223). Chichester: John Wiley & Sons, Ltd.

Kelly, G. A. (1977). The psychology of the unknown. In D. Bannister (Ed.), *New perspectives in personal constructt theory* (pp. 1–19). London: Academic Press.

Kelly, G. A. (1979). Social inheritance. In P. Stringer & D. Bannister (Eds), *Constructs of sociality and individuality* (pp. 4–17). London: Academic Press.

Mead, G. (1982a). Social consciousness and the consciousness of meaning. In H. Thayer, (Ed.), *Pragmatism: The classic writings* (pp. 341–350). Indianapolis: Hackett.

Mead, G. (1982b). The social self. In H. Thayer (Ed.), *Pragmatism: The classic writings*, (pp. 351–358). Indianapolis: Hackett.

Menand. L. (2002). *The metaphysical club.* London: Harper Collins.

Merleau-Ponty, M. (1962). *Phenomenology of perception.* London: Routledge.

Mounce, O. H. (1997). *The two pragmatisms.* London: Routledge.

Plummer, K. (2004). *Documents of life 2: An invitation to a critical humanism.* London: Sage.

Raskin, J. D. & Bridges, S. K. (Eds), (2004). *Studies in meaning 2: Bridging the personal and social in constructivist psychology.* New York: Pace University Press.

Rorty, R. (1982). *Consequences of pragmatism.* New York & London: Harvester Wheatsheaf.

Thayer, H. (1982). *Pragmatism: The classic writings.* Indianapolis: Hackett.

Warren, W. (1998). *Philosophical dimensions of personal construct psychology.* London: Routledge.

3

Reflections on the "Artistic Mentality" and Personal Construct Psychology

BILL WARREN

This chapter offers a speculative, synthetic discussion focused on elaborating some ideas in the field of philosophy and psychology of art. It attempts to clarify the notion of an *artistic outlook* and to examine the fit between this and the psychology of personal constructs.

THE ARTISTIC OUTLOOK

Barbu (1956) clarified the idea of an outlook or mentality in his discussion of a *democratic mentality*. He discussed the core psychological features of democratic outlook as *objectivity, critical-mindedness*, a sense of *leisure* or ease and a sense of one's separateness and difference, one's *individuality*. It was from this basis of recognising a link between forms of social organisation and individual psychological functioning that empirical work that produced a comprehensive account of the *authoritarian personality* and the *closed mind* was to grow (Adorno et al., 1950; Rokeach, 1960). Schiller (1793/1982) took issue with Kant who saw the aesthetic activity of mind as a relatively unimportant, secondary activity which acted merely as a type of "conditioner" or "enlivener" of the mind (Kant, 1790/1951, paragraph 49), but which added nothing to our understanding of the world. Schiller (1793/1982), however, goes well beyond Kant to give aesthetic activity a

Personal Construct Psychology: New Ideas. Edited by Peter Caputi, Heather Foster and Linda L. Viney. Copyright © 2006 John Wiley & Sons, Ltd.

much greater significance, developing the idea of *play* as best capturing what is going on in the mind when it is engaged in aesthetic activity. His conception is of a *dynamic* that is not governed by an interest in achieving some practical outcome, not operating under any imperatives. That dynamic directs us to takes things "as they are", freed from considerations of how we believe they "should be" or how we might "use" them.

For Schiller (1793/1982), the psyche in its aesthetic state "acting freely", is the "middle disposition" between sense and reason (Letter XX, ftn, p. 143), an important and dynamic feature of mind, in its own right, and not merely a "quickener" or "enlivener". Play begins with involuntary associations and, through the operation of an awareness of freedom within ourselves, it is shaped and in turn shapes our outlook and interactions with the world. In short, merely instrumental perspectives are taken over by more playful ones. Things we possess or use:

> . . . no longer bear upon them the marks of their use, their form no longer limited by merely timid expression of their function; in addition to the service they exist to render, they must at the same time reflect the genial mind which conceived them, the loving hand which wrought them, the serene and liberal spirit which chose and displayed them. . . . Disinterested and undirected pleasure is now numbered among the necessities of existence, and what is in fact unnecessary soon becomes the best part of his delight. (Letter XXVII, p. 211)

In the history of psychology, play was discussed as an important element in human development by Baldwin (1895), while Huizinga (1938/1970) focused the cultural significance of play. More recently, Meares (2000) has argued the core role of play in the development of the individual's sense of self as "flow" or "process". In his analysis, the play in which the infant engages in "babbling" and "pretend" games gives way to conversational play and to an "inner conversation", and all of these forms of playing with the world are constitutive of a sense of self, a sense of "I" and of "me". Throughout this development, what is stressed is the essential sense of freedom that is involved. Thus, too, psychological problems might be seen in terms of the absence of this quality of freedom and vitality (Meares, 2000, p. 20).

To further pin down the idea of an artistic outlook, we can come at the present question by considering what is arguably the opposite pole of the artistic mentality construct: the *technological mentality*. Within the philosophy of technology there has been an interesting discussion concerning a "technological mentality" or "technological consciousness" (Barbu, 1956; Juenger, 1949; Marcuse, 1941, 1969), which can be coupled with the idea of the "authoritarian personality" (Adorno, et al., 1950; Fromm, 1942; Kater,

1983; Rokeach, 1960; less specifically, Spear, 1970; and, more critically, Durrheim, 1997), both being fascinated by the notion of *control*.

Juenger (1949), reflecting on the Third Reich, and somewhat exaggeratedly, suggested that technology "prepares the way for the invasion ideologies"; that is, that individuals locked-on to a too ready acceptance and uncritical attitude to technology were vulnerable to accepting "off the shelf" explanations for anything outside their area of technical specialisation. Barbu (1956) is more reserved, offering three traits of his *technological consciousness*. These encompass its "elementaristic", "black and white" style which does not rest with understanding the world but exhibits an "action-anxiety" that focuses on transforming that world. A second, related feature is a lack of an ability to merely enjoy the world, in the face of a desire to master, control and shape it. The third is an attraction to the "artificial", the manufactured "which goes hand in hand with a certain detachment from nature" (p. 256).

We might note at this point Kant's early identification of the connection between beauty and goodness, and his distinction between the natural and the artificial. As to the first, Kant argues that a person who takes an interest in nature will bear the mark of a "good soul" and "when this interest is habitual, it at least indicates a frame of mind favourable to the moral feeling" (Kant, 1780/1951, Paragraph 42, p. 141). As to the second, the substitution of artificial plants and birds in, for example, a natural scene or environment to which the aesthetic judgement is addressed, will result in immediate loss of interest in the person predisposed to an habitual regarding of nature in its own terms. The artificial, being man-made, invites judgements of mere taste, which are bound up with social conventions that have little bearing on goodness. Kant here prefigures Barbu's observations that a fascination with the artificial and the man-made, and an antagonism to nature and the natural, have been identified as a feature of the authoritarian outlook and of a technological consciousness.

There is in these last ideas an interesting parallel with the connection that Meijun (2001) outlines between ecological consciousness and traditional Chinese aesthetics. Nature was held in awe and veneration by ancient Chinese artists who saw nature as "the basic and lofty principle of aesthetics", the artistic value of an object "not determined by man but by nature that transcends man" (p. 267). Again, there was in Chinese aesthetics an aversion to "possessing" beautiful things: ". . . nature had brought forth all living things on Earth but it never intended to possess them, never considered itself as their dominator" (p. 268). The ancient Chinese ecological consciousness is linked to the appreciation of the beautiful and concerned with people's *spiritual* life, whereas Western ecological consciousness focuses on the *consequences* of failing to protect the environment (for example, pollution).

Marcuse (1978) takes up questions in art and aesthetics in a fashion that is also pertinent to the present discussion. He sees aesthetics, freedom and truth as inter-related in that in transcending the particular socio-historical limitations placed on it, art's autonomy reveals the nature of "reality" as merely that which particular interests decree as reality, getting thereby beyond that to a "truer reality"; art is "subversive" or emancipatory, seeking always to go beyond the merely "given", the merely socially "sanctioned", to how things are "in fact", not how others want them to be. He emphasises the manner in which art "alienates individuals from their functional existence and performance in society" (p. 9) which stresses the exploitation of the world, and offers a non-exploitative focus on deeper, universal – as distinct from merely particular – truths. Perhaps the elevation of the aesthetic in a final turning in phenomenology made by Gadamer (1960/1975) is illustrative here and Bubner's (1981) observation on this more accessible:

> The full reality of art shows itself as a *game*, in the course of which subject and work fuse together in such a way that they seem to surrender to it . . . Without doubt tragedy furnishes the classical example of this unity of the game, becoming perceptible in the duration of the production and taking hold on the living subject. Tragedy is, according to the conception of antiquity, the manifestation of a truth which concerns everyone and for that reason takes hold of and moves the spectator. By this model, then Gadamer measures all understanding (p. 56).

Finally, it is of value to suggest a circumstantial point in the location of art as part of *culture*, which is related to but distinguished from *civilisation* (Doniela, 1987). Civilisation refers now to an achieved state of organised social life, the increase in physical comfort, improved communications, increases in personal freedom and the like (Williams, 1981). Civilisation seems to turn around humankind's practical efforts to improve conditions of living; at its base are the practicalities of life and survival. Culture, while related and perhaps even parasitic on civilisation and dependent on the existence of a leisured class, refers now to intellectual, spiritual, aesthetic effort, and to particular ways of doing things in particular groups that are more to do with *style* than with necessity. In essence, civilisation refers more to practical life, to an instrumental approach to life, whereas culture is associated with "non-use" in the practical sense. Thus is aesthetic activity, albeit circumstantially, again differentiated in terms of its disinterestedness in the mundane, daily affairs of life; though not necessarily arrogant in regard to that level of human life – as a focus of many great works of art on the grim realities of life's struggle, on working conditions or on war, will attest.

In summary, then, an artistic outlook takes the world "as it is". In a variety of thinkers who have addressed the matter, art emerges as essentially non-instrumental and non-exploitative, seeking to understand the world or things of the world *in their own terms*. The concept is illuminated by reference to an opposite outlook, the technological outlook, which seeks always to *use* the world or things of the world for other purposes, and it has its origins in the play response that has been centred in reflection on healthy psychological development. The artistic outlook is linked to the social sphere in that in interpersonal relationships egalitarianism will prevail, and individuals of this outlook will adopt a positive attitude toward nature.

PERSONAL CONSTRUCT PSYCHOLOGY

We need not here elaborate the theory of personal constructs, but can usefully locate it as growing out of developments in North American psychology which, in turn, were grounded in the philosophy of Pragmatism. In Pragmatism there was always an interest in the creative or aesthetic life of the mind, and Dewey (1934/1958) is an excellent exemplar of this. In fact, Dewey's model of human thinking embraces what might normally be thought of as "creative", and as "rational". For him, the ultimate focus of both science and art was the wide canvas of humankind's attempts to make sense of experience in the world: "The odd notion that an artist does not think and a scientific inquirer does nothing else is the result of converting a difference of tempo and emphasis into a difference in kind" (p. 15).

While Kelly (1955/1991) notes how Fixed Role Therapy essentially involves a process of creativity, creativity figures more directly in the discussion of the Creativity Cycle. This is one of the shifts in construction which the individual habitually uses in daily life; unless this habit is blocked and has to be unblocked in therapy. This Cycle involves a sequence of loosened construction followed by progressive tightening to a position of validation. Creative thinking originates in "preposterous thinking", but this must be progressively tightened otherwise that thinking remains at a level of the person merely "mumbling" to him or herself; the process of that tightening is one of hypothesis formulation and testing. Again, and now echoing that *freedom* suggested earlier as a core element of the artistic outlook, Kelly notes how that loosened construction that sets the stage for creative thinking releases "facts, long taken as self-evident, from their rigid conceptual moorings" (p. 1031).

It would seem, then, that the metaphor of a person as a *scientist* alludes to a concept of science that is closer to what might be called a "living" notion of science rather than the "formal" one (Sorel, 1906/1950). The former characterises science in a way that is closer to a genuine interest in understanding the world, an understanding freed from a total immersion in the practicalities of life and an exploitative interest in the world. Such a reemphasis allows us to understand the notion of the person as *scientist* in terms that see it encompassing a general notion of enquiry that is not different in kind from an *artistic outlook*; both approach the world with the same motivation of *understanding*. The "formal" concept of science refers to science as it had become by Sorel's time, where nothing was considered any longer in terms of its own nature and relations, but appreciated only in terms of the consequences of all enquiry for *economic* life. Indeed, relevant to our earlier discussion, Sorel draws parallels between the activity of the scientist, the artist and the warrior. The parallel is that *qua* scientist, artist and warrior, respectively, there is the pursuit of an activity "for its own sake" or "disinterestedly".

Finally, and perhaps more telling for present interests, Kelly (1955) notes:

> What we have said about the creative process applies to the way hypotheses are formed in any kind of scientific reasoning. They are formed as *predictions*. That is to say, they are designed to embrace the future rather than to embalm the past. The formulation of useful hypotheses requires the use of creative talent (p. 381).

BY WAY OF CONCLUSION

This speculative discussion synthesising various writings to illuminate an artistic or aesthetic way of approaching the world has hopefully provided a perspective that lifts personal construct psychology from too rigid an embeddedness in too rigid a notion of science.

A good ending here is to note some comments of Schiller's (1793/1982) translators:

> . . . when we come to Schiller's vision of an Aesthetic State we find there no select company of aesthetes lost in idle contemplation of music and statuary, or regaling each other with their latest poems, but a community of people, scientists, scholars, artisans, citizens, going about their ordinary affairs – but with a different quality in their attitude both to the job in hand and to each other (p. xi).

In short, the notion of the person as a scientist enshrined in personal construct psychology must be taken in terms of the "living" rather than the merely formal aspects of science. This is captured in a notion of unfettered enquiry, and entirely compatible with the type of outlook that is the *artistic outlook*. It ties in also with the type of egalitarian approach to interpersonal relations and personal relationships that can be suggested as underpinning the psychology of personal constructs from the outset (Warren, 1996), thereby focusing on the social dimension, and also paralleling the connection between beauty and goodness identified in philosophers who turn their attention to these matters.

Scientific activity and artistic activity are not the preserve of certain individuals but features of the manner in which all individuals go about their lives. The notion of *science* in the guiding metaphor of personal construct psychology embraces processes called "creative". It does this in a fashion that sees human beings now using tight, now using loose construing, always focused on making a meaning from an involvement with the world; not constrained by the limits imposed by the world, but rising above them in generating novel, even "preposterous" hypotheses about that world. At its most general, the notion of science in the metaphor of the person as scientist embraces what is here elaborated as the artistic outlook. That is, a non-exploitative outlook focused on the elaboration of meaning for one's life, and for Life, and an outlook that may be more playful than serious in the optimal case.

REFERENCES

Adorno, T. W., Frenkel-Brunswick, E., Levison, D. J. & Sanford, R. (1954). *The authoritarian personality.* New York: Harper and Row.

Baldwin, J. M. (1895). *Mental development in the child and the race.* New York: Macmillan.

Barbu, Z. (1956). *Democracy and dictatorship: Their psychology and patterns of life.* London: Routledge.

Bubner, R. (1981). *Modern German philosophy.* Cambridge: Cambridge University Press.

Dewey, J. (1958). *Art and experience.* New York: Capricorn Books. Original work published 1934.

Doniela, W. V. (1987). The aesthetic mind: Some Notes on the Psychology of Art. *Dialectic* (Journal of the University of Newcastle Philosophy Club), *29*, 28–37. (Papers from the 1986 Conference of the Australian Association for Phenomenology and Social Philosophy).

Durrheim, K. (1997). Theoretical conundrum: The politics and science of theorizing authoritarian cognition. *Political Psychology, 18(3)*, 625–647.

Fromm, E. (1956). *The sane society.* London: Routledge.

Gadamer, H. G. (1975). *Truth and method.* London: Sheed and Ward. Original work published 1960.

Huizinga, J. (1970). *Homo Ludens: A study of the play element in culture.* London: Maurice Temple Smith. Original work published 1938.

Juenger, F. (1949). *The failure of technology.* Heinsdale, Illinois: Henry Regney Co.

Kant, I. (1781). *Critique of pure reason.* Translated by Norman Kemp Smith. London: Macmillan and Co. Ltd (1964).

Kant, I. (1790). *The critique of judgement.* Translated with an Introduction by J. H. Bernard. London: Collier Macmillan Publishers (1951).

Kater, M. H. (1983). *The Nazi party: A social profile of members and leaders, 1919–1945.* London: Basil Blackwell.

Kelly, G. A. (1955). *The psychology of personal constructs.* New York: W.W. Norton and Co.

Marcuse, H. (1941). Some implications of modern technology. *Studies in Philosophy and Social Science, 9,* 414–439.

Marcuse, H. (1969). *Eros and civilization.* London: Sphere Books. Original work published 1964.

Marcuse, H. (1978). *The aesthetic dimension.* Boston: The Beacon Press.

Meares, R. (2000). *Intimacy and alienation.* London: Routledge.

Meijun, F. (2001). Ecological consciousness in traditional Chinese aesthetics. *Educational Philosophy and Theory, 33(2),* 267–270.

Rokeach, M. (1960). *The open and closed mind.* New York: Basic Books.

Schiller, F. (1982). *On the aesthetic education of man.* Oxford: The Clarendon Press. Edited and Translated and with an Introduction Commentary and Glossary of Terms by E. M. Wilkinson and L. A. Willoughby. Original work published 1793.

Sorel, G. (1950). *Reflections on violence.* Translated by T. E. Hulme and J. Roth with an Introduction by E. A. Shils. London: Collier-Macmillan Ltd. Original work published 1906.

Spear, A. (1970). *Inside the Third Reich: Memoirs.* London: Weidenfeld and Nicholson. Translated by R. And C. Winston, with an Introduction by E. Davidson.

Warren, B. (1996). The Egalitarian outlook as the underpinning of the theory of personal constructs. In D. Kalekin-Fishman and B. M. Walker (Eds), *The construction of group realities.* Malabar, Florida: Krieger Publishing Company.

Williams, R. (1983). *Keywords.* London: Fontana.

4

Personal Construct Psychology through a Poststructural Lens

PAULA EUSTACE

NINA BRUNI

Proposals of a postmodern turn in psychology (Gergen, 1994, 2001; Parker & Burman, 1993) make it appropriate to ask how Kelly's (1955) Personal Construct Psychology (PCP) sits with postmodern notions of the subject. PCP and poststructuralism, a project synonymous with the postmodern (Sarup, 1988; Warren, 1998), may, at first, appear in opposition in respect of their conceptualizations of the self. In this chapter we flag why this notion might appear so before suggesting possible sympathies, and tensions, in their respective theoretic assumptions about the self.

We focus in particular on the relationship between Kelly's (1955) conception of the self and a poststructuralist proposition of the constituted, or socially constructed, self. To this end, we consider the constitutive processes at work within nursing practice and the constitution of nurses, drawing on Paula's doctoral study for which Nina functioned as supervisor of the personal construings of nurses as professional carers (Eustace, 2004). In exploring the relationship of personal construing to the poststructuralist proposition of the (re)production of the self through discourse, we start by offering some suggestions of their possible correspondence through outlining their respective positions on the pivotal issue of the locus of subjectivity.

Personal Construct Psychology: New Ideas. Edited by Peter Caputi, Heather Foster and Linda L. Viney. Copyright © 2006 John Wiley & Sons, Ltd.

PCP AND THE POSTMODERN SUBJECT

PCP rests on premises of an unfixed selfhood and a self-in-relation – premises that also underpin postmodern theorising. Explicated in the Construction, Individuality and Sociality Corollaries (Kelly, 1955) in particular, PCP views individuals as actively producing their own identity through construing, a process that allows them to endlessly constitute and reconstitute themselves through their understandings of various experiences. Stringer and Bannister (1979) explain PCP's account of persons in relation, iterating clearly the sociality within Kelly's (1955) theory of the person:

> . . . the person, which is all that [Kelly's] psychology deals with, was only constituted in relations with others; constructs were chiefly available through interaction with others and obtained their meaning in the context of that interaction as well as through their more general and socially determined presuppositions. (Stringer & Bannister, 1979, p. xiv)

Butt (1996, p. 62) argues that the Kellian construing subject interacts intentionally through "joint venture(s)", sharing social norms and values with others in relation. Each person construes and reconstrues others, things, events, cultural material, language, and so on. While poststructuralists agree broadly with a conceptualization of the subject in relation (Davies, 2000), they view the production of self in terms of various technologies of power (Foucault, 1980) and would dispute its epistemologic centrality. However, Kelly (1955) proposes a modernist conception of the self as the locus of meaning and, in framing a "social individual", draws attention to some of the tensions between modern and postmodern positions.

THE DISCURSIVELY CONSTRUCTED POSTSTRUCTURAL SUBJECT

Whereas PCP privileges the assumption of the construction of individual meaning and holds the self as epistemologically central, the poststructuralist project sets about dissolving the subject as the centre of meaning. Belsey (1991) explains:

> Identity, subjectivity, is . . . a matrix of subject-positions, which may be inconsistent or even in contradiction with one another. Subjectivity, then, is linguistically and discursively constructed and displaced across the range of discourses in which the concrete individual participates. (Belsey, 1991, p. 597)

Poststructuralists conceive of meaning and knowledge as produced in the discursive formations of language, decentring the subject as the originator of meaning (Hekman, 1991). Without modernist notions of a universal meta-language and without universal commensurability, frames of reference dissolve and the striving for consensus in meaning becomes immaterial and arbitrary (Kvale, 1994). The integrated and grounded self of modernist discourse gives way to a fragmented and perhaps contradictory self, multi-dimensional, discursively constituting and constituted by social processes. This notion of the self of many dimensions resonates in Kelly's (1955) work. He rejects the meta-narrative in constructing the ever-construing and intentional subject and in subverting the modernist normalization of the consensual and non-contradictory self.

Yet, the notion of a decentred subject presents personal construct theorists with substantive difficulties. The poststructuralist contention of displacement, with meaning located discursively, represents a fundamental disparity in their respective discourses of the subject. One might ask whether these disparities create tensions so irrevocable that they impinge on the further elaboration of personal construct theory in the postmodern climate of contemporary psychology. We suggest here that they do not.

THE AGENTIC SELF: A POINT OF ARTICULATION

Though a different process of engagement with context and a different production of meaning mark constructivist and poststructuralist approaches, we propose that the shared focus on meaning within the two positions does allow them to mesh in useful ways. Issues of difference, such as the locus of subjectivity, may not necessarily stymie an enquiry into some form of articulation, for poststructuralism, as does PCP, claims the agency and resilience of the subject. Løvlie (1994) contends that poststructuralists aim:

> [not to dissolve] the critical subject. They are rather out to demolish ideological positions built on the idea of an epistemic subject being the centre of the world instead of being part of the text of the world. (Løvlie, 1994, p. 132)

Working within feminist poststructuralist discourse, Davies (2000) also argues against replacing the constituting with the constituted subject, proposing that agency remains integral to its conceptualization. Hekman (1991), too, maintains that, within poststructuralist discourse, an agentic entity remains resilient in a constituting world that, she argues, would otherwise determine the individual as a "social dupe" (1991, p. 47), haplessly passive in a capricious social context.

Such contentions lend support to claims of the continued relevance in a postmodern climate of the PCP proposal of the construing self as agent. Yet, for a consideration of language and its constitutive power in constructing subjects we must look to poststructuralism, and not to Kelly. Poststructuralists argue that people create a sense of self through the discursive structure of their narrative and work with proposals that, with language as the agentic medium, people construct their subject positions through discourse and relation (Davies, 2000, 2003).

We need not abandon individual human agency and subjectivity to acknowledge social constitutive forces. Kelly offers an elegant and imaginative discourse for individual action that attends to sociality and commonality in a social world. We believe, however, that poststructuralist discourse, as a way of knowing (Bruni, 1995), might enrich understandings of the construing self, in terms of social constructs and people's personal construing of them. Accordingly, we draw on narrative data from Paula's study of the personal construings of nurses as carers to suggest – through an exploration of the discursive construction of nurses as carers – that a poststructuralist examination of the formations that constitute the "caring" nurse complements the theoretical insights gained in this study through the application of PCP. This material also indicates the possibility, and power of, working with this "articulation" of seemingly disparate theories.

The study took place in Melbourne, Australia, with nurse participants recruited by advertisement from a metropolitan intensive care unit. The study complied with standard ethical requirements for human research (NHMRC, 1999). From self characterizations, each of the 5 participants offered 10 bipolar constructs that she then rated in a repertory grid of 10 provided elements (after Ellis, 1992). The grid included an "ideal self" element. We then together laddered and/or pyramided 5 of these constructs. The participants additionally offered narratives of their caring and/or uncaring experiences that feature in the data discussed here. An approach based on the deconstructive methods of poststructuralist enquiry informed the analysis of these narratives.

THE DISCURSIVE PRODUCTION OF CARING NURSES

Spivey (1997) proposes that the deconstructive method encourages new ways of reading and raises the question of who speaks in the text. Deconstructive reading offers many readings with the intention of dismantling a text's orthodoxies (Spivey, 1997), disrupting metaphysical binaries and effecting their strategic reversal. It achieves this reversal by underscoring the interdependence of such binaries (Law, 1999) – the way in which each term in the conceptual opposition contains elements of the other and depends on the other for meaning. By deciphering and challenging the oppositions and hierarchies that privilege certain meanings, deconstruction directs attention to meanings otherwise concealed and marginalized by the explanatory systems of normative consensus. A deconstructive interrogation offers to textual analysis, therefore, ways of reading that question and subvert. Deconstruction upends and undermines the interpretation of a text as a function of ideology. In so doing, it provides, as Solas (1995, p. 65) proposes, "a powerful conceptual tool for sociopolitical critique".

While deconstruction interrogates the notion of authorial voice, who speaks in the text, and allows examination of the discursive constitution of the text, constructivism has us ask how we might understand, in another way, the processes at work. Much of how the nurses in this study individually and collectively construed their practice worlds and themselves as carers in this study emerged during the laddering conversations. Their constructed identity as carers, how they made sense of their caring relationships, and their experience of caring praxis became visible. But their constitution as carers, by and in a socially constituted practice context, requires another reading – a deconstructive reading – of their narratives.

Poststructuralist considerations in this study highlighted dominant, marginal and contesting discourses (Bruni, 1995) of caring within the nurses' narratives and provided insights into the construction of self through the constituting technologies of power/knowledge relations (Burkitt, 1995). The consideration of these discursive structures adds a further dimension to the PCP-evolved data and produces a powerful lens for the exploration of the dynamics of the production, and hence of change, of the "caring" nurse.

In terms of this study, societally sanctioned, dominant discourses as institutionalized ways of speaking (Davies & Harré, 1992) create expectations of nurses to which they may feel pressure to conform. Deconstruction of their narratives indicated that these nurses embraced a number of interrelated discourses of competence and effectiveness. They often recognized the dominant institutional discourses within which they operated, and gave voice to them in seeking to position themselves as competent and effective nurses.

The first of these discourses we named "effective nursing", and the second, a competing discourse of "efficient nursing", shaped, in turn, by a discourse of "rationalist economics". We also identified a construction of "feeling good" as a discursive product of "effective nursing" and a socially sanctioned discourse of "selflessness", (re)produced in helping practices and metaphorically presented in the parable of the Samaritan helper. For the participant named Clare, whose deconstructed text we present here, the discourse of selflessness, evidenced in her helping practices, formed an important thread in shaping the discourse of "effective nursing" in which she sought to position herself.

EFFECTIVENESS AND EFFICIENCY

The competitive formation of oppositional discourses may provide the nurse with contradictory imperatives. For example, in considering the element the "ideal nurse", Clare provided a construct of "has time and thought". Her ideal nurse had the capacity, but particularly the means, to plan care and talk to patients; she structured a cohesive and consistent nursing plan rather than operating through isolated and uncoordinated activities. Clare believed, however, that the "system" penalized the nurse who sought time and thought, for, as a "real" nurse, Clare must execute her "caring" efficiently and cheaply.

According to Clare, then, she practised within economic constraints and conforming pressures, and so had less opportunity to plan her care than she would like. For her, the hospital system valued throughput, efficiency and measurable outcomes that may not, and frequently did not, derive from investments in the patient that required time (money), in particular, or deliberation. As Clare related:

> Well, they're [the hospital system] not supporting her [the nurse], they're pushing her . . . They want throughput, they want productivity . . . "Get 'em [patients] well, get 'em out the door, don't give a damn about their psychological well-being, we're not here to do that." The CEO [Chief Executive Officer] actually said that at one of those meetings . . . and he said, "That's not our problem, our job is to get them well and get them out the door, and bad luck as to what happens to them after that." That was a very clear message. And, to me, it's the message that we've [nurses] been getting for a long time.

Institutional signals about nurses' "obligations" in the face of financial restraint, time pressures and expectations of unpaid overtime formed a discourse of "rationalist economics". For Clare, this discourse competed with her construing of morally appropriate "caring" practices which she embedded in the discourse of "effective nursing". She rated herself as "impatient" on the construct "impatient–has time and thought". In discussing the explicit pole in relation to the concept of throughput efficiency, her comments suggest that nurses risk discursive formation by the powerful and dominant discourse of "rationalist economics", which submerges the marginalized –

in this context – discourse of the "effective nurse". Clare had difficulty accepting "rationalist economics" as a nursing discourse, idealizing, instead, the competence and effectiveness resulting from having "time and thought" to plan and deliver effective nursing care.

Indeed, Clare constructed herself as the nurse who, as an ideal nurse, would meet the needs of the patient but who, rather, found herself coded by contesting discourses, their rules and practices. She lived out an increasingly "impatient" compromise in just the way that she construed institutional forces would normatively produce her. She emphasized the institutional pressures that she claimed kept her from practicing thoughtful and effective nursing:

> Clare: . . . if a nurse herself is impatient and she's put in that environment, then she's not going to be able to move towards "having time and thought", she's going to get worse because she's pressured.
> Paula: Are you saying you're pressured?
> Clare: I feel pressure at work. I think we [nurses] all feel pressure at work.
> Paula: [And are you] . . . feeling influenced by this [demand for] throughput efficiency?
> Clare: Mmm. Absolutely . . . I'd be surprised if others weren't.

Time constraints formed just one of the discursive forces that Clare perceived as constraining her capacity to care for patients as she would wish. Issues of unimaginative protocols, restrictions on autonomy and expectations of conformity appeared to challenge her potential to achieve the satisfaction she sought. She answered with conviction the question of why she sought satisfaction in her nursing practice:

> *Because it makes me feel good.* It makes me feel that I am not *wasting my time*, because there *are* so *few* rewards in nursing, things like *this* [satisfaction] really matter (her emphasis).

"Feeling good" emerged as an important sentiment for all the participants, though its appeal as a form of gratification or personal reward for effort contested social constructs of the selfless helper. We consider briefly "feeling good" as a discursive product, and the competing discourses of "selflessness" and "gratification" in the next section.

SELFLESSNESS AND GRATIFICATION

A discursive construction of caring as selfless finds expression in the parable of the Good Samaritan. Selfless caring, as nursing, may stem from the monastic tending of the sick, which predates paid nursing (Nelson, 2005). A discursive construction of selflessness becomes, to some extent, part of a dominant nursing "culture" or discursive context of practice. Some nurses may identify with the notion that "genuine" caring should take place without the incentive of monetary or personal gain. The nurses in Paula's study, however, seemed to reject the discourse of "selflessness" in their helping practices. All noted, though with differing emphasis, that their acts of caring made them feel "good". Althought they may not necessarily like a patient; they understood the caring relationship to hold rewards and benefits in the forms of personal satisfaction, feeling good, or a sense of validation.

Clare explained that caring made her feel good, but emphasized that through caring she did not seek to fill a personal void, nor did she see such neediness in others as "healthy". Indeed, she rejected the notion of the selfless nurse:

> I find that there's a type of nurse, and I think its encouraged [by nursing culture], to be all things to all patients, to be intensely involved, to be self-sacrificing, to be, "Everyone else comes first before the poor old martyr". You know, this wonderful nurse that all the old ladies talk about, "She's just the *best* nurse", you know, "She does everything for you". I don't think that's the best nurse! I think the best nurse is the one who takes care of her patients *and* herself, who doesn't go home at the end of the day absolutely shattered because she's put everyone else in front of herself (her emphasis).

The selfless helper commits to altruistically helping and caring for people, notwithstanding her status within the institution as employee. Discursively constructed as the vocational nurse, the selfless carer as Samaritan helper forms a dominant discourse, here contested by a discourse of "gratification", or sought reward. Clare appropriated competing discourses; in seeking to achieve competence as a nurse as an outcome of adopting the "effective" ideal, she found her effectiveness challenged by rationalist economic imperatives. For Clare, the discourse of "gratification" leads to caring for the "wrong" reason. Nonetheless, she sought to feel good and to achieve this reward, despite carefully denying herself the motivation to do so. At the same time, Samaritanism, a rejection of the "gratification" discourse, will undo the selfless nurse, one who faces the spectre of "burnout" unless she also learns to care for herself:

> . . . she will burn out. She will end up on the heap because she cannot continue to be the mother hen to everyone. Sooner or later, she's going to get

angry and resentful of the fact that she's doing everything for everyone else, and what is she getting back?

Clare's last question suggests the oppositional imperatives of the discourses in which she participates (Davies & Harré, 1992). She has rejected the discourse of "gratification" in caring, constructing a notion of caring for the "wrong" reason. Yet, the selfless carer will suffer if she cares for the "right" reason. The rewards of feeling good may become necessary, after all, for the selfless nurse and for Clare's own satisfaction in her work, because, as she said, "[T]here are so few rewards in nursing".

In conclusion, we suggest that Kelly's work exhibits some leanings consistent with a poststructural interpretation of social processes. We have suggested the possibility of appropriating the notion of discursive practices within a constructivist worldview in the belief that it may enhance the insights educed from PCP while retaining congruence with Kelly's position. However, we have not presumed to resolve how we might come to grips with a notion of social constitution within a Kellian framework. This theorizing of an intellectual space in which an articulation can occur has suggested some intriguing possibilities while leaving unexplored a number of challenging disjunctions. Of these, the problematic of binary conceptualization – framed in dichotomies of the real-ideal, individual-universal and sign-signified – has received some attention from personal construct theorists (for example, Butt, 2000, 2001). Understandings of power/knowledge relations would present, perhaps, the most challenging of these disjunctions. And while we may choose to understand social constructs as the objects of our construing, the question as to how, constructively, we account for discursive structurings, not by their immanence but by our personal constructions of them, needs consideration. Discussion of these issues, however, lies beyond the scope of this chapter.

Despite some uncommon ground between these perspectives on (at least) the emphasis on the locus of subjectivity, possibilities exist for the beginnings of a productive articulation. The approach to construing as ways of knowing taken here draws on readings of PCP and poststructuralist theory loaded with Paula's own generative intent. But in her own reconciliation of Kelly's thesis of personal construing with the possibilities for more overtly mutually constitutive ways of knowing, we find Paula's understandings of Kelly's construction of people's meaning-making productively altered. Reflection and explorations such as those engaged in here support not just continual reconceptualization of our own ways of knowing but an ongoing interrogation of the frameworks, including PCP, that theorists adopt in exploring and explaining the constitution of human subjectivity.

REFERENCES

Belsey, C. (1991). Constructing the subject: Deconstructing the text. In R. Warhol & D. Herndle Price (Eds), *Feminisms: Anthology of literary theory* (2nd ed.), New Brunswick: Rutgers University Press.

Bruni, N. (1995). *The discursive constitution of nurse educators: An ethnography.* Unpublished Doctoral thesis, Monash University, Melbourne, Australia.

Burkitt, I. (1995). *Social selves: Theories of the social formation of personality.* London: Sage.

Butt, T. (1996). PCP: Cognitive or social psychology? In J. W. Scheer & A. Catina (Eds), *Empirical constructivism in Europe: The personal construct approach.* Gießen, Germany: Psychosocial-Verlag.

Butt, T. (2000). Pragmatism, constructivism and ethics. *Journal of Constructivist Psychology, 13*, 85–101.

Butt, T. (2001). Social action and personal constructs. *Theory and Psychology, 11*(1), 75–95.

Davies, B. (2000). *A body of writing 1990–1999.* Walnut Creek, CA: AltaMira Press.

Davies, B. (2003). Positioning the subject in body/language relations. In R. Harré & F. Moghaddam (Eds), *The self and others: Positioning individuals and groups in personal, political, and cultural contexts.* Westport, CT: Praeger.

Davies, B. & Harré, R. (1992). Contradiction in lived and told narratives. *Research on Language and Social Interaction, 25*, 1–36.

Ellis, J. M. (1992). *A personal construct approach to perceptions of care: The registered nurse and the elderly nursing home resident.* Unpublished Master's thesis, La Trobe University, Melbourne, Australia.

Eustace, P. (2004). *Caring construed: A reflective exploration.* Unpublished Doctoral thesis, RMIT University, Melbourne, Australia.

Foucault, M. (1980). Power/knowledge: Selected interviews and other writings 1972–1977. C. Gordon, L. Marshall, J. Mepham & K. Soper (trans), Gordon C. (Ed.). Brighton, UK: Harvester.

Gergen, K. J. (1994). Toward a postmodern psychology. In S. Kvale (Ed.), *Psychology and postmodernism: Inquiries in social construction.* London: Sage.

Gergen, K. J. (2001). Psychological science in a postmodern context. *American Psychologist, 56*, 803–813.

Hekman, S. (1991). Reconstituting the subject: Feminism, modernism, and postmodernism. *Hypatia, 6*(2), 44–63.

Kelly, G. A. (1955). *The psychology of personal constructs.* New York: Norton.

Kvale, S. (1994). Postmodern psychology: A contradiction in terms? In S. Kvale (Ed.), *Psychology and postmodernism: Inquiries in social construction.* London: Sage.

Law, I. (1999). A discursive approach to therapy with men. In I. Parker (Ed.), *Deconstructing psychotherapy.* Thousand Oaks, CA: Sage.

Løvlie, L. (1994). Postmodernism and subjectivity. In S. Kvale (Ed.), *Psychology and postmodernism: Inquiries in social construction.* London: Sage.

Nelson, S. (2005). Legends, legacies and lessons: 2000 years of care of sick strangers. Public lecture, The University of Melbourne, Melbourne, Australia, 3 May.

NHMRC (National Health and Medical Research Council) (1999). National statement on ethical conduct in research involving humans. Accessed 29 April, 2005 from http://www7.health.gov.au/nhmrc/publications/pdf/e35.pdf.

Parker, I. & Burman, E. (1993). Against discursive imperialism, empiricism and constructionism: Thirty-two problems with discourse analysis. In E. Burman & I. Parker (Eds),

Discourse analytic research: Repertoires and readings of texts in action. London: Routledge.

Sarup, M. (1988). An introductory guide to post-structuralism and postmodernism. London: Harvester Wheatsheaf.

Solas, J. (1995). Grammatology of social construing. In R. A. Neimeyer & G. J. Neimeyer (Eds), *Advances in personal construct psychology* (Vol. 3). Greenwich, CT: Jai Press.

Spivey, N. N. (1997). The constructivist metaphor: reading, writing and the making of meaning. San Diego, CA: Academic Press.

Stringer, P. & Bannister, D. (1979). Introduction. In P. Stringer & D. Bannister (Eds), *Constructs of sociality and individuality.* London: Academic Press.

Warren, B. (1998). *Philosophical dimensions of personal construct psychology.* London: Routledge.

5

The Joint Spatial Representation of Constructs and Elements

PRASUNA REDDY

RICHARD C. BELL

INTRODUCTION

The fundamental postulate of Personal Construct Theory (Kelly, 1955) emphasises the interdependence of constructs and elements. Since the mid-sixties, when Patrick Slater first showed that through a principal component analysis of the grid data (his INGRID program) a joint spatial representation could be obtained, such representations have become commonplace. Currently spatial representations of both constructs and elements are obtained through three different approaches, singular-value-decomposition (the generalisation of Slater's approach), correspondence analysis, and multidimensional unfolding. In this study we compare the different approaches for a number of grids, noting similarities, differences and problems.

THE SPATIAL REPRESENTATION OF REPERTORY GRIDS

Since Patrick Slater first produced an analysis of repertory grid data that generated a joint spatial representation of constructs and elements (Slater, 1964) there has been an interest in such representations. Consider for example the grid shown in Figure 5.1.

Personal Construct Psychology: New Ideas. Edited by Peter Caputi, Heather Foster and Linda L. Viney. Copyright © 2006 John Wiley & Sons, Ltd.

	A	B	C	D	E	F	G	H	I	
Warm	3.4	7.5	10.5	14.8	15.0	4.0	15.3	7.8	12.5	cool
Friendly	7.0	10.0	8.4	16.9	15.7	3.7	15.3	4.4	15.5	distant
Quiet	8.5	7.5	4.0	13.0	10.8	2.5	10.5	3.3	12.8	loud
Sharing	4.0	4.0	8.7	10.9	10.7	3.0	11.0	7.2	9.3	selfish
Attractive	5.2	2.7	13.5	7.8	10.5	8.5	11.7	13.0	4.8	ugly
Generous	9.2	4.0	9.2	5.5	4.5	8.0	5.4	10.8	6.1	stingy
Thoughtful	10.2	6.7	5.0	9.5	6.5	6.2	6.0	7.3	10.4	thoughtless
Clever	14.0	10.0	6.5	10.2	5.3	10.0	4.0	10.1	12.1	stupid
Old1	7.0	11.5	12.7	7.1	3.0	15.0	3.0	16.0	10.5	young
Insightful	14.5	9.2	16.5	2.0	6.2	15.2	8.0	18.3	5.0	uninsightful

Figure 5.1   First hypothetical grid

This grid could be analysed by a multidimensional unfolding algorithm and represented spatially as shown in Figure 5.2. The fit of this solution to the grid is excellent [stress2 = 0.015, RSQ = 1.000].

The grid could also be analysed by another algorithm, one corresponding to Slater's principal components. However this produces a different spatial configuration as is shown in Figure 5.3.

Which is correct? We can further compound the problem by considering a second grid, as shown in Figure 5.4.

If we analyse this grid by the same two methods, we obtain identical configurations, (shown in Figures 5.5 and 5.6 respectively) but reversed by method.

The unfolding solution for the first grid is extremely like the singular-value-decomposition (INGRID) solution for the second grid, while the unfolding solution for the second grid is extremely like the singular-value-decomposition for the first grid.

Seems fishy? It is. Both grids started from the same data (i.e., the same spatial coordinates for elements and constructs) – but they differed in the way the grid was formed from the data.

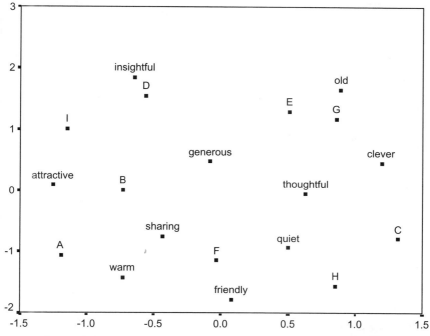

Figure 5.2 Unfolding representation of first hypothetical grid

MODELS UNDERLYING THE JOINT REPRESENTATION OF ELEMENTS AND CONSTRUCTS

Since Slater (1964) first demonstrated the data of a repertory grid could be represented by a spatial diagram that included both elements and constructs, there have been a number of alternative developments that achieve similar representations. These include other variants of factor analysis [including Horst's (1965) "basic structure with simultaneous factor solution" as in Bell (1987) and Gallifa and Botella (2000); and Eckart and Young's (1936) singular value decomposition, Bell (1998)]; correspondence analysis (Bell, 1987, 1998; Cornejo & Feixas, 1996); and multidimensional unfolding (Bell, 1983, 1994).

This last approach differs from all others. INGRID, other variants of factor analysis, and correspondence analysis, are all based on what Carroll (1972) terms a vector model. A vector model is one in which dimensional

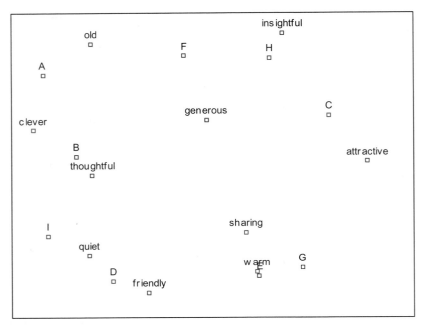

Figure 5.3 Singular-value-decomposition [INGRID] representation of first hypothetical grid

	A	B	C	D	E	F	G	H	I	
warm	6.3	4.5	4.3	2.2	1.8	5.6	1.7	5.6	3.4	cool
friendly	5.8	3.9	5.7	1.2	1.8	6.1	2.1	6.8	2.1	distant
quiet	4.6	3.6	5.5	2.1	3.0	5.2	3.2	6.0	2.4	loud
sharing	5.4	4.4	4.0	3.1	2.7	4.9	2.7	4.8	3.8	selfish
attractive	5.3	4.9	2.4	4.9	3.4	3.8	3.0	2.8	5.5	ugly
generous	3.5	4.1	3.4	4.9	4.7	3.3	4.6	3.0	4.7	stingy
thoughtful	3.4	3.5	4.8	3.5	4.3	4.1	4.5	4.6	3.2	thoughtless
clever	2.1	3.1	5.1	4.0	5.3	3.5	5.6	4.2	3.1	stupid
old	1.2	3.3	3.6	6.1	6.6	2.1	6.7	2.1	4.7	young
insightful	2.7	4.5	1.5	7.3	6.0	1.7	5.6	0.5	6.6	uninsightful

Figure 5.4 Second hypothetical grid

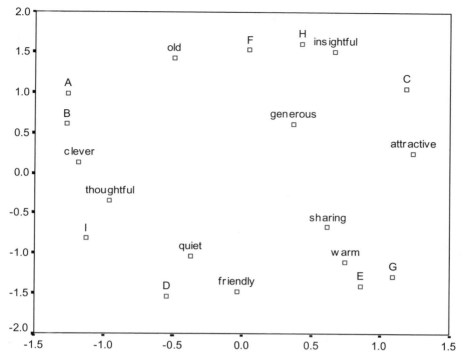

Figure 5.5 Singular-value-decomposition [INGRID] representation of second hypothetical grid

coordinates are found for elements and constructs such that the model re-creation of the grid follows from a product of the coordinates

$$G_{ij} = \sum E_{ik} \times C_{jk}$$

where

G_{ij} is the recovered grid data for element i and construct j,
E_{ik} is the coordinate for element i on dimension k, and,
C_{jk} is the coordinate for construct j on dimension k.

The unfolding model however assumes that the model recreation of the grid follows from a difference between the coordinates, such that the difference is a Euclidean distance, i.e.,

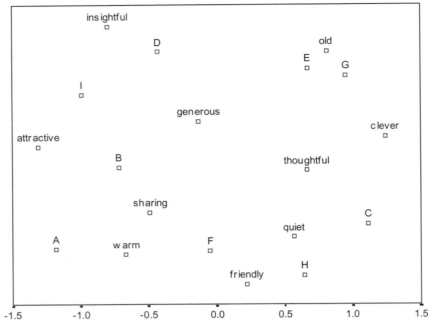

Figure 5.6 Unfolding representation of second hypothetical grid

$$G_{ij} = [\sum (E_{ik} - C_{jk})^2]^{0.5}$$

Herein lies the answer to the paradox provided by the two grids shown earlier. Both grids were formed from the same E and C coordinate matrices. The first grid was formed according to the distance model, the second according to the product model. Analysis of a distance grid by the distance model (the unfolding approach) gave the correct picture as did analysis of the product grid by the product model.

TESTING MODELS WITH REAL GRIDS

Unfortunately in the real world we do not have the underlying "true" element and construct data. We hope to uncover this from our analysis. But this contrived example shows us that the different ways of producing our spatial configurations imply different models and may distort the picture of the element-construct system.

MEANS OF COMPARISON

In order to make comparisons between different models with real data we need a criterion by which we can choose between competing models. Measuring the similarity of the configurations might be one possibility, measuring the degree to which the model fits the data might be another.

In the present study we adopted the latter approach because configural similarity approach would contain an inherent bias towards one approach or the other. Allowing the competing models to reproduce the grid according to their respective models meant that we simply had to compare the reproduced grid with the original grid. As a measure of fit we adopted a squared-correlation criterion.[1]

DATA

The data were a structured set of 120 grids collected as part of an undergraduate thesis. Each participant completed 2 grids, 1 specifying a set of acquaintances, the other a set of occupations. Both grids have fixed constructs. There were 4 treatment arrangements:

(i)   One group rated the friends grid first by construct then the occupations grid by element.
(ii) A second group rated the friends grid first by element then the occupations grid by construct.
(iii) The third group rated the occupations grid first by construct then the friends grid by element.
(iv) Finally the fourth group rated the occupations grid first by element then the friends grid by construct.

Participants were tested in small groups and close monitoring ensured that they completed grids according to instructions.

METHODS OF ANALYSIS

The grids were analysed using ALSCAL (Young, Takane & Lewyckyj, 1977) to produce the unfolding solutions. In the unfolding case, the data were treated as distances and also as reflected or reversed distances, and as

---

[1] This was the correlation between the original grid data and the derived grid – such correlations are lower than those reported by multidimensional unfolding programs such as ALSCAL where the correlation is between the optimally scaled data and the derived distances.

similarities. In the former two cases larger data values meant more dissimilar, in the latter, larger values meant more similar. If the grids were to conform to a product model, then we might expect unfolding of similarities to provide a better fit than unfolding of distances. In theory distances and reflected distances should not lead to different solutions. A version of GRID-STAT (Bell, 1998) was used to produce the singular-value-decomposition and correspondence analysis solutions.

RESULTS

The fit of the reproduced grid to the original grid is shown in Table 5.1.

It can be seen that the data in the reproduced grids from both product models (singular-value-decomposition and correspondence analysis) correlate substantially greater than do the unfolding solutions. All means were significantly different from one another.

This would suggest that processes involved in relating elements to constructs is better modelled by a product process than a distance process. However, this conclusion must be tempered by caution about the unfolding solutions.

PROBLEMS WITH UNFOLDING SOLUTIONS

Although the first grid was ably fitted by an unfolding model, more generally there have been concerns about the robustness of unfolding models using programs like ALSCAL (e.g., Borg & Groenen, 1996; Heiser, 1989; Schiffman, Reynolds & Young, 1981). However, as we have seen above this criticism was not true for the error-free data of the first grid. The spatial configuration there was recovered through the unfolding process. In real grids, however, there will be "error" which may prevent the unfolding process

Table 5.1 Fit of various methods of joint spatial representation of constructs and elements to grid data

Squared correlation between original and reproduced grid	Minimum	Maximum	Mean	Std. deviation
Singular-Value-Decomposition	0.69	0.93	0.830	0.052
Correspondence Analysis	0.69	0.93	0.826	0.052
Unfolding Reflected Distances	0.28	0.83	0.606	0.115
Unfolding Similarities	0.29	0.81	0.583	0.121
Unfolding Distances	0.34	0.84	0.553	0.118

arriving at a truly best fitting solution. Borg and Groenen (1996, Figure 5.5) and Heiser (1989, Figure 5.2) readily identify "degenerate" or false solutions by a particular configuration of points representing the rows and columns (here constructs and elements). A common degenerate configuration has the points representing constructs tightly clustered in the centre of the space and the points representing the elements distributed in a roughly circular configuration around them.

Several grids in our data produced configurations that tended to be somewhat like this degenerate pattern of points. As an example Figure 5.7 shows the solution for one such grid. Points labelled with capitals are constructs, those labelled in lower case are elements. With the exception of the construct labelled E, constructs are located in a central cluster while elements are distributed in a peripheral fashion.

Such a configuration may not be a degenerate one necessarily, although in this case the solution by means of singular-value decomposition was also one of the poorer ones [$R^2 = 0.70$]. If we examine this grid, shown in Figure 5.8 it is not easy to see why this configuration was arrived at.

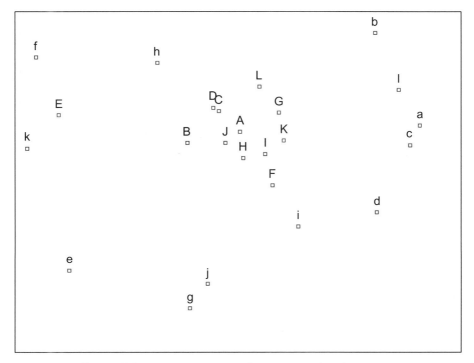

Figure 5.7   "Degenerate" unfolding solution for a grid

Constructs	Elements											
	a	b	c	d	e	f	g	h	i	j	k	l
A	1	1	1	2	4	3	3	1	1	2	1	1
B	4	1	2	2	3	3	3	1	1	3	1	1
C	2	2	4	4	4	4	5	1	2	4	1	1
D	2	2	3	3	3	1	5	1	3	4	3	3
E	3	4	3	3	2	1	4	2	3	3	1	5
F	1	2	2	1	2	5	5	4	1	1	2	3
G	1	1	2	4	4	4	4	2	3	4	4	1
H	2	4	1	1	4	3	5	3	3	1	3	2
I	1	4	2	1	4	3	3	3	2	3	4	1
J	4	2	1	2	5	2	4	2	1	2	2	2
K	1	4	2	1	4	4	4	2	1	5	5	4
L	2	2	2	4	5	4	5	2	3	5	2	1

Figure 5.8 Grid responsible for "degenerate" unfolding solution

Following in Figure 5.9 is a grid that fitted well under both product [singular-value-decomposition] and distance [unfolding] models. While the striking thing about this well-fitting grid is the prevalence of "5" ratings, it is not easy to see why this grid fits well, while the preceding grid did not.

These two grids are more formally compared in Table 5.2.

The R-squared values show the difference between the fitting and non-fitting grid – even so the non-fitting grid does not have a terrible recovery of the grid data. The mean ALSCAL vectors show the non-fitting grid to have

Constructs	Elements											
	a	**b**	**c**	**d**	**e**	**f**	**g**	**h**	**i**	**j**	**k**	**l**
A	5	5	5	5	5	5	1	4	3	1	2	2
B	5	5	5	5	5	5	1	4	3	1	1	2
C	5	5	5	5	5	5	2	5	2	1	3	3
D	4	4	4	5	5	5	1	4	2	2	3	2
E	5	5	5	5	5	5	5	2	4	4	2	3
F	4	4	5	5	5	5	4	4	4	4	2	4
G	5	5	5	5	5	5	5	3	4	4	1	2
H	3	3	4	4	5	5	5	3	5	5	4	4
I	5	5	5	5	5	5	5	2	4	4	3	3
J	4	5	5	5	5	5	5	2	5	5	3	4
K	2	1	2	2	1	1	5	1	3	5	4	4
L	1	3	2	2	3	2	5	3	2	5	5	3

Figure 5.9   Grid which produces "non-degenerate" unfolding solution

the statistics to match the "degenerate" diagram, while the fitting grid shows similarity of mean vectors for elements and constructs. The remainder of the table shows some standard statistics for the data in the two grids (obtained from GRIDSTAT).

The two grids were not really distinguished by the Average rating and the fitting grid had more similar variation between constructs and elements as evidenced by the various standard deviations, sums-of-squares, and intraclass correlation. The more poorly fitting grid had more variation among the elements than the constructs by these criteria (remembering

Table 5.2 Comparative statistics for fitting and non-fitting grid by joint spatial representation of elements and constructs

Grid statistic	Fitting grid	Non-fitting grid
Singular-Value-Decomposition R-squared	0.93	0.70
Unfolding untied Distances R-squared	0.84	0.52
ALSCAL mean element vector length	1.4614	1.8428
ALSCAL mean construct vector length	1.1550	0.5596
Average Grid rating	3.764	3.389
Average Construct Standard Deviation	1.242	1.236
Average Element Standard Deviation	1.227	1.085
Standard Deviation of Construct Means	0.537	0.378
Standard Deviation of Element Means	0.596	0.696
Construct Sums-of-Squares	41.472	20.556
Element Sums-of-Squares	51.139	69.722
Total Sums-of-Squares	275.972	244.222
Construct Intra-class Correlation	0.147	0.249
Element Intra-class Correlation	0.110	0.038
Average Root-Mean-Square Correlation between Constructs	0.588	0.380
Average Root-Mean-Square Correlation between Elements	0.605	0.298

low intraclass correlation means less similar elements). However this is precisely the configuration of elements and constructs produced by ALSCAL unfolding for this grid. The average levels of correlation were higher for the fitting grid.

FACTORS THAT AFFECT THE FIT OF SPATIAL CONFIGURATIONS OF GRID ELEMENTS AND CONSTRUCTS

The extent to which the grid statistics shown in Table 5.2 could predict the fit of the spatial configurations was tested for all 180 grids by regressing the R-squared fit measures on the grid statistics. Stepwise multiple regression showed that the Average Root-Mean-Square Correlation between Constructs and the Average Root-Mean-Square Correlation between Elements provided a significant and substantial prediction of both Singular-Value-Decomposition R-squared and Unfolding untied Distances R-squared. $[F(2,117) = 161.52$, Adjusted R-square $= 0.730$; and $F(2,117) = 97.69$,

Adjusted R square $= 0.619$, respectively]. Although in both cases the Average Root-Mean-Square Correlation between Constructs [0.683, 0.678 respectively] was more important than the Average Root-Mean-Square Correlation between Elements [0.426, 0.320], in the unfolding case this was more marked.

In examining predictors of the unfolding vector lengths (our index for degenerate unfolding solutions) we found that ALSCAL mean element vector length was most highly correlated with Average Root-Mean-Square Correlation between Constructs [$r = 0.39$], and *ALSCAL mean construct vector length* was most highly correlated with *Average Root-Mean-Square Correlation between Elements* [$r = 0.41$].

CONCLUSIONS

The analysis of the considered grid representations provided evidence for the hypothesis that product models (e.g., Singular-Value-Decomposition [INGRID] or correspondence analysis) fitted grid data better than a distance model (Unfolding). Such a finding may have implications for the way we interpret Kelly's (1955) "psychological processes" and open up personal construct theory to a more elaborated theoretical structure based on elements, perhaps reviving the speculations of Castorina and Mancini (1992) about the nature of "choice" and the role of elements in this. These findings, however, require further investigation into the nature of the unfolding methodology. While previous authors have cautioned about the tendency of multidimensional unfolding to produce degenerate configurations in these grids the failure of the unfolding model could not simply be attributed to this problem. This study also showed that the fit of any spatial models to grids is very much dependent on the relationships between the constructs, and the relationships between the elements in a grid. It follows that spatial modelling will be of little use in grids where there is fragmentation of the constructs.

REFERENCES

Bell, R. C. (1983). *Analysing repertory grid data using SPSSx 2.1.* Unpublished manuscript. Perth: University of Western Australia.

Bell, R. C. (1987). G-PACK: *A computer program for the elicitation and analysis of repertory grids* (Computer software). Melbourne: Author.

Bell, R. C. (1994). *Using SPSS to analyse repertory grid data.* Unpublished manuscript, Melbourne: University of Melbourne (revised June, 1997).

Bell, R. C. (1998). *GRIDSTAT: A program for analysing the data of a repertory grid.* (Computer software). Melbourne: Author.

Borg, I. & Groenen, P. (1996). *Modern multidimensional scaling.* New York: Springer.

Carroll, J. D. (1972). Individual differences and multidimensional scaling. In R. N. Shepard, A. K. Romney & S. B. Nerlove (Eds), *Multidimensional scaling. Vol 1 Theory* (pp. 105–155). New York: Academic Press.

Castorina, M. & Mancini, F. (1992). Construct system as a knowing system. *International Journal of Personal Construct Psychology, 5,* 271–293.

Cornejo, J. M. & Feixas, G. (1996). *GRIDCOR: Correspondence Analysis for Grid Data v. 2.0.* (Computer software). Barcelona, Spain: Authors.

Eckart, C. & Young, G. (1936). Approximation of one matrix by another of lower rank. *Psychometrika, 1,* 211–218.

Gallifa, J. & Botella, L. (2000). The structural quadrants method: A new approach to the assessment of construct system complexity via the repertory grid. *Journal of Constructivist Psychology, 13,* 1–26.

Heiser, W. J. (1989). Order invariant unfolding analysis under smoothness restrictions. In G. de Soete., H. Feger & K. C. Klauer (Eds), *New developments in psychological choice modelling* (pp. 3–31). Amsterdam: North-Holland.

Horst, P. (1965). *Factor analysis of data matrices.* New York: Norton.

Kelly, G. A. (1955). *The psychology of personal constructs.* New York: Norton.

Schiffman, S. S., Reynolds, M. L. & Young, F. W. (1981). *Introduction to multidimensional scaling: Theory, methods and applications* (p. 322). New York: Academic Press.

Slater, P. (1964). *The principal components of a repertory grid.* London: Vincent Andrews.

Young, F. W., Takane, Y. & Lewyckyj, R. (1978). ALSCAL: A nonmetric multidimensional scaling program with several individual-differences options. *Behavior Research Methods and Instrumentation, 10,* 451–453.

6

The "Inquiring Man" in the Laboratory

HARALD SEELIG

JANINA RADÓ

In traditional quantitative research it is typically taken for granted that the world can be broken down into well-defined pieces, which can be described using a handful of characteristic features. In order to test hypotheses about relations among the pieces it is sufficient to examine those characteristic features. If the experiment yields the intended results, that confirms not only the initial hypothesis but also the general assumption that the selected features provide a correct representation of the piece under investigation. If it does not, we would expect the hypothesis to be rejected. Instead of doing that, however, researchers will often try to identify influences in the experimental situation itself that may have caused subjects to react in a way that is undesirable from the viewpoint of the experiment.

Another conceivable source of errors are the personal attitudes subjects bring to the experimental situation. In quantitative research this potential problem is believed to be virtually eliminated via typical components of experimental design (which serve, among other things, to make the experimental situation opaque for the subjects[1]) and statistical procedures based on averaging across subjects.

---

[1] This approach is described and criticised by the "Kritische Psychologie" as completely excluding the subject from the design and treating experimental participants as objects (cf. Holzkamp, 1969).

Selecting the relevant variables and obeying the principles of experimental design should thus guarantee that the experiment delivers the predicted results. The "success" of an experiment, in turn, implies that any individual influences that might have been present can be considered irrelevant and there is no need to investigate them any further. But can this neglect of individual differences be considered justifiable?

From a Personal Construct Psychology (PCP) perspective, the researcher's effort to standardise the experimental situation inevitably results in a different "reality" for each research participant. Moreover, we cannot dismiss the possibility that subjects already have different attitudes, or personal constructs, about this situation upon entering it and these personal constructs affect their behaviour. This questions the basic assumptions of quantitative research in two respects. First, if such attitudes are present then we must allow that they might have an influence on the results even in experiments that do not fail. That would imply that the model that provided the basis for the experiment is incomplete or inadequate since it doesn't include these individual influences. More importantly, however, constructivists would doubt the possibility of creating a single, objective model of "reality" in the first place and therefore the examination of one model, i.e., the results of an experiment, may become meaningless.

The present study was intended to address the first of these questions. It was designed to provide evidence that participants of a typical laboratory experiment do indeed have different personal constructs about the experimental situation, and that these different "realities" map onto different patterns of performance in the laboratory experiment.

In our study 36 participants (13 female, 23 male, average age: 23.9 years, all sports students) completed first a typical biomechanical experiment, then a Repertory Grid interview that served to assess their personal construct systems. Cluster analysis of the Grid data was used to detect latent classes of similar element systems. These classes were then compared with respect to the participants' biomechanical performance. Additionally, participants' attitudes were elicited using the more established method of the Semantic Differential to provide an independent means of evaluating the adequacy of the Grid method.

The purpose of the biomechanical part was twofold. In addition to generating the quantitative data we needed for our comparison, it also created immediate experience with the laboratory situation which was expected to facilitate the elicitation of subjects' attitudes concerning this situation. Special care was taken to keep the laboratory situation as uniform as possible across subjects. It should be emphasised, however, that personal construct systems are generally assumed to be relatively stable thus the experiment itself and any differences that may have remained are unlikely to have a substantial impact on the personal construct systems subjects had *prior to* the present experiment.

The biomechanical part consisted of a typical laboratory drop jump analysis like those used in sports science to estimate an athlete's capacities and ability to perform sports specific jump movements. In this task participants stood erect on a 48 cm high platform, "dropped" down from this position and immediately tried to jump up as high as possible. The drop jump task was chosen because the movement can be easily described using only a few parameters yet it is complex enough to show the effect of psychological influences on performance. After a warm-up the subjects performed 10 jumps. Biomechanical parameters were calculated by measuring the ground reaction forces and the ground contact time electronically (via amplified piezo-electric signals from a Kistler force plate system). For each subject the following 9 parameters were calculated:

The mean (aM), the coefficient of variation (cV) and the slope of regression (sR) – each of the jumping height (jh), of the ground contact time (gct) and of the real dropping height (rdh). These parameters, especially real dropping height (which indicates any raising or lowering of the body's centre of gravity before the "drop") are seen as the ones that are most likely to show a possible influence of psychological factors.

The results obtained in this part of the study replicated the results of numerous studies in this field (see Neubert, 1999). Most importantly they show the usual pattern of coefficients for reliability, and for statistically significant dependencies between the parameters listed above and interpersonal differences like gender, experience with the drop jump task, and the participants' primary sport discipline (see Table 6.1).

The reliability of the measurements was estimated by the intraclass correlations. These were $r_i = 0,88$ for the jumping heights, $r_i = 0,81$ for the

Table 6.1 Significant dependencies between sociodemographic and drop jump data

Factor	Variable	F-value	Significance	df	eta²
Gender	aM of jh	12,623	0.001	35	0,271
primary sport	cV of jh	6,230	0.018	31	0,172
discipline	aM of gct	4,719	0.038	31	0,136
	cV of gct	5,319	0.028	31	0,151
experience	aM of jh	5,495	0.025	35	0,139
with the drop	aM of gct	7,799	0.005	35	0,206
jump task	cV of gct	5,641	0.023	35	0,142
	cV of rdh	5,792	0.022	35	0,146

Table 6.2   Elements chosen from the association experiment

German	English
Hörsaal	lecture hall
Student	student
Vorlesung	lecture
Professor	professor
Labor	laboratory
Untersuchung	investigation (scientific)
Versuch	experiment
Proband	subject (participant in an experiment)
Termin	appointment (appointed time)
Kalender	calendar
Verabredung	appointment/date
Zeit	time
Wettkampf	contest
Konkurrenz	competition
Leistung	effort

The original elements were given in German; the original stimuli appear in bold.

ground contact times and $r_i = 0{,}64$ for the real dropping height. This means that this (part of the) experiment fulfils the usual criteria in the field of biomechanical research.

Following the biomechanical experiment a Grid interview was conducted with each participant. To allow cross-subject comparison of the participants' element systems, in our interviews we used given elements. These elements were related to the laboratory situation or to the typical environment and situations of (sports) student/university life. They had been elicited in a separate association experiment where 31 participants (sports students, not the same as in the main study) were asked to respond to the 4 items (stimuli) *laboratory, lecture hall, appointment, contest*. Participants had to write down as many associated nouns as possible, in the order that the associations came to their mind. To avoid clustering effects the prescribed minimum was 15 nouns per stimulus (Strube, 1984).

Table 6.2 shows the 15 elements chosen to be included in the main experiment, namely: the 4 stimuli plus the 2 or 3 most frequent and most "spontaneous" responses to each of them[2] as indicated by the positions in the association lists (for more details see Seelig, 2001).

For the construct elicitation we used dyads that were constructed in the following way: Each stimulus item was paired with each of its associations

---

[2] One association [time] appeared for two stimuli [appointment, contest].

(s-a), as well as with each of the other stimuli (s-s). This resulted in four different stimuli-related groups of dyads (dyads that exclusively belong to one group) and a group of dyads that belong to two stimuli.

The elements and constructs were then integrated in a computerised environment and the subjects performed the rating by positioning a line on a given (distance) bar (length: 385 pixels) between 2 construct poles using mouse steering and clicking.

In part three of the experiment participants were asked to complete a semantic differential (in the same computerised environment) to rate the same elements as in the Grid interview, but this time using a set of the usual bipolarities (cf. Ertel, 1965). This allowed us to compare the two methods with respect to the reliability and validity of the cross-subject analysis (see Appendix 6.1). The results of these comparisons show that in this study the grid method can be seen as reliable and valid, that is, we can safely assume that the given elements correspond to (a) parts of the laboratory situation and (b) separate "pieces" of the (university) environment of sports students. It should be emphasised that while the semantic differentials contained a (quantitatively) standardised set of bipolar attributes the grids are based on individual constructs.

We then conducted a comparison of the individual element systems in order to find latent groups of element systems that show similar reconstructions of the relationships between the given elements.

At first each grid was analysed separately by correspondence analysis. The resulting 36 individual element systems – more precisely the elements' co-ordinates along the first 4 dimensions – were compared by cluster analysis to roughly categorise similar element systems. This way the subjects' element systems were sorted into 8 clusters (groups) of different sizes (see Table 6.3: note that cluster C 6 represents only 1 subject and is therefore excluded from further analysis).

Table 6.3   Clusters of "similar" element systems

Cluster C 1	Cluster C 2	Cluster C 3	Cluster C 4	Cluster C 5	Cluster C 6	Cluster C 7	Cluster C 8
subj.1; subj.7	subj.2; subj.8; subj.11; subj.12; subj.17; subj.20; subj.23; subj.32	subj.3; subj.10; subj.18; subj.31; subj.36	subj.4; subj.6; subj.14; subj.16; subj.21; subj.25; subj.29; subj.34	subj.5; subj.9; subj.24; subj.26; subj.30; subj.35	subj.13	subj.15; subj.22; subj.28; subj.33	subj.19; subj.27

Next we evaluated the connection between the grid data and the biomechanical data by an analysis of variance (ANOVA) which compared the subjects' biomechanical performance treating clusters as a factor (see Table 6.4). A separate test revealed no dependency between the clusters and factors like the subjects' gender, age, primary sport discipline or experience with the drop jump task.

As seen in Table 6.4 none of the differences in the biomechanical parameters between the clusters reaches statistical significance. This is partly due to the small size of the sample. However the eta^2 values in Table 6.4 show that 7.1 % to 28.0 % of the variance of the parameters can be explained by the clustering of the subjects based on their element systems. It is remarkable that these values reach the same level as the significant dependencies between the sociodemographic and the drop jump data in Table 6.1.

The results show that subjects have different element systems concerning the lab situation. Contrary to the usual nomothetic assumptions, we have found evidence that participants with "similar" element systems also perform similarly in the lab experiment. Assuming that the drop jump task is representative of biomechanical experiments and possibly laboratory experiments in general, we must conclude that subjective factors like personal constructs are an important source of influence in experimental research.

Our findings are completely in line with general PCP assumptions that each individual has his or her own personal constructs about the world and that these constructs influence his or her behaviour. As this influence is different from person to person, the results of an experiment that involves a certain set of individuals cannot be expected to generalise to a different set or to the whole population.

It is important to emphasise again that our biomechanical experiment fulfilled the criteria typically used in quantitative research. Had we not considered subjective factors, the results would have been accepted as being within

Table 6.4 Analysis of variance (ANOVA)

Variable by factor	df	F	Significance	eta^2
aM of jh *Cluster C	6, 28	0,359	0.899	0,071
aM of rdh *Cluster C	6, 28	0,593	0.733	0,113
aM of gct *Cluster C	6, 28	0,571	0.750	0,109
cV of jh *Cluster C	6, 28	1,574	0.192	0,252
cV of rdh *Cluster C	6, 28	1,741	0.148	0,272
cV of gct *Cluster C	6, 28	1,478	0.222	0,241
sR of jh *Cluster C	6, 28	0,710	0.644	0,132
sR of rdh *Cluster C	6, 28	1,322	0.280	0,221
sR of gct *Cluster C	6, 28	1,815	0.132	0,280

the range of those typical for laboratory experiments. They would have been taken to confirm the underlying quantitative model which in turn would have been regarded as an adequate representation of a portion of reality. However, as we found evidence that subjective factors were present and that they have influenced the result, this interpretation cannot be correct. What is more, we cannot be sure that results of quantitative experiments are generally free of the influence of subjective factors.

But if this is the case, can we use experiments at all to tell us something about how the quantitative model corresponds to reality? The answer is a cautious yes. Quantitative methods still have an important role in studying pieces of reality and the relationships between them. At the same time it is equally important to separate the effects of the intended experimental manipulations from those that result from subjective factors – it is only the former that we can expect to hold for the population as a whole. And clearly the presence and scope of subjective factors cannot be determined without using qualitative methods. What we need, however, is more than just including qualitative methods in the classical research paradigms. It is necessary to rethink the classical qualitative-quantitative dichotomy and to find a way of combining the two types of methods so that qualitative research can benefit from it as well. This may even open the door to a wider acceptance of purely qualitative studies.

APPENDIX 6.1

In this study we also carried out a nomothetic evaluation of the grid.

To test the reliability of the methods the grids and the semantic differentials were first analysed using INDSCAL (cf. Ahrens, 1974) over all subjects to obtain two "group element spaces" that take into consideration individual differences (weights). As Table 6.5 shows the results of the analysis are remarkably similar to the associative element groups, which had been elicited quantitatively, even though here we have assigned individual weights to each grid/semantic differential. The correspondence is not perfect, because the elements *student (Student)* and *appointment/date (Verabredung)* form a separate group in both major columns of Table 6.5.

Taking the original association groups as four categories or "traits" the reliability of these traits can be estimated by Cronbach's α. This coefficient indicates the internal consistency of a trait on the basis of the mean inter-correlation between the related items.

Inspecting the values for Cronbach's α (shown in Table 6.6) reveals that those for the grid are slightly higher than those for the semantic differential.

Table 6.5 INDSCAL analyses of the grid and the semantic differential

	Grid				Sem. differential			
	Dim. 1	Dim. 2	Dim. 3	Dim. 4	Dim. 1	Dim. 2	Dim. 3	Dim. 4
lecture hall	−1,821	−0,370	0,009	−0,962	0,105	1,907	0,599	−0,698
student	0,267	−0,113	2,113	−0,592	1,616	−0,083	0,273	1,271
lecture	−1,385	−0,423	0,131	−1,366	0,233	1,705	0,751	−0,483
professor	−1,071	−0,044	−0,028	−1,601	−0,245	1,465	1,110	0,192
laboratory	0,511	−1,408	−0,831	0,279	−0,090	0,131	−1,742	−0,261
investigation (scientific)	0,582	−1,437	−0,992	0,202	−0,769	0,289	−1,481	−0,559
experiment	0,741	−1,365	−0,825	0,334	−0,330	0,243	−1,703	0,196
subject (participant in an exp)	0,673	−1,397	1,034	0,504	1,114	0,372	−1,515	0,268
appointment/ appointed time	−0,827	0,790	−0,610	1,477	−0,186	−1,111	0,953	−1,165
calendar	−1,005	0,672	−0,145	1,628	0,171	−0,581	0,247	−1,854
appointment/date	0,836	0,450	2,210	0,307	2,134	−0,563	0,226	0,813
Time	−0,852	0,878	0,232	1,643	0,315	−1,426	0,572	−1,414
contest	1,326	1,228	−0,774	−0,451	−1,163	−1,076	0,485	1,471
competition	0,914	1,393	−0,707	−0,748	−1,556	−0,394	0,703	0,960
Effort	1,112	1,147	−0,817	−0,653	−1,350	−0,878	0,521	1,263

Table 6.6 Cronbachs α of the traits

Trait	Grid	Sem. differential
lecture hall	0.6510	0.5848
laboratory	0.8234	0.7181
appointment/appointed time	0.6328	0.4093
contest	0.8392	0.7872

In addition in both cases the values for the traits *lecture hall (Hörsaal)* and *appointment/appointed time (Termin)* are noticeably lower than the other ones. These traits contain the elements *student* and *appointment/date* which, as seen above, stand separately. Recalculating the values of the traits without these two elements yields results comparable to the other traits (0.74 and 0.72 for "lecture hall"; 0.76 and 0.65 for "appointment/ appointed time" in the grid and the semantic differential, respectively).

Thus we conclude that both methods can be seen as reliable.

Validity was investigated using a multitrait-multimethod matrix (Campell & Fiske, 1959). The matrix was created by correlating the individual inter-trait distances (Euclidean distances between the traits for each subject) in the two methods. We can estimate the validity of the traits by inspecting the intercorrelations among those traits.

> Specifically, this type of matrix is defined by the intercorrelations among several traits, each measured by several methods, and thus contains some of the information considered necessary in carrying out a validation study. In general, convergent validity can be confirmed by observing relatively large correlations between measures of the same trait based on different methods. Conversely, discriminant validity can be confirmed when the correlations are relatively low between tests, based on the same or different methods, that are intended to be indicators of distinct traits (Hubert and Baker, 1978)

Table 6.7 shows the correlations for convergent and discriminant validity for the four traits measured by the grid and the semantic differential.

To examine the validity of the resulting correlation matrix we used the statistical model proposed by Hubert and Baker (1978). Instead of heuristically comparing the correlations it is possible to examine the validity of the multitrait-multimethod matrix as a whole. The underlying null hypothesis is that the correlation coefficients in the matrix are distributed randomly. Hubert and Baker (1978) define three kinds of statistics: Γ_1 is the average of the same-trait correlations, Γ_2 is the difference between the average same-trait correlation and the average for the different traits measured under the different methods, and Γ_3 is the difference between the average same-trait correlation and the average same-method correlation. These statistics are then compared to E(aM) which is the value that would be expected if the coefficients were distributed randomly. The resulting Z-values (Table 6.8) indicate that the null hypothesis can be rejected ($p < 0.002$ for all Γs). This means that the correlation coefficients in the multitrait-multimethod matrix

Table 6.7 Multitrait-multimethod matrix

		Semantic differential				Grid			
	Traits	Lec. hall	Lab.	App.	Contest	Lec. hall	Lab.	App.	Contest
sem.	lecture hall	(0.59)							
differential	laboratory	−0.09	(0.72)						
	appointment	−0.18	0.02	(0.41)					
	contest	−0.07	0.07	−0.07	(0.79)				
grid	lecture hall	0.82	−0.20	−0.24	−0.30	(0.65)			
	laboratory	−0.16	0.79	−0.08	−0.16	−0.14	(0.82)		
	appointment	−0.28	−0.17	0.78	−0.15	−0.20	−0.17	(0.63)	
	contest	−0.23	−0.15	−0.02	0.81	−0.36	−0.30	0.02	(0.84)

Table 6.8   Characteristic values for validity

Γ_1		Γ_2		Γ_3	
$\Gamma_1 =$	0,80298283	$\Gamma_2 =$	0,98101993	$\Gamma_3 =$	0,92563093
$E(aM) =$	−0,01467078	$E(aM) =$	−0,00005868	$E(aM) =$	−0,00005868
$V =$	0,03527788	$V =$	0,05476708	$V =$	0,05476708
$s =$	0,18782407	$s =$	0,23402367	$s =$	0,23402367
$Z =$	4,35329503	$Z =$	4,19221955	$Z =$	3,95553835

are significantly distinct from a random distribution of coefficients. Therefore the measurements can be considered valid.

REFERENCES

Ahrens, H. J. (1974). Multidimensionale skalierung. Methodik, Theorie und empirische Gültigkeit. Weinheim/Basel: Beltz Verlag.

Campbell, D. T. & Fiske, D. W. (1959). Convergent and discriminant validation by the multitrait-multimethod matrix. *Psychological Bulletin, 56*, 81–105.

Ertel, S. (1965). Weitere Untersuchungen zur Standardisierung eines Eindrucksdifferentials. *Zeitschrift für Experimentelle und Angewandte Psychologie 12(2)*, 177–208.

Hubert, L. J. & Baker, F. B. (1978). Analyzing the multitrait-multimethod matrix. *Multivariate Behavioral Research, 13*, 163–179.

Neubert, A. (1999). Zur Diagnostik und Trainierbarkeit des reaktiven Bewegungsverhaltens. Köln: Sport und Buch Strauß.

Seelig, H. (2001). Subjektive Theorien über Laborsituationen – Methodologie und Struktur subjektiver Konstruktionen von Sportstudierenden. Schorndorf: Karl-Hofmann.

Strube, G. (1984). Assoziation. Der Prozess des Erinnerns und die Struktur des Gedächtnisses. Berlin: Springer.

7

Small Steps Against the Tyranny of Distance in Isolated Communities

LINDA L. VINEY

INTRODUCTION

Collecting a history of the use of personal construct ideas in an isolated community like Australia from 1970 serves a number of purposes. Normally one purpose of collecting this history is to learn from it for the future. However, given the constructive alternativism which must permeate this chapter, this can only be my view, and so the lessons too may only be mine.

I have drawn much from the very helpful history of these ideas in Victoria, Australia (Costigan, 2000). This chapter can add to Costigan's paper by dealing with something of the New South Wales and Western Australian history, as well as the Victorian. The West Australians (Stein, 2001) have also provided very useful information. There have been other attempts to encourage the sharing of personal construct ideas, such as the Australasian Personal Construct Newsletter, and the organisations that have been developed with this same aim.

My main lesson has been that the effects of geographical distance have been as threatening to the development of personal construct ideas in this vast but isolated country as they have been to so many other endeavours here.

Personal Construct Psychology: New Ideas. Edited by Peter Caputi, Heather Foster and Linda L. Viney. Copyright © 2006 John Wiley & Sons, Ltd.

SMALL STEPS AGAINST THE TYRANNY OF DISTANCE IN ISOLATED COMMUNITIES

Australia is a vast largely empty and isolated country, with most of its population in the south east corner. It is also a country in the Southern Hemisphere, when most of the world's population is in the North. In the somewhat egocentric terminology of the British Empire, Australia is not in the "East" or even the "Far East" but even further away than that. This means that distances have made it very hard for Australians to meet together to discuss personal construct ideas. This effect occurs within Australia, since the distance travelled from Sydney to Melbourne, for example, is 707 kilometres, to Adelaide is 1,166 kilometres and to Perth is as much as 3,284 kilometres. Meeting with those using such ideas overseas is also difficult, since the distance travelled from Sydney to Los Angeles is 12,054 kilometres, to Toronto is 15,544 kilometres and to London is 17,036 kilometres.

In this chapter I argue that the effects of geographical distance have been a threatening tyrant inhibiting the sharing of personal construct ideas in this country. This information should be useful to other isolated communities. I will be describing the first foundations of personal construct ideas across Australia, beginning in New South Wales, then Victoria and Western Australia. Australians at International Congresses, and then at Australasian Conferences are considered. Other attempts to encourage the sharing of personal construct ideas, such as the Australasian Personal Construct Newsletter, devised and edited by Beverly Walker and the organisations that have been developed for this same purpose will be discussed.

FIRST FOUNDATIONS

The first use of personal construct ideas appears to have been in New South Wales at Macquarie University in the School of Social Sciences. When I returned in 1970 from completing my PhD (Clinical Psychology) in Cincinnati, using both psychodynamic and cognitive ideas, I was asked to run a graduate seminar. Feeling that I had only just finished being a graduate student, I searched desperately to find something to fill the time for the whole year! When I cast my eye around my office it fell on the 1970 edition of the *British Journal of Medical Psychology* which included a report on a London-based symposium on "The Person in Psychology and Psychotherapy", which was dedicated to personal construct ideas. The symposium was edited by Miller Mair (1970), and contained some mind-boggling, challenging, creative and, ultimately extremely useful, ideas from George Kelly. In this Symposium, Al Landfield explored the congruency of construct systems of client and therapist, Jans Bonarius, Fixed Role Therapy, Joe Rychlak, dialectics, Don Bannister, theories as ways of relating to people, and Miller Mair, a conversational method of data collection. Some wonderful discussions between my graduate students and myself resulted, as did publications and completed graduate work. This experience confirmed for me the importance of the published word in communicating personal construct ideas, a lesson I bear in mind when deciding whether to put in the great effort it takes to produce a credible and hopefully useful publication.

The first publication to come from these discussions and research was in 1976, with the Cognitive Anxiety Scale developed with Mary Westbrook to measure the unique concept of anxiety developed by George Kelly (1955), using recognition that experienced events are beyond the scope of the construct system (Viney & Westbrook, 1976). The paper was published by the *Journal of Personality Assessment*. Another paper with a graduate student, Beth Freeman, followed the next year in the *Journal of Community Psychology,* on psychiatric patients' expectations of therapists (Freeman & Viney, 1977). In 1981, I published my first paper on personal construct therapy in the journal *Psychotherapy,* titled: "Experimenting with experience". In 1983, I published a report on a personal construct-based service for ill people's hospital experiences, an area, like the assessment and psychotherapeutic work, that has later been developed more fully.

The first PhD graduates using personal construct ideas in Australia seem to have been the same two young women. Dr Mary Westbrook graduated in 1976, with a personal construct study of the processes of child-bearing: "Analysing people's experiences, A study of the child-bearing year". Dr Beth Freeman graduated in 1978, with the following thesis title: "Psychiatric outpatient treatment, A multivariate analysis of alternative explanations". They both went on to teach and conduct research in Australian universities. At the same time, 1978, Janet Powell was completing with me a Masters degree through research using this approach: "Student expectations in advantaged and disadvantaged schools". Janet too went on to work in Australian universities. Also in 1977, Connie Eales completed this personal construct approach research project for a Masters on School Psychology degree: "Teacher's expectations of school counsellors".

There has now been developing more recently in New South Wales a strong group at the University of Wollongong, where we have been meeting since 1980. Today we are able to incorporate our group into the research structure of the Department of Psychology. We meet for an hour and a half weekly during term-time. Our average attendance is 14 to 16 people. There have been at least 18 PhDs from this group. In Wollongong, too, there is now the Constructive Counselling Centre, developed by Bronwyn Seaborn and me, which sees clients, runs workshops and conducts supervision. One of the most important achievements of the Centre is a fortnightly supervision group for experienced personal construct therapists.

In Victoria, the first PhD graduate using these ideas to look at Agriculture was Dr Peter Salmon, who graduated in 1978. For most of the information about Victorians, I am greatly indebted to Jacqui Costigan, who stretched her incredible memory considerably (Costigan, 2000).

Costigan also notes that Charles Langley was then doing his PhD in the USA with Dan Bieiri. The original name of the Victorian group started by Jacqui, was the Thursday Nighters, after George Kelly's tradition of discussing personal construct ideas in his home on Thursdays. Early members included Peter Salmon, Terry Cummins and Richard Bell from the University of Melbourne, Diana Taylor and Prue Brown from Monash University, Keith Stead from Churchill College, Pat Crotty from Deakin University, Don Fairhall from Ballarat College, and later, Peter Cairney and Maurice Robson from Deakin University and Bruce McAskey from Mental Health. Not only were all of these institutions represented, but also psychologists, nurses, educationalists and people in agriculture. There were around 70 people on its mailing list. An average of 15 attended the monthly meetings. The most memorable of these early meetings dealt with methodologies, focussing on grid types and analyses. Some of the other early PhDs gained in this group were by Dr Diana Taylor and Dr Peter Burgoyne. The rest of Costigan's account emphasises the importance of efforts by locals but also those visiting from Australia and overseas for a conference and to give workshops. And even at its most reduced, an average of 8 to 10 people attended the meetings. There have been at least 10 PhD graduates from this Victorian group.

In the early 70s, a parallel but almost entirely independent development of personal construct ideas occurred in Western Australia, with an emphasis completely on professional application. For this account of it, I am very indebted to Miriam Stein (Stein, 2001). In 1974, a small study group was set up by Petrice Judge in the Department of Community Services (now Family and Children's Services). Petrice later became the Chief of Psychological Services of that Department. These professionals had found that traditional psycho-diagnostic methods provided insufficient information for the complex recommendations that psychologists were required to make and would have far-reaching effects on the lives of their clients. Petrice conducted a literature search and found only a small body of relevant work. She and her group adapted what they could of the Repertory Grid using the contributions of Ravenette, Hinkle and Tshudi to develop appropriate tools. Richard Bell was also invaluable in this regard. It is apparent that it was the methods in personal construct psychology that first attracted the West Australians, like the New South Welsh and Victorians. From these earliest days, the Western Australian group has been integrative in their use of personal construct ideas. For example, they may include a family systems approach, psychodynamic methods, attachment theory, and a body of other techniques, such as behaviour analysis and guided imagery. The approaches are selected according to the perceived needs and values of the clients and the strengths of the therapists.

The Western Australian group, while geographically isolated from the rest of Australia, has continued to make sure that it has had continuing input from cutting edge personal construct ideas and methods, mostly from overseas. They are unique in this country in actually having developed a 10-week training programme in Personal Construct Therapy for Registered Psychologists. It is run by Janet Bayliss, Miriam Stein and Tony Jonikis. The programme has continued through the 1990's until this day. It is a tribute to its Convenors, that it has been able to attract students over this long period of time. The current Western Australian Personal Construct Association meets bi-monthly and continues the activities of the early group. Minutes of the group are sent to 40 active members, including clinical, counselling and organisational psychologists, and postgraduate members.

AUSTRALIANS ABROAD: OUR CONTIBUTIONS TO INTERNATIONAL CONGRESSES

No Australians appear to have been able to make the journey to the inaugural Personal Construct Congress in 1975. Jacqui Costigan was the first to make this demanding and sometimes difficult journey, it being the second one, in Oxford, in 1977. However, she reports that she found this experience incredibly useful, and has attended all of them since then. Bill Warren (University of Newcastle) was able to join her at the next one in Utrecht, Holland in 1979. In 1981, at the Congress at Brock University they were joined by me. We were at the Boston Congress in 1983, and Cambridge Congress in 1985. By that stage the very high standard of Bill's theoretical contribution was being noted, and he was invited to join the "experts". By 1983, I had begun a five year term as the Oceania Personal Construct Publication Clearing House Representative, being responsible for updating local publications on the international list each year, and was having my Congress papers published in the proceedings.

Other Australians were able to join us in the following years, including Richard Bell and Beverly Walker, at the next Congress in Memphis in 1987, and we were all able to attend those at Assisi in 1989 and Albany in 1991, and, of course, the first Congress in Australia in 1993. The selected papers from that congress have been published by the Australian Psychological Society (Walker, Costigan, Viney & Warren, 1996). The seeds of that first Australian Congress were planted back in Cambridge, when I had the unenviable task of being the only Australian at the Business Meeting proposing an Australian Congress, while Don Bannister was supporting the Italian venue. Don certainly was a formidable debater. Since then the same group of Australians, including Barbara Tooth, Julie Ellis-Scheer, Richard Bell and Beverley Walker have attended Congresses in Barcelona in 1995, Seattle in 1997, Berlin in 1999, Huddersfield in 2003 and Columbus, Ohio, in 2005. The 2001 Congress was held in Wollongong, Australia, which was very useful for Australians.

AUSTRALASIAN PERSONAL CONSTRUCT CONERENCES

The first of the Australian Personal Construct Conferences was held in Wollongong in 1983 with 70 participants, including psychologists, psychiatrists, social workers, educators and sociologists, as well as applied statisticians. The Organising Committee was a group of 11 Wollongong people, including those who are now Professor Greg Hampton, Dr Nadia Crittenden, Dr Rachael Henry, Dr Carol Preston and Associate Professors Beverly Walker and me, with Anna-Maria Tych as Secretary. Selected papers from this Conference were published (Viney, 1983). They were prefaced by the words of George Kelly (1964, cited Maher, 1979) in his paper: "The language of the hypothesis"

> Science is often understood by students as a way of avoiding subjective judgements and getting down to the hard fact of reality. But I am suggesting that the avoidance of subjectivity is not the way to get down to hard reality. Subjective thinking is, rather an essential step in the process the scientist must follow in grasping the nature of the universe (p. 150).

The papers consisted of 2 theory papers, 1 on motivation by Rachael Henry and the other on combining personal construct and Piagetian concepts from Lee Fantinel at Wollongong, as well as 2 measurement papers on Grids by Richard Bell, then still in Western Australia and Judith Brook from New Zealand. There were 10 substantive papers beginning with 3 about children and adolescents. The first of these was on crying babies, from Fay Deane and John Kirkland also from New Zealand, together with 1 on adolescent discriminations from Maurie Scott of Wollongong University, Faculty of Education, and another on adolescent runaways and their families, from the Psychology Department. Then there was further work from the Psychology Department: on religious experience from Carol Preston, moral beliefs from Rachael Henry and on illness from me. There were 2 papers from Queensland on organisational psychology: 1 on driver safety from Peter Cairney and the other on the interpersonal perceptions of systems analysts, or what we would now think of as, computer program consultants, from Adrienne Hall. The final 2 papers were on perceptions of aboriginals of their housing from Helen Ross, from the ACT and an evaluation of social work education from Ian O'Connor from Queensland. It was an uplifting and memorable experience for its participants. The grins on our faces in the 4 photographs taken testify to the extent of the validation we experienced.

There have been 12 biennial Australasian Personal Construct Conferences since 1983. The second was in Perth in 1984, again a great distance for the interested East Coast people to travel. It was organised by Richard Bell, Tony Jonikis and Petrice Judge. It clearly had the same powerful effects on its early participants. The third was in Melbourne organised by Jacqui Costigan and her group; and the fourth in Wollongong, the only site with enough people to have hosted this conference several times, largely because of the continuing strength of our group, in terms of both numbers and depth of experience. The fifth was in Adelaide, organised by Alan Stewart; and the sixth in Wollongong again. The seventh was in Sydney; hosted by Pam Bell and Sue Nagy. The eighth was in Canberra, but this was essentially organised by the Wollongong Group. The ninth was in Brisbane, organised by Barbara Tooth; and the tenth was in Bendigo organised by Julie Ellis-Scheer. The eleventh was in Sydney, organised by Bill Warren and the twelfth was in Melbourne organised by Richard Bell and Prasuna Reddy. These conferences have continued to attract some very gifted participants from a similar range of professions; and they have also continued to apply personal construct ideas very fruitfully in a wide range of areas. They have also continued to provide much needed validation of the construing and values of the people who attend.

THE AUSTRALASIAN PERSONAL CONSTRUCT NEWSLETTER AND OTHER CONTRIBUTIONS

A very important mitigator of the effects of distance on the spread of personal construct ideas here was the Australasian Personal Construct Psychology Newsletter, first published in 1986. Beverly Walker has been solely responsible for the 4 issues each year since then, resulting in 72 issues so far. This has now also become the organ of what has become the Personal Construct Psychology Interest Group of the Australian Psychological Society. Each issue contains a range of material ranging from articles on European and American Conferences attended, personal articles, latest publications and methodologies, websites and information about Australasian conferences, training programmes and workshops. The immediate circulation of the Newsletter is 20, but for the wider interest group it is currently about 150, a very large number with whom to communicate regularly and frequently.

It is also important to make clear that there have been other contributions to the sharing of these ideas in Australia through work on committees, without pursuing all the details. For the first interim committee, the Convenor was Beverly Walker, Barbara Tooth was Secretary, Bill Warren was Treasurer and Linda Viney a committee member. Then Richard Bell took over as Convenor, with Beverly as Newsletter Editor and Jacqui Costigan as the Victorian group representative and later with Miriam Stein as the West Australian representative. Today there are two parallel committees, the general one and the Australian Psychological Society Interest Group one. The current committee is: Bill Warren (Convenor), Barbara Tooth (Secretary), Chris Stevens (Treasurer), with Beverly Walker, Richard Bell and Miriam Stein as members. The contribution of these people to the spread of personal construct ideas is much appreciated.

AUSTRALIA'S DISTANCES IN THE TWENTY FIRST CENTURY: THE TYRANNY REDUCED

Fortunately, there are now available desk top computers that make possible communication through e-mail and the World Wide Web. The Australasian Personal Construct Psychology Newsletter that is so important can now be accessed through e-mail. The major current PCP websites and newsgroups are listed below. These processes make it possible for Australians to access methodologies and conduct research with Australians and those in other isolated communities, and also with people overseas who use personal construct ideas. This helps to reduce our isolation; but distances are still large. Access to these computing processes is also available in all Australian universities; but is not necessarily so in the government services, although that is becoming more common. The 14th International Personal Construct Psychology Congress, too, was still essential to reducing our Australian sense of isolation and distance.

REFERENCES

Costigan, J. (2000). The Victorian Personal Construct Association: Its history over 17 Years. In J. Ellis-Scheer (Ed.), *Proceeding of the Ninth Australasian Personal Construct Conference*. Bendigo: Latrobe University.

Freeman, R. B. & Viney, L. L. (1977). Patients' expectations of the therapist role. *Journal of Community Psychology, 5*, 372–379.

Kelly, G. W. (1964). The language of hypothesis: Man's psychological instrument. In B. Maher (Ed.), *Clinical psychology and personality* (pp. 147–162). New York: Kreiger.

Mair, J. M. M. (1970). The person in psychology and psychotherapy: An introduction. Symposium on The Person in Psychology and Psychotherapy. *The British Journal of Medical Psychology, 43*, 197–206.

Stein, M. (2001). History of the Personal Construct Psychology Association in Western Australia. Perth: Personal Communication.

Viney, L. L. (1983). Australasian *Personal Construct Psychology Conference 1983: Selected Papers*. Wollongong: University of Wollongong.

Viney, L. L. & Westbrook, M. T. (1976). Cognitive anxiety: A method of content analysis for verbal samples. *Journal of Personality Assessment, 40*, 140–150

Walker, B. M., Costigan, J., Viney, L. L. & Warren, W. (1996). *Personal Construct Theory: A Psychology for the Future*. Melbourne: Australian Psychological Society.

PCP Web Sites and Newsgroups (Thanks to Dr Heather Foster)

Personal Construct Psychology database http://www.psyc.uow.edu.au/research/pcp/citedb/index.html

Information about personal construct psychology http://www.pcp-net.de/info/homepages.html

Encyclopaedia: The Internet Encyclopaedia of Personal Construct Psychology http://www.pcp-net.org/encyclopaedia/

PCP E-journal
Personal Construct Theory and Practice: An Internet Journal devoted to the Psychology of Personal Constructs http://www.pcp-net.org/journal/

Regional Networks

Australasian Personal Construct Group (APCG) http://www.pcp-net.org/aus/

Constructivist Psychology Network (CPN) (North America) http://www.constructivistpsych.org

European Personal Construct Association (EPCA) http://www.pcp-net.org/epca/

German PCP Group (DPPK) http://www.pcp-net.de/dppk/

Italian Constructivist Psychology and Psychotherapy Group (AIPPC) http://www.aippc.it/

Newsletters and Newsgroups (Mailing Lists)

Internet-ional Newsletter http://www.pcp-net.de/info/news.html

Australasian Newsletter http://www.psyc.uow.edu.au/research/pcp/apcn/index.html

Constructivist Chronicle (North America) http://www2.newpaltz.edu/~raskinj/CCIndex.html

Mailing List (jiscmail, ex-mailbase) http://www.jiscmail.ac.uk/lists/pcp.html

Grid User Group (EnquireWithin) http://groups.yahoo.com/group/RepGrid/

SECTION II

Assessment and Understanding

8

Therapeutic Artistry: Evoking Experiential and Relational Truths[1]

LARRY M. LEITNER

As I have wrestled with rationed care and reductionist, "empirically violated" (Bohart, O'Hara & Leitner, 1998), manualised "treatments", I have become increasingly concerned that this version of so called therapy is being seen as something you "do" to a client, not a way of being with another human being. In this chapter, I will describe some ways that good personal construct psychotherapy (Leitner, 1988) facilitates and celebrates the healing power of the relational encounter in the therapy room. In this approach, the therapist is an "improvisational artist" (Bohart, 2001), not a technician.

As I explore the artistry of the psychotherapist, I hope to not further entrench the simplistic construct of "artist versus scientist". This construction, all too often applied in a reified and literalistic way in psychotherapy writings, leaves gifted therapists stuck. They can decide that they are "scientists" and use manualised "treatments" that the "data say" (it is impossible, from a Personal Construct Psychology (PCP) perspective, for "data" to "say" anything) work for this disorder. However, rejecting that shallow intellectual sterility leaves the therapist vulnerable to an "anything goes" lack of intellectual rigor seen all too often in therapies that claim to be artistic.

[1] This Chapter is based upon the Keynote Address given at the International Congress on Personal Construct Psychology, Wollongong, NSW, AUSTRALIA, July, 2001. All clinical material has been distorted to maintain anonymity. I would like to thank Lara Honos-Webb and especially April Faidley for their comments on earlier drafts of this chapter.

Contrary to either of these options, the therapeutic creativity of the "artistic" therapist can spring from a theory that is at least as intellectually rigorous as that of therapists who call themselves "scientists".

Specifically, I will focus on two areas: evoking the client's lived experiential truths and creatively using the unique personal material in therapy to help the client experience vital relational issues. Finally, I will distinguish between true therapeutic creativity and an anti-intellectual acceptance of an anything goes mentality. Hopefully, when I am done, therapists (and non-therapist researchers also) can be comfortable with and proud of their artistic use of the therapy relationship without feeling like they must also be comfortable with therapies like past life regression, crystals, channeling and some of the farther reaches of transpersonal psychology!

EVOKING EXPERIENTIAL TRUTHS

If the conversation of therapy talks *about* life, but does not touch the core meanings and powerful emotions that accompany being alive, it is intellectualised and superficial. The most central experiences of a client's existence are not brought into play in the therapy room. On the other hand, if interventions can vividly evoke a client's lived experience, therapy can be life changing. Thus, speaking in a way that evokes for the client the deepest and most powerful experience of being alive is a vital part of therapeutic artistry. It is no wonder that Kelly (1955/1991a, 1955/1991b) emphasised the necessity of therapists being skilled in the use of language. In this section, I will discuss poetic language, the creative use of metaphors and symbols, and the resurrection of hope from the wreckage of past traumas.

POETIC LANGUAGE

Language is as important to a psychotherapist as it is to a poet (Faidley & Leitner, 2000). Through the creative use of language, the therapist can help the client think the unthinkable and know the unknowable. In other words, language, properly chosen, can access feelings and experiences that the client may be only vaguely aware of and bring to a verbal level what has been symbolised, but not spoken. A well-chosen word, a turn of phrase, the form given to an inquiry or a reflection, can mean the difference between an average response and a profound one. In this regard, the language the therapist uses must meet two major requirements.

First, the language must evoke the experiential truths of the client's life. I use the term "experiential truth" because it captures the way that a good therapist's words capture the client's experience of truth – not necessarily "truth" in the objective and realistic sense of that term. When the therapist is in tune with, resonating with, intuiting the process of the client, the words chosen deepen the experience of the truths of the client's life.

For example, consider Jean, a woman who presented for therapy hallucinating the word "slut". In my therapy with Jean, we traced the origin of the hallucination to her horror at needing to leave her marriage, resulting in a marked decrease in her symptom. Later, she began to wonder whether she was a "slut" like the voices had said. As she talked about how her parents felt about issues like divorce, non-marital sex, and so on, I said, "One of the horrors of your life is that you always feel that you have to prove that you are not evil. You never have had the gift of just being able to trust that others care for you". This intervention helped move Jean from the content of her fears to the process of living her life petrified that she was unlovable. This issue, implicit in much of Jean's experience, had not been brought to a higher level of awareness prior to my intervention.

In addition to evoking experiential truths, the therapist's language must be able to reflect these truths in ways that open up options for growth, transformation, or transcendence. Implicit in the interaction with Jean described above is that life would be fuller if she could assume that others care for her. She does not have to change her parents' views on extra-marital sex to have a rich life. Rather, if she can find the courage to overcome her decision to believe that her worth is contingent on proving her goodness, she can be freer. Language for evoking such truths should be carefully chosen. Many people need to numb themselves to experience due to the implicit horrors of their constructions of their lives (Leitner, 1999b, 2001). Language that can help the client get beyond the numbing tendency can be most therapeutic. For example, consider my use of the term "horror" when I was speaking to Jean – "One of the horrors of your life is that you always feel that you have to prove that you are not evil". I could have said, "Your style is to . . ." or "one of the things you tend to do is . . ." However, the term "horror" gets beyond mere technical descriptions, no matter how accurate, to the underlying experiential truth for her. She had lived her entire life under the construction of proving her worth and decency to others. Evocative language uses terms that can highlight and accentuate the experiences of life.

In that regard, therapists need to look beyond specific content to the horrors, the tragedies, and the heroic nature of individual lives. Horrors do not have to be Post Traumatic Stress Disorder (PTSD) causing mutilations; tragedies do not have to be great romantic betrayals; heroism does not have to show itself on battlefields. Rather, every life has places of overwhelming pain; places where the best intents, hopes, and dreams have crashed upon the rocky shoals of "reality"; places where sacrifices have been made; places where courage and integrity have shone through darkness and misery. My language, as a therapist, needs to be couched in words and forms that can evoke these experiences.

The ROLE relationship of life-changing psychotherapy has no room for phoniness and manipulation. This implies that my language, highlighting and accentuating these personal/universal experiential realities, needs to be consistent with my experience of the client. In other words, I have to experience my client's triumphs and tragedies, aspirations and despairs, dreams and devastations. If I can achieve/maintain optimal therapeutic distance (Leitner, 1995), I can readily experience my client's deepest emotions. I can become a finely tuned instrument, resonating with and accentuating my client's inner experience. The specific words I choose to illustrate this resonance can then flow spontaneously from my best experience of what it is like to be this human being.

METAPHORS AND SYMBOLS

Metaphors and symbols play a vital role in evoking experiential truths (Faidley & Leitner, 2000). None of the metaphors used in the preceding section are literally TRUE. The therapist is not, literally, a violin, cello, or some other finely tuned instrument, for example. Hopefully, however, metaphors point us toward a greater experiential truth. Often metaphors can serve as ways the therapist can hold overwhelming emotions. Metaphors and symbols also can be vital means of connecting with the experience of clients in therapy or drawing attention to unexplored aspects of experience. Because these ways of symbolising experience point us toward deeper experiential truths, they often evoke felt meanings that have been at a low level of awareness. As such, they help the therapist help the client become more alive in the therapy room.

For example, Diane entered therapy due to feelings of low self-worth and inadequacy. Soon thereafter, she began to make vague references to an abusive relationship with her husband. However, she never really elaborated on these references, despite my repeated attempts to explore the matter. As we dealt with this refusal to elaborate, Diane mentioned that her husband helped her decide ahead of time what issues she would discuss in therapy and had her give him a detailed description of each therapy session. She construed that as his involvement and concern for her therapy. I described him as acting more like a therapy supervisor than a spouse. This intervention heightened her vague sense of unease about his invasion of her therapy. (Note, by the way, the use of the term "invasion" to metaphorically elicit a sense of his inappropriate blurring of her separate individuality.)

Creativity in the use of symbols also can help the therapist evoke a client's felt reality. For example, at one point in my therapy with Jean (the woman hallucinating "slut"), we were speaking of her dependency on and fears of me. She was quite concrete and literal about these feelings. I pointed out that, behind the feelings were issues about whether I could be her "good mother", as opposed to the one that had allowed her father to rape her. The symbolism of "good mother", with its connotations of love, protection, and non-sexual holding, evoked a deeply felt response in Jean. She began to cry and talked openly of her desire to trust me, in addition to her fears of doing so.

CONNECTING PAST TRAUMAS TO PRESENT EXPERIENCE

As events continue to injure and overwhelm a person, the emotional demands of honoring those injuries can become more than the person can tolerate (Kelly, 1955/1991b; Leitner, 1999a). At that point, most people numb themselves emotionally to the implications of their meaning-making system (Leitner, 1999b, 2001). However, because emotionality is the basis of our process of being alive (Leitner, 1985), this numbing results in our losing awareness of the links *from* these past injuries *to* our present experience. The ultimate outcome, particularly for more seriously injured persons, is an experience of life in which horrific fears, anxieties, hallucinations, obsessions, compulsions, etc. seem to have appeared "out of the blue".

A gifted therapist, through the creative use of language, can help reconnect present experiences to past devastation. This process of reconnecting is, in and of itself, powerfully therapeutic. The client no longer has to feel bizarre, inadequate, or defective, having experiences that seem to own him. Rather, experiences can be seen as desperate, even courageously creative, solutions to the most unsolvable of life injuries (Leitner & Celentana, 1997). The client can experience the self less as a victim of life and more as someone who might be able to come to solutions today that were impossible yesterday.

We can see this again in my therapy with Jean. As we explored the roots of her hallucinatory experiences, we began to deal with experiences of systematic sexual abuse and torture. However, because the sexual experiences were the only times she experienced any semblance of caring, the part of her that was frightened, alone, and emotionally needy was willing to participate in the abuse. Other parts of her, horrified at the decision to participate, viewed her as a "slut". At this point, the basis of her hallucinatory experiences became clear to her.

Our work with this matter was not done yet. Creative use of language does more than just connect present experiences to past traumas. It makes the connection in a way that leads to *hope*. As we sorted out this material, I said, "You were so little, so needy, that you felt you had no choice but to cooperate with a terrible situation. However, together, you and I can sort this out and come to ways of viewing your decisions that are less damning to you. It will take time and hard work but, together, we can do that". Jean was very frightened about the prospect of reliving these experiences. They had almost destroyed her once. I told her that we could delve into them at her pace, that I would not ask her to go faster than she could tolerate. I then told her an old Southern saying: "Joys shared are doubled; sorrows shared are halved. The first time, you were alone when you went through these horrors. This time, we will be together".

Notice how the material in this vignette does more than just explain the cause of the hallucinations. It explains them in a way that implies a way out of her distress. It also explains them in a way that talks about the importance of the connection between us, aggressively offering my person as a connecting force, a holding support. The material also shows my respect and trust of Jean (e.g., we can go at her pace, we can do it, etc.). Finally, it provides her with an experience of someone who can genuinely empathise with a part of her she has viewed as totally despicable.

In summary, the use of language to evoke the client's deeply felt "truths" about life lies at the heart of the therapeutic encounter. Absent this artistic gift, therapy will be sterile, intellectualised, and, at best, merely change peripheral structures. It is no wonder that therapists need to continually foster their creative development throughout life (Leitner & Faidley, 1999). As a matter of fact, I would go farther: good therapeutic training programs ought to require exposure to great literature and the arts at least as much as they require exposure to things like the "biological bases of behavior", the "cognitive bases of behavior", the *DSM*, and other "scientific" requirements.

USING PERSONAL MATERIAL TO DEAL WITH ROLE RELATIONSHIP ISSUES

The fundamental human struggle between the need to connect deeply with an other and the need to retreat from intimacy to protect oneself from the terrors of relational connection is the major theoretical underpinning of experiential personal construct psychotherapy. Creative interventions can link the client's specific personal material to this basic issue, thereby helping the client grapple with this essential dilemma of existence. This linkage is based on our definition of treatment – the application of theory to distress (Leitner, Faidley & Celentana, 2000). Thus, the experiential personal construct therapist listens to the lived experience of clients with an ear toward construing the ROLE relationship implications of these experiences. The ability to tie personal issues into these general, universal, struggles allows the client to see the relationship between present experience and past traumas, with the powerful therapeutic implications of this link described above. In addition, the therapist's ability to do this can help the client feel less bizarrely idiosyncratic; the client's struggles, while unique, also are based upon universal struggles with humanness.

In this section, then, I will deal with the art of listening for ROLE relational material in the client's life as well as listening for ROLE relational material in the actual therapeutic ROLE relationship. However, before beginning, I want to emphasize yet again that therapeutic artistry demands interventions that evoke the lived experience of the client. In other words, if I intervene in ways that lead to theoretical, intellectual, discussions of ROLE relationship issues, I am failing my client. Rather, the interventions have to be made in a way that evokes the felt terror, devastation, hopes, or dreams of the human being struggling with needing to connect deeply with others and to protect the self from potentially dangerous others.

THE ART OF LISTENING FOR ROLE RELATIONSHIP MATERIAL

Therapist genuineness, creativity, and optimal therapeutic distance (Leitner, 1995; Leitner & Faidley, 1999) are essential to the art of listening for ROLE relationship material. However, in life changing psychotherapy, the therapist must search out and encounter the client's *current areas of aliveness*. I speak of "current areas of aliveness" because different issues can be salient at different times. "Aliveness" gets to process, change, emotionality and vitality. The area of aliveness is where the client is growing *at that moment*. Technically speaking, "finding the client's aliveness" is a way of saying that we need to find the place where the current elaborative choices are being made. Therefore, the operative therapeutic question for me at the beginning of the session is, "Where is my client's aliveness today?"

While it is easy to become overwhelmed and confused by the material presented, in many ways, finding the area of client aliveness is a ridiculously easy task. If I start from the firmly held hypothesis that clients begin with the most relevant material for the day, I often immediately can see the aliveness the client brings to the session. Early in the session, I listen quietly, asking myself, "What makes this material so vital that the client chooses to start the session with it?"

Sometimes this question leads me to seemingly contradictory places. For example, it might be so vital precisely because it is so sterile and impoverished. The vitality, the aliveness, is the client's fear of trusting me with rich vulnerabilities. This leads me to the client's fears of connecting with me. At other times, the vitality might be tied to needs for reassurance that the relationship with me is safe enough to move deeper into felt experience. Can I be trusted to constantly care even when the client has been away from me for the time between sessions?

For example, George started his second session by talking about his wife's betrayal of him in ways that implied that I knew how she had injured him. However, we had not discussed these things in our previous session. I instantly hypothesised that George struggled with being able to recognise the separateness, the individuality, of others. His experience was real and powerful and he, at some level, assumed that all others somehow knew all about his experience. As we clarified this style, I was able to say, "One of the tragedies of this way of being for you is that, if others get confused by this, they may withdraw. That limits your ability to connect with others and leaves you more alone than you want to be".

Later in the therapy relationship, after the client has had experiences of moving quickly to the growing edges of the meaning-making system, therapists can be free to ask more directly about areas of aliveness. Simple questions like, "What's up for you today?", "Where are you today?", or "What's going on right now?" often can start the process of the session. Commenting on initial sighs, shifts in posture, etc. also can start the process.

However, finding the current area of aliveness is just the beginning of the therapeutic encounter. The therapist also must find ways to explore the personal issues behind the aliveness. For example, as we explored George's implicit assumption that his experience was all that was real, we got to the ways his mother invaded his inner world (reading his diary, sneaking into his room to see what he was doing, listening in on his phone calls, reading his mail). Thus, a powerful person in George's life was affirming constructions of intimacy as a fusion of self and other such that independence, uniqueness, or separateness was not really possible.

This work clearly emphasises connecting past traumas to present experience. However, it connects the traumas to present experience in a particular way. George became aware of the ways that his struggles with ROLE relationships are limited by the ways he has construed these traumas. In other words, my interventions tied experiential personal construct theory to George's uniquely personal experience.

Together, we could now explore the ways he had drawn boundaries between self and other in his life. The drawing of boundaries between self and others is both vitally important and ambiguous. Within the safe confines of the therapy room, George could struggle with whether he needed to draw those boundaries at a different spot. The emotionally alive material of George's life is worked on in ways that are theoretically comprehensible.

As another example, let us return to Jean. As we explored her marriage and her desires to leave it, she became quite afraid of making a mistake. What if he was actually "good enough" and it was just her "craziness" that made her think she could have more? What if her desires for more were just romantic beliefs in finding perfection? These fears were explored and felt very deeply by both of us. In the context of doing that, I could say to her, "No one is exactly like us or completely different from us. That makes figuring out whether someone is just too different from us awfully confusing and scary". In other words, we used her terrors to talk about the issue of *discrimination*, the construing of differences between self and others and evaluating whether those differences will injure you (see Leitner, Faidley & Celentana, 2000; Leitner & Pfenninger, 1994).

These interventions are consistent with our definition of treatment as the application of theory to distress. Each intervention allows the client to struggle over an important aspect of the theory of connection versus separation in ROLE relationships. However, these interventions were chosen out of an infinite variety of potential responses because I listened to the material from within the framework of experiential personal construct psychotherapy. The balance here shows the powerful connection and separation inherent in the therapeutic ROLE relationship. The client's aliveness is the essential issue here while the therapist's professional constructions facilitate the work of the therapy. Both persons bring important, essential, vital aspects to the encounter in the therapy room. Absent either one the therapy becomes a façade.

THE ART OF LISTENING FOR THERAPEUTIC ROLE RELATIONSHIP MATERIAL

As I have stated on many occasions previously (e.g., Leitner 1995, 1997), the relationship between therapist and client is, in many ways the primary crucible in which therapy occurs. Therapists who discount this aspect of psychotherapy deny their clients a significant opportunity to use the therapy relationship as a living laboratory for risking profound personal change. Therefore, it is important for the therapist to develop the ability to listen to the client's experience with an attitude toward attending to the implications of the material for the encounter occurring in the therapy room.

ROLE relationships are fundamental to life. When seeking therapy, the client is deciding to risk trusting the therapist with the most central despairs and fears. Not surprisingly, then, the client will need to determine what sort of human being the therapist is. In so doing, the client is actively wrestling with how extensively to connect with the therapist, how much to trust, how deep this relationship can become. In other words, the client is sorting through the complex, ambiguous, frightening, rewarding process of elaborating a ROLE relationship with the therapist.

Implicit in this discussion, then, is the hypothesis that there constantly will be material relevant to the therapy ROLE relationship in the material discussed in therapy. It behooves the therapist to always listen to the client with this hypothesis in mind. Sometimes, this material is obvious in what the client says. For example, Tom refused to discuss his sexual history with me because he did not know whether to trust me with that material or not. This made the issue of discrimination a central focus of therapy – how could he decide whether I was trustworthy or not? What would happen if he decided I was and was wrong? What would happen if he decided I wasn't and was wrong?

At other times, the therapist needs to listen to the process behind the client's material to see the therapeutic ROLE relationship implications. For example, when Jean originally presented, she needed to protect herself by presenting a confusing picture of disorganisation and hallucinations. As she determined she could trust me to engage her deepest fears, she was able to talk more directly about the issue with her husband and the hallucinations decreased. Even when the client-therapist relationship is not being directly discussed, the creative therapist can, through monitoring this process, make important inferences about the relational struggles in the therapy room.

In addition to always assuming the presence of material relevant to the therapy ROLE relationship, therapists can listen to the client's relational history to make inferences about the therapeutic ROLE relationship. Examples include relationships with other therapists, physicians, bosses, parents, and significant others (See Leitner, 1997, for a discussion of this issue). Connecting this previous relational history to the therapy relationship can be quite important. For example, after Jean reported a decrease in hallucinations (in the second session), we began to discuss the ways she often quickly trusted others and then regretted it. She had become sexually involved with her future husband on their first date and later felt like she had to marry him because of that. After I reflected her tendency to trust, then get scared and withdraw, I said, "It will be interesting how that tendency shows itself in our relationship. My hunch is that you will get scared and withdraw from me".

If I can maintain optimal therapeutic distance, I often can have experiences of my client that can help us talk about the process of connecting versus withdrawing from me. For example, as we talked about George's experience of his mother's invasions, I became aware of feeling angry and afraid, feelings I do not often experience in the therapy room. I wondered why I was experiencing these feelings now, with George. This enabled me to share with him my fantasy that a part of him was so enraged by his mother's actions that he was afraid of viciously attacking her. When this intervention was powerfully affirmed (complete with fantasies of mutilating her body), I asked, "What stopped you from sharing this with me before I brought it up?" This question led to his uncertainty that I could be strong enough to engage his rage without panicking.

Notice how, with George, I did not share my feelings of anger and fear. Rather, I used them to move us toward an aspect of our relationship that had not been discussed. At other times, sharing the content of my experience can be powerfully therapeutic. For example, with another client, much more intact than George, I experienced fear. I said to him, "When you talk about this issue, I feel afraid. I very rarely feel fear in the therapy room. What do you think is going on that leads me to feel afraid?" This question led us to the client's fear that he was so angry he could kill someone. Again, we then could discuss what it said about our relationship that he could not share that with me openly and spontaneously.

All feelings I have about my client can be vital clues to the unfolding therapy relationship. However, recognising such feelings often is difficult. I encourage therapists to spend some time actively fantasising about their clients in order to attempt to access some of these submerged communications about the nature of the therapy relationship. Obviously, once accessed, another aspect of therapeutic creativity is how to deal with the communications. As seen above, sometimes they can be discussed directly; at other times they can be used without directly sharing the feelings. Deciding which approach will be most effective for a particular client demands thoughtfulness and humility.

Finally, therapists need to master the art of what I call "relaxed vigilance" and "tactful aggression" in discovering and utilising the therapeutic relationship to facilitate client growth. These terms emphasise the contradictory nature of being a therapist. My ability to be relaxed with my client allows the therapy world to be safe and comfortable. However, while being relaxed, I also vigilantly guard and protect the therapy relationship. Any possible threat to it is confronted and dealt with. So, even if it seems only hypothetical, I may raise the issue. I often have clients who, after a relatively short period of therapy, start to joke with me about this vigilance. For example, Jean came in once and said that she was ready to talk about the dreams she had about her father's sexual abuse. However, she also mentioned that, while driving to her therapy appointment, she had heard the hallucinations again. She already knew that I would want to deal with the hallucinations since they often were ways she retreated from me. I would focus on our relationship first and foremost.

The seemingly contradictory term "tactful aggression" illustrates the ways I use the unfolding therapy relationship. True therapeutic artistry uses aggression in the classic Kellian sense. I actively engage and elaborate my understanding of the client's experiential world. However, this engagement is done tactfully, sensitively, never asking for that which cannot be given. Always inviting the client deeper, never forcing. My clients can then appreciate my simultaneous respect for their distress and my firmly held belief that, together, we can confront what was once unimaginable.

TRUE THERAPEUTIC ARTISTRY

Experiential personal construct psychotherapy, based so firmly within Kelly's personal construct psychology, demands true therapeutic creativity. In this final section, I will briefly distinguish between true therapeutic artistry and the intellectually sloppy views of artistry that can be seen in aspects of experiential therapies today. I will make this distinction by describing Kelly's creativity cycle, still one of the more misunderstood aspects of his theory. It is a cycle that begins with loosened constructions and ends with tightened and validated constructions. Implicitly, he argues that all of therapy, indeed all of life, is a creative process (see Leitner & Faidley, 1999). As with all aspects of his theory, Kelly's words were chosen carefully when describing the creativity cycle. As we will see, the creativity cycle can separate true therapeutic artistry from both treating "patients" technically and from the fringes of some psychologies today.

LOOSENING

The use of the loosening component of the cycle can be seen throughout this chapter. When loosening, I am suspending judgments and allowing the fertile chaos (Kelly, 1955/1991a) of my experience of the client's life take over. I reduce objectivity, heighten subjectivity, and could care less about the "truth" of the hunches I develop. For example, I did not try to tighten and affirm or reject any hypotheses about the "truth" of my anger and fear when listening to George above. Absent loosening, therapy remains a technical doing to people, not a creative being with them. Not surprisingly, many of the intellectually rigorous but emotionally sterile schools of applying manualised treatments to people minimise therapeutic loosening. Leitner and Faidley (1999) describe the loosening component more systematically.

TIGHTENING

However, creative artistry demands more than mere loosening. At some point, I need to tighten my construing and actually engage a real live client in a real live world and determine whether these ways of understanding my client are useful. My ways of engaging the client need to be clear, concise, understandable and consistent. I cannot stay vague, ephemeral, and inconsistent. (This aspect of the creativity cycle separates true artistry from some of the looser "pop psychology" approaches.) Again, Leitner and Faidley (1999) describe this process in more detail.

VALIDATION

Further, creativity is more than a cycling from loosened to tightened constructions. Kelly makes it very clear that the tightened constructions need to be validated. In other words, I can have tightened constructions about past lives, spirit quests, or what have you and not be creative. Creativity demands that these constructions be validated by real clients in the real world of human distress and suffering. Many "theories" of human suffering fail at this particular test of creativity. Some of these theories discount and ignore the experiences of people who invalidate the theory. Obviously, when evidence invalidating a theory is discounted while evidence in support is unquestioned, you have a case for intellectual sloppiness.

More to our point, though, if psychology and psychotherapy are to be about respecting the lived experience of humans, we cannot discount that experience when it invalidates our beliefs, no matter how centrally held. We owe it to our clients (and ourselves) to honor their experience as the only true validation of our theories of the distress, despair, and hope of the human soul. True creativity demands true courage from us, a willingness to test and, if necessary, abandon beliefs so near to our hearts that we feel parts of us are being lost. However, absent that courage, we either are technicians or touchy feely amateurs. Our clients, those persons who entrust their very beings to us, demand and deserve something more.

REFERENCES

Bohart, A. C. (2001, August). The therapist as improvisational artist. Paper presented at the annual meeting of the American Psychological Association, San Francisco, CA.

Bohart, A. C., O'Hara, M. M. & Leitner, L. M. (1998). Empirically violated treatments: Disenfranchisement of humanistic and other psychotherapies. *Psychotherapy Research, 8*, 141–157.

Faidley, A. J. & Leitner, L. M. (2000). The poetry of our lives: Symbolism in experiential personal construct psychotherapy. In J. W. Scheer (Ed.), The person in society: Challenges to a constructivist theory (pp. 381–390). Gieben, Germany: Psychosozial-Verlag.

Kelly, G. A. (1991a). *The psychology of personal constructs: Volume I: A theory of personality.* London: Routledge (originally published 1955).

Kelly, G. A. (1991b). *The psychology of personal constructs: Volume II: Clinical diagnosis and psychotherapy.* London: Routledge (originally published 1955).

Leitner, L. M. (1985). The terrors of cognition: On the experiential validity of personal construct theory. In D. Banister (Ed.), *Issues and approaches in personal construct theory* (pp. 83–103). London: Academic.

Leitner, L. M. (1988). Terror, risk, and reverence: Experiential personal construct psychotherapy. *International Journal of Personal Construct Psychology, 1*, 261–272.

Leitner, L. M. (1995). Optimal therapeutic distance: A therapist's experience of personal construct psychotherapy. In R. Neimeyer & M. Mahoney (Eds), *Constructivism in Psychotherapy* (pp. 357–370). Washington, DC: American Psychological Association.

Leitner, L. M. (1997, July). Transference and countertransference in experiential personal construct psychotherapy. Presented at the International Congress on Personal Construct Psychology, Seattle, WA.

Leitner, L. M. (1999a). Levels of awareness in experiential personal construct psychotherapy. *Journal of Constructivist Psychology, 12*, 239–252.

Leitner, L. M. (1999b). Terror, numbness, panic, and awe: Experiential personal constructivism and panic. *The Psychotherapy Patient, 11(1, 2)*, 157–170.

Leitner, L. M. (2001). The role of awe in experiential personal construct psychotherapy. *The Psychotherapy Patient, 11(3, 4)*, 149–162.

Leitner, L. M. & Celentana, M. A. (1997). Constructivist therapy with serious disturbances. *The Humanistic Psychologist, 25*, 271–285.

Leitner, L. M. & Faidley, A. J. (1995). The awful, aweful nature of ROLE relationships. In G. Neimeyer & R. Neimeyer (Eds), *Advances in personal construct psychology* (Vol. III) (pp. 291–314). Greenwich, CT: JAI.

Leitner, L. M. & Faidley, A. J. (1999). Creativity in experiential personal construct psychotherapy. *Journal of Constructivist Psychology, 12*, 273–286.

Leitner, L. M. & Faidley, A. J. (2001). Disorder, diagnoses, and the struggles of humanness. In J. R. Raskin & S. K. Bridges (Eds), *Studies in meaning: Exploring constructivist psychology*. (pp. 91–121). New York: Pace University Press.

Leitner, L. M., Faidley, A. J. & Celentana, M. A. (2000). Diagnosing human meaning making: An experiential constructivist approach. In R. Neimeyer & J. Raskin (Eds), *Construction of disorders: Meaning making frameworks for psychotherapy* (pp. 175–203). Washington, DC: American Psychological Association.

Leitner, L. M. & Pfenninger, D. T. (1994). Sociality and optimal functioning. *Journal of Constructivist Psychology, 7*, 119–135.

9

Diversity and Multiculturalism in Psychotherapy: A Personal Construct Perspective

DEREK C. OLIVER

MARK W. SCHLUTSMEYER

Approaching psychotherapy from Kelly's (1955) personal construct perspective offers a way of thinking necessary for appropriate engagement of individuals from culturally diverse, marginalised or unempowered groups. The application of constructivist ideas (e.g., constructive alternativism, ROLE relating, sociality) to a framework for psychotherapy addressing the experiences of such individuals will be discussed. A primary advantage of using a constructivist approach to multicultural psychotherapy is that it reflects a worldview held by the therapist and not a therapeutic "technique". Furthermore, the primacy of individual experience is inherent in work with all individuals; thus one does not have to shift lenses or change therapeutic style when working with diverse clients.

Approaches to psychotherapy that honor, respect and fully appreciate the experience of diverse individuals must be developed and incorporated if mental health practitioners are to continue to provide effective services in an ever-changing world. In the current context, the authors construe diversity and multiculturalism in psychotherapy as an endeavor in working with individuals whose experiences may be fundamentally different than those within the "empowered" group of a culture, especially when the therapist is part of that empowered group. This context includes issues related to ethnicity,

Personal Construct Psychology: New Ideas. Edited by Peter Caputi, Heather Foster and Linda L. Viney. Copyright © 2006 John Wiley & Sons, Ltd.

cultural background, sexual orientation, gender and socioeconomic status. We will use the phrases "diverse" and "multicultural" interchangeably to denote those who construe themselves as "marginalised" due to these factors – acknowledging up front that such language itself may be problematic given the different political, social, linguistic, and experiential meanings these terms have for different individuals. It must be noted that the ideas discussed herein are representative of issues encountered by the authors within the cultural milieu of the United States, but we believe these ideas are applicable across contexts.

Effective approaches to psychotherapy should address a way of thinking about the experiences of diverse individuals rather than "multicultural techniques" or manualised ways of thinking about such groups – which may be little more than the propagation of extant stereotypes. Although prescriptive techniques for multicultural sensitivity may contain some validity when applied to large numbers of individuals within a group, we distort the human experience when we assume that any specific technique will apply equally to each individual (Leitner, Begley & Faidley, 1996). This sets up a dilemma for therapists: on one hand it is crucial to acknowledge differences and engage them as a way of thinking in therapy. On the other hand, it is important to avoid approaching diversity in ways that sidestep personal meaning by being rigid, stereotyped, or oversimplified. We believe this dilemma can be addressed by viewing the therapeutic endeavor through the lens of George Kelly's (1955) personal construct psychology and one of its theoretical descendants, experiential personal construct psychotherapy (Leitner, 1988).

MULTICULTURALISM: A PERSONAL CONSTRUCT APPROACH

Of primary importance to our construction of multiculturalism is Kelly's (1955) basic notion of constructive alternativism: in essence, there is an objectively real universe in which we live, but as individuals we can only know it to the extent that we construe it; these constructions are constantly open to revision and replacement. Although we interpret the world in certain ways, it is possible to change those interpretations. For example, based on my experience as a fifth-generation Anglo-American, it may be easy to fall into the trap of construing the experience of a third generation Asian–American as one in which "she should be acculturated by now". However, in doing so I may fail to understand the reasons why she has not "acculturated" and the sense of coherence that results in continuing to adhere to customs found in the culture of origin. Situations may arise which may cause me to revise my understanding of this person. If I discuss with her the importance of holding these customs and beliefs so deeply, I may become more empathic to the processes contributing to the development of her constructs. The necessity of fostering openness to the revisions of one's constructs is the first aspect of our personal construct approach to multiculturalism.

Working from Kelly's (1955) fundamental postulate – that one's thoughts, behaviors, feelings, values, and other psychological processes are dictated by the way events are anticipated based on past experiences – points to the second key aspect of our approach to multiculturalism. This is the working assumption that an individual's culture is defined as the pool of experiences upon which future anticipations will be based. Some of these experiences may feel communal and shared (e.g., participating in a group religious service) while others may feel more individualised (e.g., a feeling of ostracism at a family gathering). This way of thinking about culture prevents the use of rigid assumptions that general cultural trends apply to each person within a particular cultural group. For example, although Asian cultures are typically seen as valuing a collectivist rather than an individualist mindset, a given individual's experience of that collectivist mindset may not necessarily lead her to value it the way others do. When working with individuals, assumptions about the shared aspects of culture should be balanced with an understanding that each individual experiences and anticipates those shared events differently. Our broad definition of culture suggests that all interactions should be construed as multicultural interactions, although some feel distinctly more so than others.

The third and final key aspect of our personal construct approach to multiculturalism is related to Kelly's (1955) sociality corollary and the notion of core role constructs. The sociality corollary defines "social" relationships as interactions in which one person construes the construction process of another person. Of primary importance is how the sociality corollary relates to the core role constructs of the individual. Core role constructs are those that are central to the individual's identity and existence; they bestow upon the person his or her most profound sense of personal meaning. Intimacy in social relationships increases as individuals construe one another's core role constructs. This leads to the third key aspect of our multicultural approach, which is the belief that multicultural social interactions heighten intimacy by directing attention to core role constructs. Even simply looking at someone who seems culturally different can evoke intimate core beliefs – the roots of my experience are so different from yours that we do not even look to be the same kind of person! Because of this heightened intimacy, multicultural interaction provides many opportunities for core validation and core invalidation.

MULTICULTURALISM AND PERSONAL CONSTRUCT PSYCHOTHERAPY

Ivey (1995) noted that psychotherapy could be construed as an endeavor in liberation in which therapists are involved in "helping clients learn to see themselves in relation not only to themselves but also to cultural/contextual influences" (p. 53). One's identity develops on many planes and is multi-systemic. To understand the core role constructs of the individual and to aid in achieving this liberation, all the forces of identity development must be accounted for – personal, family, cultural, and historical. In other words, how have past experiences led to the current way in which events are anticipated? Personal construct therapy focuses on engaging the individual explicitly around this process of development (i.e., assessing the experiential antecedents of present constructs and understanding their implications for current and future functioning). Such engagement becomes a validation of core role constructs associated with the innermost meanings of one's iden-tity. Personal construct therapy thereby seeks liberation from roles and expectations that are often imposed upon marginalised individuals. Thus, personal construct psychotherapy not only respects the experience of the individual as primary and "real" from the perspective of constructive altern-ativism, but also "seeks to inform the individual as to how the social and historical past, present, and future affect cognition, emotion, and action" (p. 54).

Sampson (1993) has elaborated ways in which unempowered persons have been denied voices and the ability to make autonomous decisions about their identity. Given this lack of agency in establishing identity, reluctance to "acculturate into the mainstream" is quite understandable. Even if one assumes marginalised persons did want to completely acculturate (certainly a questionable assumption itself), the lack of acceptance and validation afforded them by dominant society may preclude this possibility. On those occasions when their voices *are* heard, it is typically when speaking with the constructs imposed upon them by the dominant culture rather than from their own experiences and subjectivity. For example, issues of significance to African–Americans are not only underrepresented in research, but "when-ever they are represented, they are presented in the terms controlled by the dominant groups rather than in their own terms" (Sampson, 1993, p. 1220). How can one construe a true sense of personal identity when the terms of such personal identification and the voicing of that identity are dictated by others?

EXPERIENTIAL PERSONAL CONSTRUCT PSYCHOTHERAPY

The lack of validation experienced by many individuals within such groups can be addressed using Leitner's (1988, 1995a, 1995b; Leitner & Dunnett, 1993) Experiential Personal Construct Psychotherapy (EPCP). This approach focuses on ROLE relating, which is inherently tied to the sociality corollary and core role constructs. ROLE relating occurs when we reciprocally allow our core role constructs to be known to one another. To the extent that another person construes the processes by which I maintain the deep personal meanings that are central to my existence and identity (and vice versa), we may engage in a profound and meaningful interpersonal relationship. However, due to the threat and terror of possible invalidation of my core constructs in ROLE relating, I may choose to avoid such relationships, retreating to the safety–yet–meaninglessness that comes with living a life lacking in such relationships. Participating in ROLE relationships rather than retreating from them provides life with richness and profoundness of experience. This process is inherently one of deep emotional content. Thus EPCP, as a therapy that helps one construe distress as a means of avoiding possible core invalidation through ROLE relating, is loaded with intense emotion and profound meaning.

Experiential Personal Construct Psychotherapy can be directly applied to the experiences of marginalised individuals in therapy. If someone has experienced extreme marginalisation, how could he or she possibly risk investing in a ROLE relationship? When the vast majority of persons in mainstream society make no effort to understand a minority person's core role constructs, is it even likely that such persons will engage in many ROLE relationships outside of their own immediate group? The concepts of "threat" and "terror" do not exaggerate the position felt by many minorities and marginalised persons in attempting to engage in meaningful relationships in a society that is often either unable or unwilling to provide core validation.

Such individuals may not only construe themselves as less powerful within a given society, but may also experience the more powerful or dominant members of the society as unable or unwilling to understand their experience of the world. They may even create meanings based upon the expectation that their experiences will be discounted or ignored and thus retreat from meaningful interpersonal relationships (Leitner, Begley & Faidley, 1996). Sadly, efforts to avoid the massive core invalidation that accompanies marginalisation may be labeled "pathology" by mental health professionals. For example, one of the authors worked with an African–American client who was so accustomed to being labeled as paranoid by health professionals that he was completely embarrassed to describe his symptoms. Retreats from ROLE relationships may be manifested in countless ways: impulsivity or passivity (to keep from getting close enough to the other to engage in intimate social processes governed by the sociality corollary), depression (which drains energy resources needed for committing to ROLE relating), fragmented personalities (to keep the totality of one's existence from being invalidated). Personal construct therapy construes these strategies as natural human responses to marginalisation and the ensuing threat of core invalidation – as opposed to clear indicators of "pathology."

Experiential Personal Construct Psychotherapy makes explicit use of sociality and ROLE relating a primary facilitator of movement in therapy. By participating in an environment in which the therapist and the client can engage in the process of ROLE relating, the client can actively overcome the ways in which avoidance of ROLE relationships has led to inner emptiness. Active engagement in ROLE relating within the therapeutic environment allows the individual to reconstrue the world as one in which emptiness and meaninglessness are not necessary. This is in large part achieved through optimal therapeutic distance: active engagement of the feelings of the other from an empathic perspective while simultaneously acknowledging the separateness of the other's constructions as self-owned and not belonging to you (i.e., the therapist) (Leitner, 1995a).

When working with diverse or marginalised clients, optimal therapeutic distance is often difficult to achieve; the relationship that develops may be one in which therapist and client are actually "therapeutic strangers" (Leitner, 1995a): the therapist – due to overt or covert influences – is unable to connect at a core role level and engage in a relationship founded upon sociality. For the majority of therapists who work with minority clients, this can have detrimental effects in therapy; the individual feels further removed and rejected by a member of the dominant society. This is not to imply that such rejection is intentional; it may be attributed to the therapist's lack of awareness of his or her own ethnocentrism, lack of understanding of subtle forms of racism or sexism, or focus on a presenting problem without paying proper attention to cultural or other systemic factors. However, even unintentional or subtle forms of indifference to cultural differences may have a significant impact on the individual client and the therapeutic relationship.

ROLE RELATIONSHIPS AND THE VALIDATION OF CULTURAL EXPERIENCE

ROLE relating necessitates a key focus on an experiential understanding of the individual, including constructions of the culture of origin and experiences of invalidation by the empowered majority as well as an understanding of the meaningfulness that is derived through an individual's current construction of the world. By contrast, cognitive therapies, for example, may discount the importance of the meaning system found in present constructions of the world and aim merely to "fix distortions" without empathically and experientially subsuming the client's process of meaning-making. When applied to work with marginalised individuals, this "fixing of distortions" is subtly yet inherently based upon constructions of the world that are rooted in acceptance of the values of the dominant culture as more "correct" than those of the marginalised culture. Judith Katz (1985), for example, has noted that many therapists are unaware of the cultural values that they bring into the psychotherapeutic endeavor and as such act as "perpetuators of cultural oppression" (p. 615).

As a brief example, one of the authors experienced these struggles during his time as a psychotherapist within a prison setting with a diverse population of individuals. He found that therapy participants often interacted in ways that other mental health professionals were labeling as defensiveness, resistance, and minimisation. One African–American client initially referred to the therapist as a "pampered white male" who would not be able to understand and relate to his personal experiences. From a personal construct perspective, this minority client may have quite legitimately expected therapy to be yet another instance of marginalisation, misunderstanding and persecution. Such expectations are understandable because many approaches to therapy typically view certain thought patterns and behaviors as "correct" and others as "distorted". In fact, other components of the individual's rehabilitation program specifically sought to "fix distortions". For this client and therapist, however, discussion of differences in their cultural backgrounds and experiences, and exploration of ways in which the therapist might better understand the client's ways of construing his world, allowed a much different understanding to emerge. An empathic and mutually respectful relationship was able to develop.

Kelly's (1955) choice corollary is important for understanding how EPCP fosters these kinds of relationships in the multicultural therapy context. The choice corollary states that an individual construes the world in ways that he or she anticipates will lead to further extension and definition of the overall meaning system. This corollary presumes that people make choices that they

feel will improve the goodness-of-fit between the world and their anticipations of it. If a psychotherapist is not mindful of the choice corollary, he or
she may hesitate to address the elaboration of "growth choices" related to
core role constructs associated with ethnic or group identity. This hesitation
may be due to a lack of awareness regarding personal biases that arise in
working with such individuals, or because the therapist construes such issues
as "marginal" to the presenting problem. Issues of cultural identity and bias,
however, may indeed be primary even if the presenting problem is couched
in other terms.

For example, if mistrust toward others is employed by an Hispanic–
American as a mode of retreating from ROLE relating (remembering that
retreat in this manner is seen as more rewarding and elaborative than ROLE
engagement if we accept the choice corollary), the therapist may fail to
understand the meaningfulness of this choice and may choose to focus on
"symptom reduction" rather than construct and meaning elaboration. The
individual will often (rightly) construe this therapist's response as destruct-
ive invalidation of his or her position, which has developed due to lack of
validation and support from the dominant majority to begin with. This continued invalidation perpetuates his choice of retreat and avoidance of ROLE
relating and further contributes to impoverished relating. Thus, it is
imperative of a therapist to engage the patient in his or her own personal
meanings rather than retreating from the experience of the individual. The
therapist's self-awareness of personal biases is of crucial importance so that
such biases do not obstruct the process of coming to understand the client's
ways of making meaning.

EPCP AS A MULTICULTURAL WORLDVIEW

An experiential personal construct approach to psychotherapy with diverse
populations is consistent with ethical imperatives advocated by various
authors. For example, Sue et al. (1992) outlined a conceptual framework for
competency in cross-cultural counseling. Of primary importance is understanding the worldview of the culturally different client involved in this
process is the recognition of how race, culture and ethnicity affect how
one's processes are "psychologically channelised", to use Kelly's (1955)
terms. Essential to this engagement is, among other issues, respect for the
client's religious beliefs and conceptualisations about mental health; awareness of institutional barriers, sociopolitical influences and the implications
of family networks and hierarchies; and awareness of one's own biases,
stereotypes and preconceived ideas about a group. None of these considera-

tions is met if the therapist is not able to fully subsume the experience of the other and engage in deep ROLE relating with the individual. EPCP requires, by definition, that the totality of the client's experiences be respected in the establishment of the therapeutic relationship. Optimal therapeutic distance in such situations is based upon a ROLE relationship in which the therapist is empathic to the processes of construing and meaning-making associated with cultural influences, coupled with a mutual awareness by both parties that the therapist may never be a part of that culture.

One of the most beneficial aspects of EPCP is that one works with all individuals in the same manner without finding it necessary to adopt another lens when working with a person of another race, religion, sex, socioeconomic group, and cultural group. If the therapist is truly able to engage from a personal construct perspective and value the processes of human meaning making, he or she will be able to work comfortably and competently with a culturally diverse or marginalised individual. Such engagement is reflective of a personal worldview held by the therapist and not a "therapeutic hat" that is taken off at the end of the hour. If multicultural sensitivity is used as a strategy or technique, the client will perceive a less than genuine validation of the human experience and ROLE relationship will be preempted.

SUMMARY AND CONCLUSION

Approaching the therapeutic relationship from a personal construct framework offers many advantages from which to conduct culturally-sensitive psychotherapy. Its primary tenet is respect for the primacy of the experience of the individual and the honoring of the construction system of the client to facilitate an empowering ROLE relationship. We have argued that marginalisation of diverse clients may create barriers to individual understanding in therapy that may not be overcome by more common multicultural awareness "techniques" alone. Personal construct therapists attempt to address these barriers through genuine engagement with clients' personal meanings. From a construct perspective, this manner of engagement is inherent in work with all individuals; therefore, one does not have to shift perspectives, refocus, or change therapeutic style when working with someone from a culturally different group. In fact, to rely on such shifts may damage the relationship. The client is aware of the genuineness of the engagement and may in fact reject a therapist he or she felt was adopting a specific role that was not coherent with the therapist's value system. In our view, a therapist's multicultural sensitivity must therefore be experienced by both the client and the therapist as a tacit and deeply-held worldview.

REFERENCES

Ivey, A. E. (1995). Psychotherapy as liberation: Toward specific skills and strategies in multicultural counseling and therapy. In J. G. Ponterotto, J. M. Casas, L. A. Suzuki & C. M. Alexander (Eds), *Handbook of multicultural counseling*. Thousand Oaks, CA: Sage Publications.

Katz, J. H. (1985). The sociopolitical nature of counseling. *The counseling psychologist, 13*, 615–624.

Kelly, G. A. (1955). *The psychology of personal constructs* (2 vols). New York: Norton.

Leitner, L. M. (1988). Terror, risk, and reverence: Experiential personal construct psychotherapy. *International Journal of Personal Construct Psychology, 1*, 251–261.

Leitner, L. M. (1995a). Optimal therapeutic distance: A therapist's experience of personal construct psychotherapy. In R. A. Neimeyer & M. J. Mahoney (Eds), *Constructivism in psychotherapy*. Washington, DC: American Psychological Association.

Leitner, L. M. (1995b). Dispositional assessment techniques in experiential personal construct psychotherapy. *Journal of Constructivist Psychology, 8*, 53–74.

Leitner, L. M., Begley, E. A. & Faidley, A. J. (1996). Cultural construing and marginalised persons: Role relationships and ROLE relationships. In D. Kalekin-Fishman & B. M. Walker (Eds), *The construction of group realities: Culture, society, and personal construct theory*. Malabar, FL: Krieger.

Leitner, L. M. & Dunnett, N. G. M. (1993). *Critical issues in personal construct psychotherapy*. Malabar, FL: Krieger.

Sampson, E. E. (1993). Identity politics: Challenges to psychology's understanding. *American Psychologist, 48*, 1219–1230.

Sue, D. W., Arredondo, P. & McDavis, R. J. (1992). Multicultural counseling competencies and standards: A call to the profession. *Journal of Multicultural Counseling and Development, 20*, 64–88.

10

Making Sense of Dementia

SALLY ROBBINS

MIKE BENDER

INTRODUCTION

The story of the book of Genesis articulates my personal starting point in
exploring the experience of the phenomena called dementia. In essence it
says that even in paradise, in perfect happiness, humans choose the pursuit
of knowledge and understanding rather than the continuation of that happy
state. Perhaps the American Bill of Rights got it wrong then; "the pursuit of
happiness" may not be the be all and end all. It seems to me that this is the
archetypal expression of the Choice Corollary; "a person chooses for himself
that alternative in a dichotomised construct through which he anticipates the
greater possibility for extension and definition of his system" – even if it
means being cast out of paradise.

Given this, what sense can I make of a life in dementia, when abilities fail
and memories fade, until it seems impossible to build experiences into a
coherent whole? The very thought challenges my deepest held beliefs about
the purpose of existence. Viney (1993) reminds us of the "severe threat" and
guilt feeling that can be experienced by therapists "who are reminded that
they too may be older, ill, and even cognitively impaired one day". When
I am with these people I experience this, and I also have a sense of
Fragmentation, since for myself I fear that a life like theirs may not be
worth living, and yet when I am with someone who is having such experiences I feel that their life is.

Personal Construct Psychology: New Ideas. Edited by Peter Caputi, Heather Foster and Linda L.
Viney. Copyright © 2006 John Wiley & Sons, Ltd.

In recent years Tom Kitwood made the subject of dementia his own, and indeed no '90's work on dementia is complete without its Kitwood references. Fundamentally Kitwood talked about Personhood, the essential quality of humanity:

> The time has come . . . to recognise men and women who have dementia in their full humanity. Our frame of reference should no longer be person – with – DEMENTIA, but PERSON – with – dementia. (Kitwood, 1997, p. 7).

He emphasises the importance of the relationships that people with dementia experience:

> To see personhood in relational terms is, I suggest, essential if we are to understand dementia. Even when cognitive impairment is very severe, an I-Thou form of meeting and relating is often possible. (Kitwood, 1997, p. 12).

The task of trying to reconstrue dementia within a Personal Construct Psychology (PCP) framework which we are attempting is essentially one of building a bridge between existing ideas on dementia in the literature, such as those of Kitwood, and the PCP world of understanding and facilitating change, and incorporating our own experiences in the process. Perhaps the issues involved can be best envisaged if we consider one person's experience. If we start then, with the story of a real person, who I shall call Jennie. Her experiences trouble and challenge me, and they represent in full measure the phenomena I want to understand better.

In just over three years I have seen Jennie change from a woman in work and coping with a home and family, to someone who is not always able to acknowledge or react to the presence of others and who screams frequently through her waking day. I struggle to make any sense of this.

In this chapter we present some attempts we have made to make that sense.

THE EXISTING THEORIES AND PROBLEMS WITH THEM

In essence the current mainstream view of dementia comes from medicine and can be summarised as involving a reification along these lines:

> Dementia is an illness, or a cluster of illnesses, which can be distinguished from normality and from each other. Research work is concentrated on endeavouring to find drug treatments and cures for the illness (NICE 2001), and there are some non-curative things which can help a bit. Dementia usually starts small but moves on inexorably until you die.

Over the last 30 or 40 years there have grown up alongside these medical understandings of dementia a range of psychological approaches to the issues. To a large extent these have centred on attempts to do something useful to help people with these problems, but in doing this they put forward explicit, or sometimes implicit, ways of understanding what is going on. Reality Orientation (Woods, 1992), Reminiscence (Bender et al., 1999; Butler, 1963), Validation Therapy (Feil, 1994) and Person Centred Dementia Care (Kitwood & Bredin, 1992) are the most influential examples of such psychological approaches.

By their nature our theories constrain us. We are indeed psychologically channelised. In emphasising one thing we neglect another. Our own efforts will be equally flawed in this way.

The medical theories have led to therapeutic nihilism for most of the last century, and even with the arrival of "anti-dementia" drugs there is still a lack of room in this approach for any other therapeutic input. The presumption, as with the medical approach to depression, is that the psychological manifestation is caused by neurotransmitter malfunctions, and if we can just manipulate these enough, all will be well. Perhaps the most troubling aspect of the medical theory is its classic demonstration of a construct system defended by hostility. Mike Bender (Bender, 1998; Bender & Wainwright, 1998) has articulated the problems thoroughly and clearly.

The psychological theories differ from the medical in many ways. Clearly they explicitly avoid the therapeutic nihilism, but certainly Reality Orientation and Reminiscence have quite restricted ranges of convenience.

Validation Therapy is drawn up in a very preemptive and constellatory way. The combination of its style of construing and its content makes me feel that it is disrespectful to the people it talks about. Finally, in Person Centred Dementia Care, Kitwood and colleagues do indeed link biomedical research with the personal and social context, as Kitwood (1997) aimed, but the system remains quite loose, and at times simplistic. Much of the theory remains quite general in nature, with most of the subordinate level of construing remaining unclear.

THE EXPERIENCE OF DEMENTIA

"I am going mad"

"Am I going mad?"

"I feel useless"

"It's so annoying"

"I feel so stupid"

"They're making a fuss"

"I don't know what you are talking about"

"I used to be able to . . ."

These are the sorts of things that people say to me when I meet them to discuss problems with memory, particularly when they come for an initial appointment at our Coventry Memory Clinic. Often they repeat the statements, elaborate on them, give examples. Sometimes they cry. Their sense of cumulative and unexpected invalidation is palpable. Over and over again they find that something expected by them, their friends, their relatives, you, me and the dog has not happened . . . and for no obvious reason. This is truly terrible. They are anxious, fearful and threatened, and rightly so. They do not know when they can trust themselves and often a fragmented sense of self is apparent; "I am capable, can and have done this, that, and the other, but sometimes – often even, it doesn't work – I am useless".

For some people the impact on their sense of self of all this invalidation seems to be cushioned by their relationships with others. I have noticed this happening with several of the people I have known over some years but it is well illustrated by one man in particular I recall; let's call him Alf. When I met Alf and his wife his cognitive abilities were really quite poor. He could remember very little of what was said or of what happened during the day. He had no idea what time it was or what day, and quite often he would struggle to express himself, losing words or losing track of what he wanted to say. At times these things troubled him, and his wife was consistently troubled by his repetitive questions, as he tried to fill in the gaps in his awareness. His ability to engage with me and others, and to interact socially and appropriately remained strong, despite this loss of verbal skill, but all the time he was aware of not remembering much.

In spite of these experiences he was generally quite cheerful. In part he was able to console himself about his memory losses by saying he had not been much good at school and by rehearsing some old facts which he could remember, thus minimising the apparent extent of his decline. The contact with us was driven by his wife's hope that we could do something to help rather than any impetus from him. To me though, it seemed that most of his sense of well being was drawn from his relationship with his wife. His close loving relationship with her seemed to help him to maintain an active sense of himself in relation to her and to others: Kitwood's personhood in action

I think. I think this is more than the phenomena that Kelly referred to as some psychological functions being more disturbed than others, and as "certain formalised social skills" being relatively preserved (Kelly, 1991, Vol 2, p. 256). I think Alf shows "an awareness of validation of (his) core structure" (McCoy's [1977] definition of love, p. 109) which helps him to overcome the fragmenting influence of the other invalidations he experiences. Alf and his wife can co-create and preserve a sense of "true self" for him which is slightly apart from the self that relies on doing and achieving – or indeed not doing so.

Epting (1977) suggested that "love is a process of validation and invalidation which leads to the best elaboration of ourselves as complete persons" (p. 52). I think this extended description also works well for what I am trying to describe in Alf, since it is the preservation of a sense of a complete self, in the face of a multitude of invalidating experiences from outside their relationship that is at issue. From moment to moment, on minor issues, he seems to use the subtle responses of his wife to guide his behaviour, using her judgement to supplement his own. These responses can be invalidating as well as validating, and are equally valuable in both forms. The fundamental validation of his core structure is secure and so he is free to experience some invalidation in subordinate construing without this impacting too much on his sense of self.

There is a tendency in theorising about dementia because of the language of "validation therapy" and of person centred dementia care to value only the validating (in PCP terms) responses, which I think misses out half the story.

SOME ATTEMPTS TO UNDERSTAND DEMENTIA USING PCP

Clare Morris (2000) tells us:

> In my view we need a model of the person that can be applied equally to the person with dementia at all stages of the disease; family and formal caregivers; and you and me. A framework to describe the process of therapy, and which integrates the eclectic influences of the cultural revolution in dementia care. Personal Construct Psychology is such a framework. (p. 23)

Kelly, as ever, made a good start on this. In his chapter on Disorders of Transition (Kelly, Volume II, 1991 pp. 222–264) he outlines two, and maybe a third "well documented facts" about "conditions of organic deficit".

First, he says that "in cases of organic deterioration or injury some broad types of psychological functions are disturbed more than others". He says this relates to "greater loss of memory for recent events" as opposed to relatively preserved vocabulary and certain language skills, even after sharp impairment of problem solving, and "retention of certain formalised social skills long after social sensitivity has been blunted".

Second he noted that "the physiologically handicapped person tends to constrict his field of spontaneous elaboration" and he linked this to "rigidity", "perseveration", and "general ineptitude in changing the course of one's thinking". Earlier, Kelly stated

> When one minimises the apparent incompatibility of one's construction systems by drawing in the outer boundaries of one's perceptual field, the relatively repetitive mental process that ensues is designated as 'constriction" (Vol 1, p. 352).

Third he says that some clinical psychologists notice a link between people referring to organic impairment in testing and actually having it. Kelly reckons this suggests the person's areas of recent spontaneous elaboration (Kelly, 1991, Vol 2, pp. 256–257).

He describes the task of the "organically deteriorated person" as reconstruing himself:

> in a constricted world, using as his point of departure the constructs which were once richly documented, and gradually substituting them for constructs dealing with new content and with new and limited ranges of convenience.

He is also characteristically clear on the role of the therapist – to help the client to develop:

> constructs that will bridge the past, the present, and the future, even though, for this particular client, the events of these periods may seem markedly different from each other.

He tells us directly:

> The life role must be firmly established . . . it is extremely important that the significance of his earlier life be carefully preserved and enhanced. The therapist must help him develop a sense of personal history and destiny that will help him to see his life role as something far more than the little daily orbit that he taps out with his cane.

Sometimes I wonder why I bother trying to work things out for myself, when I discover Kelly so neatly and succinctly anticipating reminiscence therapy and the so called revolution of bringing personhood into dementia care by so many years.

On the more specific issues of the construing of such people, Kelly introduces the idea of a "deteriorated construct" – "one that has become relatively impermeable". He says these are common in "organic and aged cases".

Finally, he concludes this section with a brief warning on differential diagnosis which I think many colleagues would benefit from considering. He notes that the "organic picture" is one of "attempted reconstruction which may ensue from other handicaps as well". He says that this picture might also be seen in someone with a "deep-seated feeling of inadequacy", or with "a toxic disturbance", or with a "psychological handicap or trauma" as well as in truly "organic cases". As a result he cautions us to "consider the constricting behaviour as the client's own attempt to make an adjustment to his changing situation".

Elsewhere, in Volume 1, Kelly (1991) talks explicitly about the issue of forgetting:

> In order for an experience to be remembered or perceived clearly it must be supported within a system of constructs. (p. 348)

He explains that as constructs and structures are changed some elements drop out whilst others are more prominent as the goodness of fit changes or the range of convenience alters. This obviously works well for the forgetting of old material, and is perhaps particularly appropriate for forgotten things from childhood. Finally he tells us that in the normal run of psychotherapy:

> When an idea is mislaid because the person has no place to file it, it need not be forever lost. Usually there is enough systematic structure surrounding it to keep it from escaping altogether.

Morris and Kelly, then, give us a starting point in considering dementia from a PCP point of view. In the autumn of 2000 Bender and I drew up a list of the sort of examples people described to us when they were talking about their problems with memory and related issues (Robbins & Bender, 2000). We drew this together into what Bender termed "A taxonomy of unexplained losses". As we looked at them they seemed to cluster into a number of groups which we might make sense of in slightly different ways. The first cluster seemed to concern the capturing of new information, but others concerned more varied functions. I reproduce our list below:

A TAXONOMY OF UNEXPLAINED COGNITIVE LOSSES

Cluster 1

- Can't remember messages
- Can't remember instructions
- Can't remember recent conversations
- Can't remember where I've put things

Cluster 2

- Forgetting what I want to say
- Repeated questioning
- Anxiety at separation – perhaps so bad that the partner "ceases to exist" if they go to the toilet, so the door has to be kept open
- Excessive slowness of response, though eventually the right response is produced
- Variability in ability across a short time span – being "on the blink"

Cluster 3

- Putting things in very odd places – e.g., bacon in the washing machine
- Failure to successfully complete a sequence of very well learnt behaviours, such as making tea
- Failure to do what used to be easy – e.g., an accountant unable to sign a cheque
- Failure to recognise family members
- Misidentifying family members
- Incoherent speech which makes little or no sense to listeners

Cluster 4

- Paranoid ideation – burglars or the partner has moved papers

Cluster 5

- Unlikely accusations of infidelity

Cluster 6

- Social withdrawal, even when social competence and relationships are apparently maintained
- Flatness of affect – that which used to please and motivate no longer does – shown granddaughter's scholarship says "Very nice, What's for tea?"

Cluster 7

- Restlessness and wandering

Cluster 8

- Panic at failure to accomplish previously easily undertaken behaviours, such as seeing friends and relatives
- Anxiety at anticipation of a previously easily undertaken behaviour, like going to town

These brief descriptions can mean different things with different people, depending on the situation. What is reported as failure to identify family members, for example, may concern a difficulty in naming them, or might be a loss of "normal" reaction to them. We might discover that the reaction normalises when the person speaks, as if the difficulty lies in visual recognition but is corrected when more information in different modalities is available. When faced with one of these brief descriptions of behaviour we might therefore want to say "It depends!" until we have more detail. Whilst acknowledging that in the particular case we need to ask more and to listen carefully, to make sure we have a good understanding of what the person means when they say these things, I think it is possible to draw some conclusions about what is going on, at least under certain circumstances.

The single uniting factor in the list that we drew up from what people tell us is happening to them is the experience of invalidation. What follows that experience depends on what construct has been invalidated, how it is being used, where it is in their system, and how it relates to the rest of the system; that is to say, there might be a whole range of different outcomes. Any number of outcomes, anxiety, fear, threat, guilt, shame, constriction, or indeed aggression, may be identified, depending on how the so-called invalidation is experienced for that person at that time.

If the construct is being used loosely the event may not even be experienced as invalidation. Consider, for example, the event of dropping something. A juggler may accept dropping things at times; perhaps the overall "batting average" is more important than the individual event (tight superordinate with looser subordinate constructs). However, if the construct were to be tight and perhaps linked by regnancy to core constructs, then we may experience guilt, shame and threat, as the event invalidates a core self construct and dislodges the person both from their own and from their understanding of others views of themselves. Someone whose family experiences Huntington's Disease might have this reaction if they drop something, trip up or shake unexpectedly; this invalidating experience is likely to be more salient to them and to their view of themselves than it would be to others. In this case even a single instance of clumsiness is likely to be much more meaningful than it is to the rest of the population, since Huntington's Disease is characterised by involuntary movements and small problems with movement and gait are often early signs that a person is developing symptoms which will increase and eventually incapacitate them. Since this disorder is inherited through a dominant gene, people often live for years with the fear of developing it and in the knowledge that there is a 50 % chance that this will happen. At the same time they are perhaps living with, or in contact with, other family members who have the disease, and thus very painfully aware of the symptoms and their significance.

In attempting to look at this in more detail, and in order to identify some patterns which PCP can further illuminate, I will consider in turn the clusters in the taxonomy presented earlier.

Cluster 1

- Can't remember messages
- Can't remember instructions
- Can't remember recent conversations
- Can't remember where I put things

Fundamentally these experiences are characterised by a failure to incorporate new information. The general function is there, the old information is there, but the latest examples are either missing or inaccessible.

There may be a few things going on here. Overall, this bit of the system is functioning in a looser way; it has an identity but using it can lead to a range of predictions which vary from time to time – now you remember/now you don't. Kelly tells us that loose construing is often preverbal (Kelly, 1991 Vol. 2, p. 365). Certainly if some of the constructs concerned are preverbal this is likely to affect the way they operate, with normally easy or verbal labels being less easy to access, for example. Quite often in these situations the person retains some sense, a feeling or a general idea but not the detail or the verbal label. Dalton (1985) reminds us of a similar phenomenon noted by Bartlett (1932) in his experiments on memory:

> people seldom took the situation detail by detail, but rather tended to get a general impression of the whole, on the basis of which they constructed the probable detail. This was the case whether the material was verbal narrative, pictures or faces. (Dalton, 1985, p. 8).

From this it seems that some more general aspects of memory function may be working normally, but that it is the construction of the subordinate specifics which is the problem.

There also seems to be some issue of permeability/impermeability in this situation. Is the new information perhaps not included in the relevant construct at all? In this case the construct may have become less permeable. Perhaps we have some of Kelly's (1991) "deteriorated constructs" making themselves felt. This issue is probably most easily illustrated by the fourth example – *can't remember where I put things*. Suppose the event is my forgetting that I have put my newly arrived Tesco vouchers in my handbag. Where are they? Has someone taken them? I have a, probably detailed but not updated, list of what is in my handbag. The construct, perhaps something like: "things in my handbag . . . stuff I've got" elsewhere stands, but its operation has changed so that it is distinctly less useful.

To continue looking at these first four experiences, we might begin to ask what else is happening. One possibility is that there is constriction in the perceptual field. Kelly (1991) has already warned us to look out for constriction in spontaneous elaboration. If fear or threat is being experienced there may be a corresponding constriction in the perceptual field in order to minimise the apparent incompatibility of having some constructs suddenly and unexpectedly invalidated, so that the information we are expecting to see later was not available for construing in the first place. Many people who are experiencing problems with memory and other mental functions certainly do express feelings of fear and threat, not surprisingly, as we have seen. If there is constriction in the perceptual field this might then lead to a situation in which new experiences and pieces of information are not incorporated into the system, a gap in memory.

Maybe it is also worth invoking the Choice Corollary in this respect; perhaps taking in this new information is not perceived as extending or further defining the persons system . . . so they choose not to. This may sound glib, and perhaps is a non sequitor; "people forget because . . . they don't choose to remember!" This point is difficult to express well, but Peggy Dalton's (1985) paper might assist. She tells us that in Bartlett's (1932) thinking about why some memories are dominant and others less so or missing he hypothesised that they were related to the individual's "appetite, instinct, interests and ideals". This expresses more accessibly my sense that some failures of memory are related to a lack of salience in the materials and/or the situation.

To recap then, I am suggesting that when someone says "I can't remember messages and instructions, and I keep forgetting recent conversations and where I have put things" then we might begin to consider whether;

  (i) parts of the system are operating loosely
 (ii) parts of the system have reduced in permeability
(iii) constructs have deteriorated
(iv) there is constriction in the perceptual field (perhaps linked to threat), and
 (v) whether or not there is some other aspect of life that is more salient – which led to a choice to focus on that rather than to retain the information in the context of a perception that memory is constructed and that detail is dependent on the general impression. If we can begin to see, for an individual person, whether these constructions of memory and forgetting fit, then we can begin to engage with them in developing a shared understanding of what is happening. This might make the situation less scary for both of us, counteracting some of the threat and anxiety we both feel. We might also begin to see if any of the psychotherapeutic approaches we use in other domains can be usefully extended to help in this one. If I am able to work on in this way I can ask myself – Can I dilate this far? Is my system permeable enough? and Do the constructs remain useful if I do? If I can proceed with this then my own journey to know continues.

Cluster 2

- Forgetting what I want to say
- Repeated questioning
- Anxiety at separation – perhaps so bad that the partner "ceases to exist" if they go to the toilet, so the door has to be kept open
- Excessive slowness of response, though eventually the right response is produced
- Variability in ability cross a short time span – being "on the blink"

Moving down the list which Bender and I constructed, I would suggest that forgetting what you want to say, repetitive questioning, anxiety at the partner's absence and excessive slowness may be seen as extensions of these same ways of construing events; Looseness, Impermeability, Constriction and Choice. They too hinge on an unexpected gap in the person's knowledge of recent events; if what I have said, what you said, and where you have gone are inaccessible, then what I was going to do or say in response is also hard to pinpoint. In the same way as the first four examples, in these circumstances it would be all too easy for bits of information to slip through the mind's net, or even to fail to register in the first place, because of a combination of a greater tendency towards looseness and the use of preverbal construsts, changes in construct permeability, constriction, and a lack of salience in the task. In such circumstances the person might become very slow and deliberate in their functioning in an attempt to maximise the tightness of their construing.

Cluster 3

- Putting things in very odd places – e.g., bacon in the washing machine
- Failure to successfully complete a sequence of very well learnt behaviours, such as making tea
- Failure to do what used to be easy – e.g., an accountant unable to sign a cheque
- Failure to recognise family members
- Misidentifying family members
- Incoherent speech which makes little or no sense to listeners

This next cluster of six losses may also be seen as different manifestations of loosening in previous tight constructs or clusters of constructs. If we take the bacon example, there are not very many appropriate things to do with bacon . . . put in shopping bag, put on supermarket checkout, put in fridge, put in frying pan, put under grill, put on plate, put on kitchen table to be chopped – and a few more. Which is right and when depends on the superordinate about the activity, e.g., shopping or cooking. If we introduce looseness we might get the wrong combinations of activity or a greater variety of elements – instead of fridge we get "things in kitchen with doors" perhaps, or we operate on the tacit/kinaesthetic/procedural level of the feel of opening the door and putting the bacon in (usually) the fridge.

Clare Morris (1999, p. 28) talks about a similar disability in her article on visual impairment and problems of perception. She notes that some people have difficulties with the meanings of the perceptions they make; with the associative aspects of objects. In such a situation the person can see and feel the object but may not know what it is, and/or what implications this has. Even if I know something is bacon, I may not be able to access the other meaningful constructs linked with this, including perhaps the superordinate ones about objects which go in the fridge. Equally, I may know the bacon is a cold pink packet of something, and the fridge is a white metal box, but not be able to connect these perceptions more meaningfully. Somehow I cannot move around my pre-existing system so that my construing has greatly reduced meaning and utility. These remarks would obviously apply equally well to the recognition of family members, and perhaps to the cheque signing if it is linking the presence of the cheque with the act of signing which is the problem.

The other aspect of the previously invoked changes in construction which seems particularly relevant here is the Choice Corollary issue. My own experience of "doing funny things" and misplacing objects suggests that this usually occurs when I am preoccupied, i.e., when I have chosen to deal mainly with some other issue. I think that at such times the rest of my construing is looser. I wonder if the mistakes which people with cognitive losses make are in part due to an exaggerated form of this. Certainly under threat the person might tend to constrict their perceptual field and to tighten their construing in the area in focus. This might then leave less capacity for dealing tightly in more peripheral areas of the perceptual field, in this case the face, or the bacon.

Cluster 4

- Paranoid ideation – burglars or the partner has moved papers

When we consider the issue of paranoid ideas that someone has stolen or moved things, it appears initially to be a hostile reaction. Kelly (1991) defines hostility as:

> the continued effort to extort validational evidence in favour of a type of social prediction which has already been recognised as a failure (Vol 2, p. 7).

Some validation or invalidation about the whereabouts of the object concerned has been available, but the person is acting as if this is not so. However, I think it may well be inaccurate to think of this behaviour as hostile, since the words "has already been recognised as a failure" beg the question "has it?". Certainly if, for example, a decrease in permeability means elements have not been construed as expected by the person's system, then it is as if the incident has never happened to them. In this case the most reasonable way for that person to understand what is happening is that someone else has moved the object.

Furthermore, if the here and now situation includes some sense of feeling silly, and of others doubting one's word, then the issue of whether someone has done this on purpose, perhaps as a joke or trick, might well arise. If we add to this mix that it is highly probable that the person is feeling more anxious than is his or her norm, he or she may well have shifted his or her position on some kind of capable–vulnerable construct. If, moreover, they had previously construed others as potentially malign it is then a very short step to "I didn't do it . . . so someone must have . . . and they meant to . . . they have taken advantage of me while I'm feeling weaker".

Cluster 5

• Unlikely accusations of infidelity

Unlikely accusations of infidelity fit to some extent with the cognitive errors already discussed. They could well be related to the problems in face or person recognition mentioned earlier. For example, if my husband is kissing a family member who is not recognised, or is misrecognised, then the question "What is he doing with her – and why?" might be quite reasonable. If I hug my brother when I see him that will probably fit with a certain area of construing, but if I open the door to the Betterware man and do the same it might lead to some quite different conclusions.

An alternative understanding of this behaviour goes back again to a change in construct permeability, but this time a change to greater permeability in constructs that have been impermeable for a long time. Early in a relationship we might think that our partner is attracted to others as much as she or he is to us. As time goes on we perhaps develop the idea that she or he now only fancies us, or fancies us more than others. This idea is likely, I would suggest, to be linked to some sense of self. This sense of self is likely to change if we experience repeated invalidation of core construing. So if I am different, then perhaps my expectations of close relationships are also open to change. It seems to me that if the Beatles can write a whole song around the "will you still need me . . . when I'm sixty four?" theme, and so many of us act out our insecurity about relationships as we age, by dying our hair and trying to appear unchanged, it should not surprise us that someone with failing mental abilities feels similarly unsure of their relationships.

Cluster 6

- Social withdrawal, even when social competence and relationships are apparently maintained
- Flatness of affect – that which used to please and motivate no longer does, so when shown granddaughter's scholarship says "Very nice, What's for tea?"

With the issues of social withdrawal and flatness of affect we are probably back with constriction. A move to simplify social contacts should help to minimise apparent contradictions in construing, and in doing this others play less of a role in our lives. The other point about the flatness of affect in response to good news about a granddaughter is that a normal reaction relies on the simultaneous connection of a whole range of constructions; those concerning scholarships, those concerning the granddaughter, those concerning the educational context of local schools and predicted attainment, and those concerning how we communicate with our family at the very least.

Cluster 7

- Restlessness and wandering

The wandering example is perhaps the most difficult in our list, since this phrase is used to describe a vast range of different behaviours in my experience. In some places I have worked, you are called a wanderer if you stir at all from your chair. However, if we consider repetitive walking which we cannot make sense of to be "wandering" I think this is often an attempt by the person themselves to make sense of their experience; literally a search for meaning when the immediate environment and one's own position do not make sense. As such we might characterise it as aggressive behaviour, aimed at actively elaborating the person's system.

Cluster 8

- Panic at failure to accomplish previously easily undertaken behaviours, such as seeing friends and relatives.
- Anxiety at anticipation of a previously easily undertaken behaviour, like going to town.

Finally we come to the panic and anxiety items in our list, and I think by this time they seem eminently sensible. This whole experience is one of being unsure whether we have the wherewithal to cope with what life will contain next. This constant anxiety will progress into fear and threat if and when more superordinate construing is undermined by the appreciation of invalidation, e.g., "If this bit of my system is looser perhaps other bits are too – and I don't know it!"

SYNTHESIS – THE STORY OF JENNIE

If any of this is to be of use in thinking about dementia and working with the people affected it needs to be applicable to particular people in their particular circumstances. With this in mind, I turn to my experiences of Jennie, and consider her situation from the "outside in".

I met Jennie through the Coventry Memory Clinic early in 1998 when she was 52. At that point she was living at home with her husband and sons, and working as a school teacher. She had a very active involvement with the church. She was finding it difficult to remember and keep track of all the things she needed to in her working life. She had driven herself to the initial appointment alone, and was not herself particularly concerned about her problems. When she found some of the testing difficult she explained it by saying, for example, that she had never taken much notice of history and so did not know the answers.

In the Clinic we estimated that she had originally had a high level of ability, and there seemed nothing much in the anxiety and depression area. She was physically and emotionally in good shape. There were some queries about her hormonal balance, but these were not excessive. Her new learning was poor, suggestive of some impermeability in the relevant constructs, and her poor recall of commonly known old information appeared to show some loosening in her construct system. The other thing I noticed was her difficulty in zipping up her jacket when it was time to leave. I was not sure if this could best be understood as loosening, leading to a lack of precision in the nonverbal constructs involved, or as impermeability, so that the new instance of zip-doing-up was not incorporated into the existing set of such events, but was generally inclined to see it as the former.

I met with Jennie and her husband to review the outcome of their visit to the Clinic. I confirmed that we thought her memory was poorer than it should be, given all the information we had collected. Jennie seemed unconcerned and did not want to discuss the findings in any depth. It was clear she did not want to hear any more. It was difficult to know quite how she experienced this. It would be easy to see this as constriction, as a way of avoiding the impact of information incompatible with the rest of her view of herself.

Her husband told us in confidence that Jennie's mother had had similar difficulties before her death, but Jennie had not reported this when asked. To date, Jennie has never discussed her own view of her situation with anyone. I have always respected Jennie's position on this but have felt more inhibited and unsure of my role in relation to her as a result. It makes it more difficult to be sure of my role with Jennie, with so little direct validation of my approach.

The next time I met Jennie the picture was much the same, but more extended. She was getting more upset about her memory lapses, and would have spells of two or three days when she had particular difficulty managing her clothes. The only new feature was a difficulty in doing things in the kitchen which involved complex movements and sequencing, particularly if she had to use both hands in a co-ordinated way. It seemed she could not translate into physical action a set of complex tacit constructions when accuracy of the action and precise timing were needed in both hands. Sometimes this would improve if her husband told her what to do with each hand. Whereas we can hesitate or make a slight slip in our speech without losing the communication, if the same sort of thing happens with actions in the kitchen the whole sequence fails – the food is not transferred from pan to plate, or the ingredients are not included and stirred adequately. She had taken early retirement from her job, having returned to work after the long summer break and not been able to function adequately.

I did not see Jennie and her husband again for some months, until September 1999 when the second of her sons left home to go to college. In the meantime she had been prescribed Rivastigmine, and her husband had reported some improvement in spontaneous speech and in the range of language she used after this. He also felt that her memory for day to day events and her ability to talk about them showed some improvement.

The departure of her son left Jennie at home alone much more and she was finding this difficult, particularly as she could no longer tell the time from the clock, and therefore did not know how long it would be before her husband returned from work. She knew when she wanted to know the time and would look at the clock, but what she saw made no sense to her. She was unable to incorporate new experiences of looking at the clock into her existing knowledge base of constructs about how to tell the time. It seemed that parts of this construct system had also become less permeable. Unable to anticipate what the day would bring,–"Is it lunchtime? Will he be home soon?–And should I be doing something?", Jennie began to experience periods of anxiety. After some delay I managed to get a talking watch in the form of a key chain. Jennie could clip it to her clothes and when she pressed the button the time was spoken. This intervention was based on the idea that

Jennie might still have an understanding of time, though not the ability to read a clock, and, like many other people in similar positions, she might be able to learn a new routine if prompted enough. In part this succeeded, but the effect was not great enough. The problems of being alone at home escalated. I think Jennie's experience of anxiety was too great and too frequent to be endured. With the help of one of our social workers, Jennie began to go out to a day care centre run by the Alzheimer's Disease Society once a week and to have carers visiting several times a day.

For some months these arrangements were quite successful, as long as the transport to the day care centre ran on time, so that Jennie was not anxiously awaiting it too long. The day care centre was a great hit. Jennie described it as a "club" and enjoyed the pub lunches and outings she was involved in. She was able to use her abilities in relationships and her familiarity with social situations such as meals and at those times she was free of anxiety. Clearly, she was still able to extend her life to interact with new people in new situations. She was able to remember the general feeling of enjoyment and relaxation when we spoke about the "club". Gradually though, more problems emerged at home. Jennie began to have occasional epileptic fits. She had difficulty recognising the carers and would sometimes get very angry and attack them. She also got more difficult for others to help, particularly with dressing, and would get aggressive and frightened. I think that, faced with a relative stranger in the house she was surprised and frightened, having failed to incorporate her acquaintance with them into an increasingly impermeable construct system. By then, she was at times operating as if none of the recent changes had happened in her life and on such occasions reacted to an "intruder" as she would have years previously. She could not make sense of her own disabilities, or of others' attempts to help, and she could not predict what would come next. Her "normal" predictions based on her impermeable constructs were invalidated, and she reacted with anger.

After this Jennie began to attend the day hospital, where there are a range of staff, who are familiar with problems such as Jennie's, to care for her. Attempts were made to make the support at home more robust so that she could continue to live there, but eventually she was admitted to the hospital ward in October 2000.

When I met with her there she would sometimes say a few words to me and respond to my approach by raising her eyes to me and occasionally smiling. Mostly though, she would potter around talking to herself, and I found it difficult to know what was engaging her. Clearly, she had not stopped her attempts to make sense of the world, but there was an increasing lack of commonality between her construing and mine, and my attempts at sociality were increasingly unsuccessful.

It was decided that she would be best cared for in a specialist unit some miles away, but to date no funding has been available for her. Jennie has therefore remained on the acute ward. Some days her distress is frequent and overwhelming. She hits out at others and seems very frightened. Her sense of anxiety, fear, threat and hostility, perhaps amounting to Leitner's (1985) description of "terror", are palpable. The additional aspect of guilt in Leitner's "terror" is not so directly apparent now, but was certainly very obvious when my conversations with Jennie were more extensive. The experience of those around her, of failing to connect psychologically with her in any helpful way, is very painful. Sometimes it is difficult to see any response from her to anything done or said. At these times it feels there is a complete lack of sociality. I find it very difficult to be with her like this because of my own sense of failure and horror. For a while she was screaming continually through her waking hours, but thankfully, a reduction in medication improved this. Since then she has screamed less frequently and it has been more possible to communicate with Jennie again. My colleague, who saw her just after this change, tells me that when she greeted her Jennie held out her hand and said "Help me".

REFERENCES

Bartlett, F. C. (1932). *Remembering: A study in experimental and social psychology.* Cambridge, UK: Cambridge University Press.

Bender, M. P. (1998). *What happens when you stop using the concept of "dementia"?: a post-disease approach.* Paper given at the Gerontological Research Network Seminar Southampton University, Thursday 12th November.

Bender, M., Bauchham, P. & Norris, A. (1999). *The therapeutic purposes of reminiscence.* London: Sage.

Bender, M. P. & Wainwright, A. (1998). *Dementia: reversing out of a dead end.* PSIGE Newsletter November.

Butler, R. (1963). The life review: an interpretation of reminiscences in the aged. *Psychiatry,* 26, 65–76.

Dalton, P. (1985). *Remembering as reconstruction: A personal Construct view of memory.* Paper submitted for the Diploma in Personal Construct Psychology (Therapy and Counselling) May.

Dalton, P. (1992) Living in the present: the experience of amnesia. *Changes 10(3),* 213–221.

Epting, F. R. (1977). The loving experience and the creation of love. Paper presented at the Southeastern Psychological Association Hollywood Florida. Quoted in F. R. Epting 1984 *Personal Construct Counseling and Psychotherapy,* p. 52.

Feil, N. (1982). *Validation: the Feil method.* Cleveland, Ohio: Edward Feil Productions.

Kelly, G. A. (1991). *The psychology of personal constructs* Volumes 1 and 2 Routledge.

Kitwood, T. (1996). A dialectical framework for dementia. In R. T. Woods (Ed.), A *Handbook of the Clinical Psychology of Ageing* (pp. 267–282). Chichester: John Wiley & Sons, Ltd.

Kitwood, T. (1997). *Dementia reconsidered: the person comes first*. Buckingham: Open University Press.

Kitwood, T. & Bredin, K. (1992). *Person to person: A guide to the care of those with failing mental powers*. Bradford Dementia Research Group.

Leitner, L. M. (1985). The terrors of cognition: On the experiential validity of Personal Construct Theory. In D. Bannister (Ed.), *Issues and Approaches in Personal Construct Theory*. London: Academic Press.

McCoy, M. M. (1977). A reconstruction of emotion. In D. Bannister (Ed.), *New Perspectives in Personal Construct Theory* (pp. 93–124). London: Academic Press.

Robbins, S. E. & Bender, M. P. (2000). *A highway of diamonds with nobody on it – applying Personal Construct Theory to understand dementia*. Discussion paper at a peer supervision meeting PCP and Dementia, Edgeware Community Hospital December.

Viney, L. V. (1993). *Life stories: personal construct therapy with the elderly*. Chichester: John Wiley & Sons, Ltd.

Woods, R. T. (1992). What can be learned from studies on reality orientation? In G. Jones & B. Miesen (Eds), *Care-giving in dementia* (pp. 121–136). London: Routledge.

11

Psychotherapists' Theoretical Orientations as Elaborative Choices

DAVID A. WINTER

FINN TSCHUDI

NICHOLAS GILBERT

INTRODUCTION

The field of psychological therapy presents a bewildering array of choices for the budding psychotherapist, as indeed for the client who is seeking therapy. At last count there were nearly 500 such therapies (Karasu, 1986), and the number is rapidly growing. Since research still indicates that most therapies are roughly equally effective (Wampole et al., 1997), how does the practitioner who wishes to enter this field, or the prospective therapy client, choose between them? From a personal construct theory perspective, such a choice, like any other, would be expected to be based upon anticipated possibilities for the extension or definition of the individual's construct system. In view of the threat which therapists often seem to experience when their favoured models are challenged, and the occasional vehemence of their disputes with those of different orientations, it might also be expected that preferences for therapy reflect individuals' core constructs.

Some indirect support for this position has been provided by a research programme which commenced over 30 years ago, initially to explore

Personal Construct Psychology: New Ideas. Edited by Peter Caputi, Heather Foster and Linda L. Viney. Copyright © 2006 John Wiley & Sons, Ltd.

resistance to the introduction of a therapeutic community in a traditional psychiatric hospital. This provided consistent evidence that the attitudes and preferences of both staff and clients concerning psychiatric and psychological treatment reflect individuals' "personal styles" (Caine & Smail, 1969; Caine, Wijesinghe & Winter, 1981; Caine & Winter, 1993; Winter, 1990). Specifically, staff who favour, or choose to practise, more structured, directive treatment approaches have been found to be more outer-directed and conservative than those who favour less directive, more interpersonally-focused approaches. There have been similar findings with clients, whose personal styles (as assessed by measures of direction of interest and conservatism) have also been found to be reflected in features of their personal construct systems, scores on measures of openness to experience and convergent/divergent thinking, the nature of their presenting symptoms, and their response to different forms of therapy.

A further body of research has demonstrated that in clients (Lyddon & Adamson, 1992; Neimeyer et al., 1993), behavioural scientists (Johnson et al., 1988), and psychotherapists (Arthur, 1999, 2000; Schacht & Black, 1985), individuals' "worldview" reflects their preferences for theoretical orientations, those with a mechanistic worldview preferring a behavioural, and those with an organicist worldview a constructivist, developmental, or psychodynamic, approach. Arthur's (2000) study also found differences on various other aspects of epistemological style and personality between cognitive-behavioural and psychodynamic therapists. In addition, the therapeutic practices of psychotherapists (Vasco, 1994) and the therapeutic preferences of students and psychotherapists (Lyddon, 1989; Neimeyer & Morton, 1997; Neimeyer, Saferstein & Arnold, 2005) have been found to reflect the extent to which their epistemological orientation is constructivist or rationalist.

Our study examined differences between therapists of different orientations using measures of both personal styles and philosophical beliefs, allowing investigation of the relationship between these domains. The use of the repertory grid technique also allowed exploration of therapists' constructions of their own and other therapeutic approaches, and examination of the extent of commonality of their construing within and between orientations. The inclusion of a group of personal construct psychotherapists in the study provided an opportunity to examine their distinctiveness from therapists of other orientations.

Specifically, the hypotheses investigated were that:

(i) outer-directedness is related to rationalist philosophical beliefs;
(ii) therapists of different theoretical orientations differ in inner-directedness, personal construct, humanistic, and psychodynamic

therapists being the most inner-directed and cognitive-behavioural therapists the least;

(iii) therapists of different orientations differ in philosophical beliefs, personal construct, systemic, and humanistic therapists being the most constructivist and cognitive-behavioural therapists the most rationalist; and,

(iv) there is greater commonality of construing of therapists within therapeutic orientations than between therapists of different orientations.

METHOD

PARTICIPANTS

Invitations to participate were sent to the following psychotherapists on the National Register of the United Kingdom Council for Psychotherapy (numbers agreeing to participate are indicated in parentheses):

- 118 analytical psychologists (11);
- 42 cognitive-analytic therapists (5);
- 160 randomly selected cognitive-behavioural therapists (13);
- 281 humanistic therapists, stratified to include each particular humanistic orientation (33);
- 150 hypno-psychotherapists (15);
- 63 neuro-linguistic psychotherapists (8);
- 37 personal construct psychotherapists (9);
- 150 randomly selected psychodynamic psychotherapists (11);
- 152 randomly selected systemic therapists (12).

The overall response rate was 9.9%.

MEASURES

Participants were asked to complete:

- a questionnaire requesting demographic information and details of the respondent's therapeutic orientation and experience;
- the Direction of Interest Questionnaire (DIQ) (Caine et al., 1982), high scores on which indicate inner-directedness;

- the Therapist Attitude Questionnaire-Short Form (TAQ) (Neimeyer & Morton, 1997), which includes rationalism and constructivism scales;
- a repertory grid in which, as indicated in Figure 11.1, 16 therapeutic approaches and an ideal approach were rated on 18 supplied constructs drawn from the literature on psychotherapy and optional elicited constructs. Grids were analysed by the principal component analysis of FLEXIGRID (Tschudi, 1998), from which various measures were extracted, and the MULTIGRID package (Tschudi, 2001) was employed to examine the mean grids of therapists of different orientations and to provide various other calculations.

RESULTS

RELATIONSHIPS BETWEEN MEASURES

As predicted in hypothesis (i), inner direction of interest was found to be significantly inversely correlated with rationalist philosophical beliefs ($r = -0.45$; $p < 0.01$). Its lack of correlation with the measure of constructivist beliefs ($r = -0.06$) is consistent with the lack of evidence of the predictive validity of the TAQ Constructivism scale in previous research.

Various significant correlations were also found between grid measures and other variables. Of most interest were:

- the relationship between outer direction of interest and a more unidimensional construct system, as indicated in a low percentage of variation accounted for by the second principal component of the grid ($r = 0.29$; $p < 0.05$);
- a relationship between number of years since the completion of training and degree of satisfaction with the therapist's own treatment orientation, as reflected in a low distance between the grid element referring to this orientation and the "ideal treatment approach" element ($r = -0.44$; $p < 0.01$);
- a relationship between rationalist beliefs and favourable constructions of behaviour therapy and cognitive therapy, as reflected in the distances between these elements and the "ideal treatment approach" element (both $rs = -0.42$; $p < 0.01$);
- a relationship between constructivist beliefs and a favourable construction of existential therapy ($r = -0.31$; $p < 0.05$).

Elements

1. Behaviour therapy
2. Cognitive therapy
3. Psychoanalytic psychotherapy
4. Analytical psychology
5. Gestalt psychotherapy
6. Transactional analysis (TA)
7. Psychosynthesis
8. Existential psychotherapy
9. Cognitive analytic therapy (CAT)
10. Psychodrama
11. Personal construct psychotherapy
12. Neuro-linguistic programming (NLP)
13. Systemic therapy
14. Client centred therapy
15. Hypno-psychotherapy
16. Group analysis
17. Your own preferred approach (if not included in the above list)
18. An ideal treatment approach

Constructs

1. Deterministic–indeterministic
2. Elementaristic–holistic
3. Apersonal – individually focused
4. Realistic–idealistic
5. Extraspective–introspective
6. Aims for corrective treatment goals – aims for creative treatment goals
7. Focuses on conscious awareness – focuses on unconscious awareness
8. Objective–subjective
9. Mechanistic–contextualist
10. Unstructured treatment sessions – highly structured treatment sessions
11. Authoritarian therapeutic relationship–democratic
12. Impersonal–personal
13. Concerned with the past – concerned with the present and future
14. Has a weak evidence base – has a strong evidence base
15. Ineffective–effective
16. Unlikely to be harmful – potentially harmful
17. Would feel uncomfortable to employ – would feel comfortable
18. Would not wish to be treated by – would be happy to be treated by

Figure 11.1 Elements and constructs in the repertory grid

DIFFERENCES BETWEEN ORIENTATIONS ON QUESTIONNAIRE MEASURES

As indicated in Table 11.1, cognitive-behavioural therapists were found to be significantly more outer-directed than therapists of all other orientations. Psychodynamic therapists were the most inner-directed, and significantly more so than hypnotherapists. A similar pattern emerged on the Rationalism Scale (see Table 11.2), cognitive-behavioural therapists being more rationalist than all other groups except hypnotherapists, who in turn were more rationalist than all the remaining groups except neurolinguistic psychotherapists. Perhaps surprisingly, in that they are classified within the UK Council for Psychotherapy as constructivists, neurolinguistic psychotherapists were more rationalist than psychodynamic, personal construct, and humanistic therapists. Systemic therapists were also more rationalist than psychodynamic therapists. No significant differences between the groups emerged on the TAQ Constructivism Scale.

DIFFERENCES BETWEEN GROUPS ON REPERTORY GRIDS

As expected, on the repertory grid most therapists tended to view their own approach more positively (i.e., as more similar to an ideal treatment approach) than did therapists of other orientations. Table 11.3 presents

Table 11.1   Differences between therapists on the direction of interest questionnaire

Orientation	N	Mean	SD
Cognitive-behavioural	13	14.69	4.66
Hypno-psychotherapy	14	19.00	5.84
Systemic	12	19.67	4.27
Analytical psychology	11	20.73	4.17
Neuro-linguistic	8	20.75	4.53
Cognitive-analytic	6	20.83	5.53
Humanistic	32	21.09	4.45
Personal construct	8	22.50	4.11
Psychodynamic	10	23.50	4.09

Analysis of variance revealed a significant difference between orientations: $F(8, 105) = 3.50$, $p = 0.001$. LSD tests indicated the following significant differences:
• cognitive-behavioural therapy less than all other orientations
• psychodynamic psychotherapy greater than hypno-psychotherapy.

Table 11.2 Differences between therapists on the therapist
attitude questionnaire

Rationalist Scale

Orientation	N	Mean	SD
Cognitive-behavioural	13	27.08	3.97
Hypno-psychotherapy	15	26.03	3.65
Neuro-linguistic	8	22.19	3.16
Systemic	12	19.71	4.61
Analytical psychology	11	18.95	4.50
Cognitive-analytic	5	18.60	5.55
Humanistic	33	17.39	4.75
Personal construct	9	16.22	6.02
Psychodynamic	11	15.27	3.55

Constructivist Scale
No significant differences between therapists were observed.

Analysis of variance revealed a significant difference between orientations: $F(8, 108) = 11.70$; $p < 0.001$.
LSD tests revealed the following significant differences:
• cognitive-behavioural greater than all orientations except hypno-psychotherapy
• hypno-psychotherapy greater then all orientations except CBT and NLP
• neuro-linguistic greater then psychodynamic, personal construct and humanistic
• systemic greater than psychodynamic.

the mean distances of the ideal treatment approach and their own approach
from other approaches for the personal construct psychotherapists, where
distances are normed so that the expected value is 1. Somewhat surprisingly,
given that cognitive analytic therapy has roots in personal construct theory,
personal construct psychotherapists saw it as further from the ideal treatment
approach than did therapists of all other orientations except psychodynamic
therapy. This is perhaps consistent with Freud's (1914) notion of the
"narcissism of small differences". Personal construct psychotherapists
also tended to view their own approach as more distinctive, in terms of
its distance from other approaches, than did other therapists. In this regard,
the most consistent difference from therapists of other orientations was
that these all saw personal construct psychotherapy as significantly
more similar to psychoanalysis ($F = 4.63$; $p < 0.001$). Psychoanalysis
was, in fact, the treatment approach viewed by personal construct
psychotherapists as least similar to their own, followed closely by
behaviour therapy. By contrast, personal construct psychotherapists

Table 11.3 Mean element distances of therapeutic approaches from ideal treatment approach and personal construct psychotherapy in the grids of personal construct psychotherapists

	Distance from			
	Ideal approach		Personal construct therapy	
	Mean	SD	Mean	SD
Psychoanalysis	1.44	0.29	1.60	0.32
Behaviour therapy	1.41	0.32	1.56	0.34
Analytic psychology	1.31	0.28	1.43	0.41
Cognitive therapy	1.21	0.21	1.32	0.26
Group analysis	1.20	0.49	1.23	0.31
Hypnotherapy	0.95	0.39	1.11	0.20
TA	1.09	0.37	1.08	0.23
CAT	1.07	0.33	1.09	0.32
Gestalt therapy	1.03	0.41	1.05	0.24
Psychosynthesis	0.92	0.31	0.96	0.16
Psychodrama	0.88	0.26	0.91	0.11
Systemic therapy	0.68	0.36	0.88	0.30
Client centred therapy	0.82	0.20	0.82	0.16
Existential therapy	0.75	0.23	0.77	0.27
NLP	0.77	0.26	0.74	0.23
Personal construct	0.42	0.20		

viewed themselves as having most in common with neurolinguistic and existential psychotherapists, perhaps not surprisingly as these are the other orientations represented in the Experiential Constructivist Section of the UK Council for Psychotherapy.

Differences and commonalities between the grids of therapists of different orientations were examined further using Tschudi's (2001) MULTIGRID package. This allowed the construction of a mean grid for the therapists as a whole as well as for therapists within each orientation. The plot derived from principal component analysis of the mean grid of the whole group is shown in Figure 11.2. The first principal component of this grid differentiated therapies in terms of whether they were introspective, holistic, individually focused, contextualist, and had creative treatment goals or extraspective, elementaristic, apersonal, mechanistic and corrective. The placement of the therapies indicated that this could be regarded as a "humanistic" versus "cognitive-behavioural" dimension. The second component was

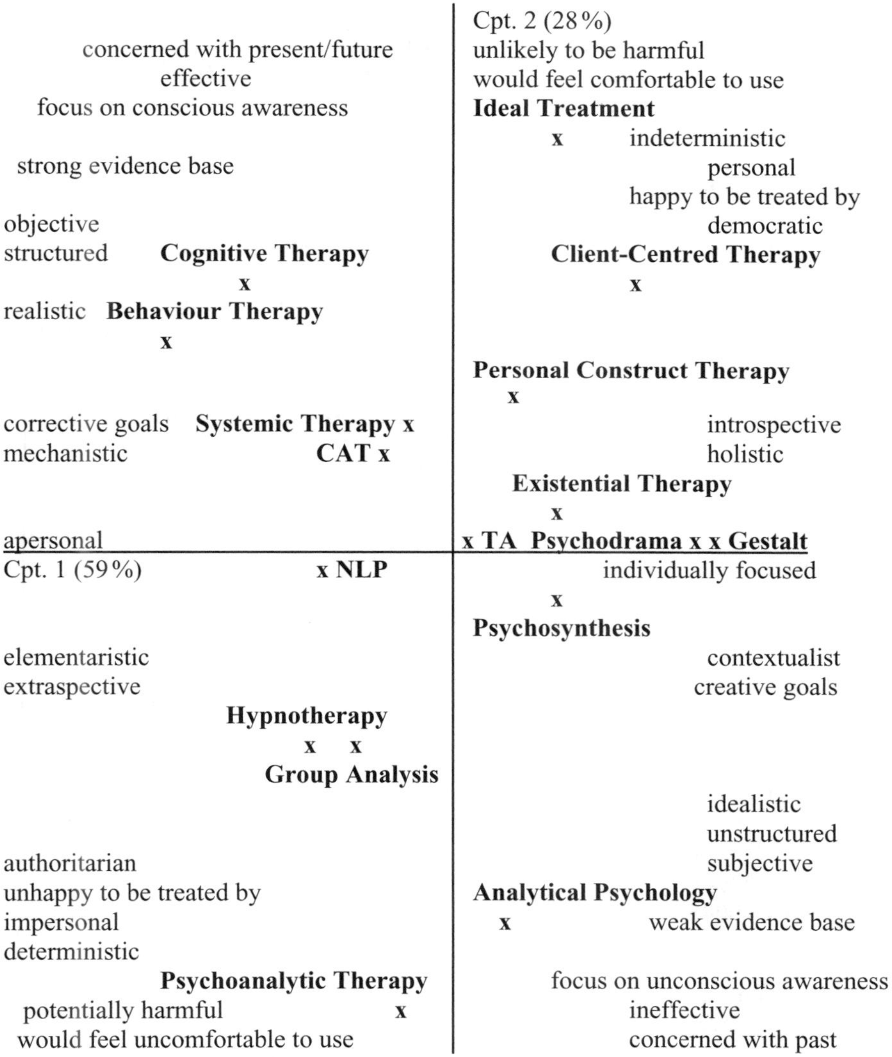

Cpt. 2 (28%)

concerned with present/future
unlikely to be harmful
effective
would feel comfortable to use
focus on conscious awareness   **Ideal Treatment**
                                         x   indeterministic
                                                personal
strong evidence base   happy to be treated by
objective   democratic
structured   **Cognitive Therapy**   **Client-Centred Therapy**
                      x   x
realistic **Behaviour Therapy**
                 x
                                         Personal Construct Therapy
                                                x
corrective goals   **Systemic Therapy** x   introspective
mechanistic   **CAT** x   holistic
                                         Existential Therapy
                                                x
apersonal   x TA Psychodrama x x Gestalt
Cpt. 1 (59%)   **x NLP**   individually focused
                                                x
                                         Psychosynthesis
elementaristic   contextualist
extraspective   creative goals
                      Hypnotherapy
                          x   x
                      Group Analysis
                                                        idealistic
                                                        unstructured
authoritarian   subjective
unhappy to be treated by   **Analytical Psychology**
impersonal   x   weak evidence base
deterministic
                  Psychoanalytic Therapy   focus on unconscious awareness
   potentially harmful   x   ineffective
   would feel uncomfortable to use   concerned with past

Figure 11.2 Plot of elements in construct space from principal component analysis of therapists' mean grid

concerned with whether therapies were effective, had a low potential to harm, felt comfortable to use, and were more concerned with the present and future and with conscious awareness. Client-centred and cognitive therapies were viewed in these terms and contrasted with analytic therapies. The constructions of humanistic therapists may have been over-represented in this mean grid since they contributed approximately a third of the grids on which

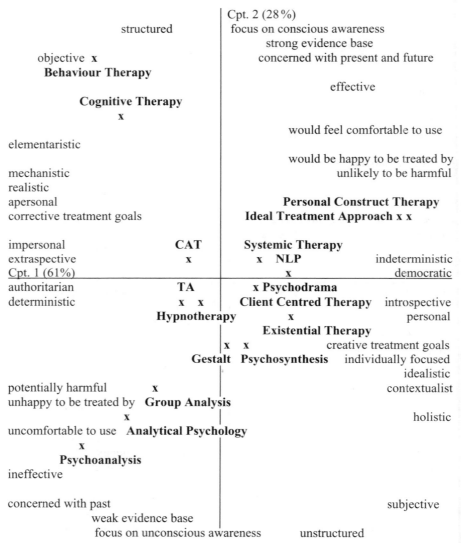

Figure 11.3 Plot of elements in construct space from principal component analysis of personal construct psychotherapists' mean grid

it was based. However, if the mean grid of the personal construct psychotherapists is considered separately (see Figure 11.3), it can be seen not to differ greatly from that of the group as a whole except for the more extreme placement of personal construct psychotherapy on the first principal component, where it is contrasted with both cognitive-behavioural and analytic therapies.

Table 11.4 provides the mean correlations between the groups of grids and, in the diagonal, the mean within group correlations. It can be seen that the former correlations tended to be lower than the latter, indicating that, as predicted, there was greater commonality of construing within than between orientations. If those orientations where less than four grids were available are excluded, personal construct psychotherapy is the most homogeneous group in terms of commonality of construing and cognitive-behaviour therapy the least. Table 11.5 provides the correlations between the mean grids, and indicates that the construing of the personal construct psychotherapists had greatest commonality with that of the neurolinguistic and humanistic therapists and least with that of the more analytically oriented therapists. The fact that there was a much higher mean correlation (0.57) between the mean grids than between the individual grids (0.31) indicates the structure in the data.

A more detailed examination of the commonality of construing within the sample is possible by drawing upon the criteria proposed by Bell (2000) for

Table 11.4 Mean correlations within (in diagonal) and between groups of grids

	CBT	Psy	Hum	PCP	Sys	Hyp
CBT	**0.33**	0.22	0.24	0.29	0.30	0.26
Psychodynamic	0.22	**0.45**	0.36	0.28	0.31	0.26
Humanistic	0.24	0.36	**0.38**	0.33	0.33	0.29
PCP	0.29	0.28	0.33	**0.47**	0.37	0.31
Systemic	0.30	0.31	0.33	0.37	**0.38**	0.31
Hypnotherapy	0.26	0.26	0.29	0.31	0.31	**0.35**

Table 11.5 Correlations between mean grids

	NLP	PCP	Hyp	CBT	Sys	Hum	CAT	Psy
PCP	0.69							
Hypnotherapy	0.58	0.63						
CBT	0.44	0.61	0.63					
Systemic	0.55	0.66	0.62	0.63				
Humanistic	0.58	0.69	0.67	0.60	0.70			
CAT	0.47	0.53	0.53	0.55	0.49	0.66		
Psychodynamic	0.47	0.51	0.54	0.47	0.58	0.78	0.62	
Analytical	0.32	0.39	0.44	0.48	0.53	0.67	0.60	0.71

Table 11.6 Results from principal component analyses of element correlation matrices of each construct

Construct	Variance of Cpt. 1	Differentiation
Indeterministic	20.88	0.59
Holistic	22.87	0.69
Individually focused	20.20	0.46
Idealistic	28.43	0.62
Introspective	24.77	0.66
Creative treatment goals	18.37	0.72
Focus on unconscious awareness	23.01	0.88
Subjective	20.52	0.66
Contextualist	25.30	0.87
Structured treatment sessions	30.15	0.67
Democratic therapeutic relationship	20.08	0.85
Personal	22.73	0.59
Concerned with present and future	26.40	0.90
Strong evidence base	27.37	0.84
Effective	34.04	0.81
Potentially harmful	45.91	0.96
Would feel comfortable to use	22.94	0.63
Would be happy to be treated by	20.81	0.26

testing the commonality of particular constructs. His method involves carrying out principal component analyses of the element correlation matrices of each construct in turn, and examining the variance accounted for by the first component in each of these analyses, as well as a ratio indicating the differentiation between the first and subsequent components. As shown in Table 11.6, the first of these measures provides limited support for the commonality of construing in the group since only for 1 construct was the size of the first principal component below 20%, the criterion for unidimensionality suggested by Reckase (1979). This measure indicated greatest commonality for constructs concerning the potential harmfulness and effectiveness of therapies and whether treatment sessions are structured. Lowest commonality was indicated for constructs concerning whether treatment goals are creative or corrective, whether the therapeutic relationship is democratic, whether therapy is individually focused and subjective, whether the respondent would be happy to be treated by the therapy, and whether the therapeutic approach is deterministic. A somewhat different pattern emerged using the measure of differentiation, but again this suggested greatest commonality for the construct concerning potential harmfulness, as well as for that concerning the temporal focus of the therapy, and lowest commonality for constructs concerning whether the approach is deterministic, personal, individually focused, and one by which the respondent would be happy to be treated.

ANALYSIS OF ELICITED CONSTRUCTS

The previous grid analyses all focused upon participants' ratings of therapies on the supplied constructs. In addition, two approaches were adopted in analysing the constructs elicited from participants. In the first of these, a grid was created of different participants' ratings of the elements on their elicited constructs. One hundred and twenty three constructs were included in this grid, which was analysed in two halves. The constructs loading most highly on the first two principal components from each of the resulting two analyses are presented in Table 11.7. In both of these grids the first components essentially contrasted cognitive-behavioural approaches, described by such construct poles as "symptom focused" and "technique focused", with analytic approaches, described by construct poles such as "very time consuming" and "trains via apostolic succession". In both grids, cognitive-behavioural and analytic approaches were similarly placed on the second component, and contrasted with constructivist and some humanistic approaches. The constructs loading highly on this component largely concerned humanistic issues, such as the importance accorded to the individual client, as well as issues related to the breadth of the approach. The similarity between the results of the analyses of the two grids provides some indication of the reliability of the procedure.

The other approach adopted to the analysis of the elicited construct poles was that 2 of the authors of the chapter independently divided them into a number of categories. They then discussed their classifications, and agreed upon a taxonomy which, as shown in Figure 11.4, consisted of 16 categories, all except 1 of which were divided into subcategories. Definitions were written for each category and subcategory (these may be obtained from the first author on request). The two authors concerned then reclassified all of the construct poles in terms of this category system. Examination of the reliability of the coding of the first 1,298 construct poles elicited revealed a very respectable kappa of 0.67 for the 16 superordinate categories. The codings of the senior author of all the 2,087 construct poles elicited, which were made blind to the therapeutic orientation of the respondent, were used in the subsequent analysis. This revealed a highly significant difference in the content of the constructs used by therapists of different orientations (chi square = 410; $p < 0.001$). As can be seen in Table 11.8, over a quarter of construct

Table 11.7   Constructs loading most highly on first two components from elicited construct grids

---

Grid 1

Component 1

private practice model – public service model
measurement is not useful – measurement can be useful
trains via apostolic succession – trains via practical input
noncollaborative approach – collaborative approach
no evidence based research – evidence based research
no focus on current problem – focus on current problem

Component 2

connectedness – fragmented
hopeful – helpless
cross-culturally responsible – Western culture based
client feels important – client is part of a process
beneficial – not beneficial
client can disclose to therapist – can't disclose to therapist
flexible boundaries – tight

Grid 2

Component 1

non-collaborative experience – collaborative experience
doesn't apply to range of problems – applies to range of problems
time open–time limited
not limited by time – time limited
feeling – thinking
only privately available – free to client

Component 2

broader than interaction – looking at style of interaction
less interpretive – heavily interpretive
process focused – content focused
constructs also vital – behaviour detailed
open to person to person dialogue – not open to dialogue

---

poles concerned either focus on an aspect of the client's functioning or the therapeutic relationship. Although most groups of therapists differentiated approaches highly on the basis of these 2 construct categories, other categories revealed more distinctive, and predictable, preoccupations of particular orientations. For example, the cognitive-behaviour therapists used a large number of constructs concerning technical aspects of therapy, the psychodynamic therapists showed a particular concern with psychodynamic structure and processes, the personal construct psychotherapists were concerned with personal meaning, and the systemic therapists, not unpredictably, focused on the social context of therapy. Despite the current climate of

1. Usefulness

2. Structure

3. Focus on aspect of the client's functioning

4. Concern with the therapeutic relationship

5. Concern with psychodynamic structure and process

6. Concern with personal meaning

7. Concern with treatment goals

8. Concern with personal growth, wholeness and choice

9. Concern with social context

10. Technical approach

11. Concern with theory

12. Temporal focus

13. Reflexivity

14. Value judgements

15. Self reference

16. Other

Figure 11.4 Content categories for therapists' constructions of therapies

evidence-based practice, the therapists were relatively unconcerned with the usefulness of therapy, and neither did they show any great concern with theoretical issues. Several of them were not averse to making value judgements concerning other approaches, often seeing these in less than complimentary terms, as reflected in such construct poles as "crap therapy", "long winded, old fashioned", "Procrustean", "heavy on waffle, light on outcome data", and "loony theory". The reader may wish to guess which therapies were described in these terms by therapists of which orientations.

Table 11.8   Percentage of construct poles in each category

	Total	CBT	Psy	Hum	CAT	PCP	NLP	Sys	Hyp
					Therapists				
Usefulness	4.6	7.9	5.9	3.4	3.3	1.8	6.7	1.3	7.9
Structure	8.5	15.0	9.5	7.0	**12.3**	5.0	7.5	5.2	**16.1**
Focus	**13.6**	**15.4**	10.5	13.9	13.9	15.8	10.2	**22.7**	6.9
Relationship	**13.5**	**16.6**	**18.8**	14.5	9.0	7.7	**12.9**	10.4	10.1
Psychodynamics	**10.3**	6.3	**20.4**	8.6	10.7	7.2	10.2	9.7	10.1
Meaning	6.0	2.8	2.3	6.6	4.9	**13.5**	4.1	7.8	6.3
Goals	3.5	5.1	1.0	4.2	0.8	3.2	6.8	5.8	0.5
Growth	4.7	0.0	2.3	7.3	5.7	5.0	8.8	1.3	4.2
Social	9.9	7.5	6.9	**11.1**	8.2	**15.3**	6.8	**20.8**	2.1
Technical	6.4	**15.7**	4.9	7.6	2.5	7.2	4.1	3.2	7.9
Theory	3.4	3.2	4.6	2.7	2.5	5.0	2.7	1.3	4.8
Temporal	4.9	3.6	4.6	5.3	5.7	5.9	1.4	1.9	9.0
Reflexivity	0.1	0.0	0.0	0.0	0.0	0.5	0.7	0.6	0.0
Value	5.8	5.9	5.6	3.7	9.0	6.8	**10.9**	4.5	7.4
Self reference	4.0	1.6	1.0	3.2	**11.5**	0.5	5.4	3.2	**13.8**
Other	0.7	0.8	1.6	0.7	0.0	0.0	2.0	0.0	0.0

The 3 categories used with most frequency by each group are highlighted in bold type.

THERAPEUTIC PREFERENCES

A further indication of respondents' evaluation of other therapies was provided by examining their responses to questions asking them to which therapies they would never refer a client and which they would opt for if they were a client. Table 11.9 indicates the mean number of times therapists in each orientation mentioned a therapy to which they would never refer. If this can be regarded as a measure of intolerance of other approaches, it can be seen that the psychodynamic psychotherapists were the most intolerant and the Jungians, neurolinguistic and personal construct psychotherapists the most tolerant. As can also be seen in Table 11.9, nearly a third of the approaches to which respondents would never refer fell within the humanistic spectrum.

However, a somewhat different picture is presented when considering which approaches these therapists would choose if they were clients. Although previous research has indicated that therapists generally seek personal therapy within their own orientation (Norcross, 1990; Norcross et al., 1988), in this sample, as can be seen from Table 11.10, nearly half of the

Table 11.9   Mean number of therapies to which therapists in each orientation would never refer

Psychodynamic	2.20
Cognitive-analytic	1.83
Cognitive-behavioural	1.62
Humanistic	1.28
Hypno-psychotherapy	1.14
Systemic	1.08
Personal construct	0.50
Neuro-linguistic	0.25
Analytical psychology	0.00
Therapies to which respondents would not refer	
Humanistic	31.75 (expressed as percentages of total of therapies to which they would not refer)
Neuro-linguistic	15.08
Hypno-psychotherapy	14.29
Psychodynamic	13.49
Cognitive-behavioural	10.32
Personal construct	5.56
Group analysis	3.97
Analytical psychology	3.17
Cognitive-analytic	1.59
Systemic	0.79

therapists (46.93 %) would have opted for another orientation. In this regard, humanistic approaches were particularly popular, being chosen by a quarter of the therapists who would seek therapy within an orientation other than their own. Not unpredictably, the constructivist therapists, namely neurolinguistic and personal construct psychotherapists, were most likely to experiment with alternative orientations. More surprising was the willingness of some cognitive-behaviour therapists to undergo therapies which might be considered to contrast markedly with their own orientation, 3 opting for a Jungian approach, 1 for psychodynamic psychotherapy, 5 for a humanistic therapy, and 3 for cognitive analytic therapy.

CONCLUSIONS

Our findings provide further support for the view that psychotherapists' preferences for particular orientations are based upon those core aspects of construing which are tapped by measures of personal style and epistemological

Table 11.10 Percentage of therapists who would choose personal therapy of an alternative orientation

Neuro-linguistic	66.67		
Personal construct	62.50		
Hypno-psychotherapy	60.87		
Systemic	50.00		
Analytical psychology	50.00		
Cognitive-behavioural	48.00		
Psychodynamic	46.67		
Humanistic	33.87		
Cognitive-analytic	33.33	**TOTAL**	**46.93**
THERAPIES CHOSEN FROM OTHER ORIENTATIONS (as %)			
Humanistic	25.00		
Analytical psychology	17.86		
Psychodynamic	11.90		
Group analysis	10.71		
Cognitive-behavioural	8.33		
Neuro-linguistic	8.33		
Cognitive-analytic	7.14		
Systemic	4.76		
Hypno-psychotherapy	3.57		
Personal construct	2.38		

orientation, and they demonstrate the continued value of the DIQ and TAQ Rationalism Scale in research in this area. The dichotomies assessed by these measures have interesting similarities, which will be examined in further research, with Silvan Tomkins' (1995) proposed polarity between "normative" and humanistic ideologies, which he relates to the left and right sides of the brain respectively.

The questionnaire measures which we used do not tell the whole story, however, as is indicated by the position of personal construct psychotherapists, who, while being differentiated as predicted on these scales from cognitive-behaviour therapists, could not be distinguished from analytically oriented therapists. It was only when the specific domain of their constructions of different therapeutic approaches was considered that the distinctiveness of personal construct psychotherapists from analytic therapists was demonstrated, as were their greater commonality of construing with more constructivist therapists, and their particular concern with personal meaning, in marked contrast to psychodynamic therapists. These latter findings have demonstrated the role which repertory grid technique may play in research on psychotherapists, and in particular the versatility of MULTIGRID analysis of groups of repertory grids, and the possible utility of our taxonomy of constructs concerning therapy.

REFERENCES

Arthur, A. (1999). Clinical psychologists, psychotherapists and orientation choice: does personality matter? *Clinical Psychology Forum, 125*, 33–37.

Arthur, A. (2000). The personality and cognitive-epistemological traits of cognitive behavioural and psychoanalytic psychotherapists. *British Journal of Medical Psychology, 73*, 243–257.

Bell, R. C. (2000). On testing the commonality of constructs in supplied grids. *Journal of Constructivist Psychology, 13*, 303–311.

Caine, T. M. & Smail, D. J. (1969). *The treatment of mental illness: Science, faith and the therapeutic personality.* London: University of London Press.

Caine, T. M., Smail, D. J., Wijesinghe, O. B. A. & Winter, D. A. (1982). The Claybury selection battery manual. Windsor: NFER-Nelson.

Caine, T. M., Wijesinghe, O. B. A. & Winter, D. A. (1981). *Personal styles in neurosis: Implications for small group psychotherapy and behaviour therapy.* London: Routledge and Kegan Paul.

Caine, T. M. & Winter, D. A. (1993). Personal styles and universal polarities: implications for therapeutic practice. *Therapeutic Communities, 14*, 91–102.

Freud, S. (1914). On narcissism. In S. Freud, *Collected works.* London: Hogarth Press.

Johnson, J. A., Germer, C. K., Efran, J. S. & Overton, W. F. (1988). Personality as the basis for theoretical predilections. *Journal of Personality and Social Psychology, 55*, 824–835.

Karasu, T. B. (1986). The psychotherapies: benefits and limitations. *American Journal of Psychotherapy, 40*, 324–343.

Lyddon, W. J. (1989). Personal epistemology and preference for counseling. *Journal of Counseling Psychology, 36*, 423–429.

Lyddon, W. J. & Adamson, L. A. (1992). Worldview and counseling preference: An analogue study. *Journal of Counseling and Development, 71*, 41–47.

Neimeyer, G. J. & Morton, R. J. (1997). Personal epistemologies and preferences for rationalist versus constructivist psychotherapies. *Journal of Constructivist Psychology, 10*, 109–123.

Neimeyer, G. J., Prichard, S., Lyddon, W. J. & Sherrard, P. A. D. (1993). The role of epistemic style in counseling preference and orientation. *Journal of Counseling and Development, 71*, 515–523.

Neimeyer, G. J., Saferstein, J. & Arnold, W. (2005). Personal construct psychotherapy: epistemology and practice. In D. A. Winter & L. L. Viney (Eds), *Personal construct psychotherapy: Advances in theory, practice and research.* London: Croom Helm.

Reckase, M. (1979). Unifactor latent trait models applied to multifactor tests: Results and implications. *Journal of Educational Statistics, 4*, 207–230.

Schacht, T. E. & Black, D. A. (1985). Epistemological commitments of behavioral and psychoanalytic therapists. *Professional Psychology: Research and Practice, 16*, 316–323.

Soldz, S. (1989). Do psychotherapists use different construct subsystems for construing clients and personal acquaintances? *Journal of Social and Clinical Psychology, 8*, 97–112.

Tomkins, S. S. (1995). Ideology and affect. In E. Demos (Ed.), *Exploring Affect. The Selected Writings of Silvan S. Tomkins*. New York: Cambridge University Press.

Tschudi, F. (1998). Flexigrid. Oslo: Tschudi Systems Sales.

Tschudi, F. (2001). Multigrid. Oslo: Tschudi Systems Sales.

Vasco, A. B. (1994). Correlates of constructivism among Portuguese therapists. *Journal of Constructivist Psychology*, 7, 1–16.

Wampole, B. E., Mondin, G. W., Moody, M., Stich, F., Benson, K. & Ahn, H. (1997). A meta-analysis of outcome studies comparing bona fide psychotherapies: Empirically, "All must have prizes". *Psychological Bulletin*, *122*, 203–215.

Watson, S. (1999). How do therapists construe clients, other therapists, and researchers? Paper presented at 13th International Congress on personal construct psychology, Berlin.

Winter, D. A. (1990). Therapeutic alternatives for psychological disorder: personal construct psychology investigations in a health service setting. In G. J. Neimeyer & R. A. Neimeyer (Eds), *Advances in personal construct psychology*, vol. 1. New York: JAI Press.

12

A Personal Construct Theory View of Professional Identity

JULIE ELLIS

The aim of this chapter is to highlight how a Professional Identity could be described in Personal Construct Theory (PCT) terms. The focus is on its application to help in the understanding of the processes involved in forming and maintaining a Professional Identity, particularly, for the 60 nurse participants of a study on Professional Identity.

THE STUDY

This study was undertaken with 60 nurses (30 first year students and 30 expert nurses with an average job experience of 15 years), in which repertory grids were used to collect data on participants' constructions of their professional selves.

The analysis used to identify groups of professional identity was complex and resulted in a Professional Identity Orientation for each participant in the study. Data included in this Professional Identity Orientation included:

- Proportion of Variance on the first component in the Principal Components Analysis,
- Proportion of variance of every construct,
- Correlations between constructs, specifically significant relationships between the construct Caring/Not caring and other constructs elicited,

---

Personal Construct Psychology: New Ideas. Edited by Peter Caputi, Heather Foster and Linda L. Viney. Copyright © 2006 John Wiley & Sons, Ltd.

- Standard Euclidean distances between elements, particularly focussing on the similarity or dissimilarity between elements, such as Self as a Nurse, and Ideal Self as a Nurse.
- Cosines between constructs and elements, indicating association of constructs and elements. To describe the elements, the three constructs with the highest cosines were used (Ellis, 2000).

PROFESSIONAL IDENTITY ORIENTATION

Content analysis of the Professional Identity Orientation for each participant therefore, did not simply categorise construct poles but included the above information, and the aim was to identify themes represented by this group of nurses and to represent equilibrium between the idiographic and the nomothetic approaches to understanding human nature (Allport, 1961, in Shaughnessy & Zechmeister, 1994).

THE TYPES OF PROFESSIONAL IDENTITY

Six types of professional identity were identified: an "immature" identity that occurred mainly in the students' group, a "patient-oriented" professional identity (with more students than experts sharing this professional identity), an achievement-oriented identity (more experts than students), a conflict-oriented identity, a social justice-oriented professional identity and a balanced professional identity (with only experts in the last three groups – see Table 12.1).

PROFESSIONAL IDENTITY

CONSTRUING A PROFESSIONAL IDENTITY

How do people construe or anticipate their future professional selves? This question could be asked of young people who are attempting to decide on a career, as well as professionals who are or should be contemplating changes to their professional roles. For some people, the choice of a career is made early in life, and this provides opportunities for anticipation and construing of how the role might be. Information may be gleaned from family and friends, from books, newspapers and television. Therefore, slowly, an anticipatory position is built up. For these people, undertaking studies in their chosen role or commencing in the work place means facing the task of

Table 12.1   Six types of professional identity of nurses – distribution in the 2 groups of nurses

	Student nurses	Expert nurses
Immature	**17**	**3**
s: immature, nice, development-focused	9	2
p + s: immature	3	–
p + s + w: nondescript, undifferentiated	5	1
Patient-oriented	**11**	**5**
p: caring, support	5	1
p + s: patient-focussed and open	3	4
p + w: integrated	3	–
Achievement-oriented	**2**	**7**
w: achievement, ambition, performance	2	3
w + p: holistic ambition	–	1
w + s: balanced achiever	–	3
Crisis and conflict	**–**	**10**
s: *crisis, conflict, dilemma*	–	6
p + w: *conflicting*	–	2
p + w + s: *anxious, unhappy*	–	2
Social justice-oriented	**–**	**2**
p: *social justice-focused*	–	2
Balanced	**–**	**3**
s: *balanced*	–	1
p + w + s: *balanced, integrated, mature*	–	2

S = Self focus; P = People focus; W = Work focus.

having their previously developed anticipations confirmed and developing means of defending their already existing constructs against the danger of invalidation. This implies modifying their construct systems continually as they encounter new elements of work practices.

This seems to be the case with the patient-oriented group of students, and possibly also with the few achievement-oriented ones. They have a discernible Professional Identity that may be rooted in earlier (childhood) experiences. However, for others, decisions are made regarding future professional roles without opportunity for anticipation and construing. This occurs for many reasons and for many people in our society. They then face the situation where they are forced to start defining constructs and construct systems while also dealing with the new role or studying for the role.

The student nurses in this study were 18–20 years old and had been students for only 8 months. They had selected nursing as a career, but knew very little about it. They were more interested in enjoying themselves and having a good time. However, they would eventually spend many weeks in the hospital environment where they were expected to be able to construe that environment and many of the things that are happening therein. It is probable that they faced many anxious moments during these times in the hospital. "Anxiety is the recognition that one is inescapably confronted with events to which one's constructs do not adequately apply. It is the recognition that the events with which one is confronted lie outside the range of convenience of one's construct system" (Kelly, 1991, p. 366).

It is possible that some of these students found the anxiety too much to bear, and left. Kelly (1991) proposes that the Fragmentation and Modulation Corollaries, "taken together, assume that one can tolerate some incompatibility, but not too much" (p. 366).

From a PCT perspective, anxiety is neither good nor bad. It does "represent an awareness that one's construct system does not apply to the events at hand. It is, therefore, a precondition for making revisions" (Kelly, 1991, p. 367). But this does not mean that the more anxious a person, the more the person is likely to make an effective revision of constructs. A person can be so anxious that they "rush about" and cannot concentrate on reconstruing.

CONSTRUCTION OF A PROFESSIONAL IDENTITY

Not all people working successfully in a professional environment share the same Professional Identity. As their personalities and their ways of coping with the demands of work are different, they may develop different ways of construing themselves professionally. Sometimes this may result in different career choices within the same profession.

It would normally be expected that a person working in a professional role for a number of years would have developed a useful construct system that helps him or her deal with his or her role on a day to day basis. They would normally have had the opportunity to anticipate most events that occur in their work role. Their construct systems would or should help them deal with the difficult situation encountered by developing ways of dealing with them by "construing their replications" (Kelly, 1991, p. 35). They do this by using previous experiences to make sense of and develop ways of dealing with new events that are similar to past events. It would then be expected that as each person tests out their expectations of their professional role, then those anticipations will be either validated or invalidated. If the anticipations are validated, then there will be a strengthening of the anticipation and the constructs concerned. If the anticipations are invalidated, the person will need to modify those predictions and constructions. In this way, several anticipations may be appropriate in each event, and the person will have developed ways of responding to the various outcomes of the event. Each person will choose those constructs and construct poles that are most meaningful for them and help them to anticipate future events. For example, like the outcome of their responses to and decisions made about professional activities.

The choice made by the person will maximise the degree to which their professional world can be predicted. Each person has some essential reason for the choices made, and the critical choice is made on the basis that it provides the greatest possibility of extension or definition of the system in an ongoing movement towards personally-relevant meaning. For extension to occur, the choice made allows further construing to take place, that is, a person's choices are open to revision. By definition, the choice made allows the system as it already exists to be confirmed. The problem is that this may not always happen for nurses. If they have not really developed a useful Professional Identity construct system, then they will have to rely on their personal construct system, which is more than likely to conflict with their professional role. The opposite could also be true. A person whose personal identity is closely linked to their professional identity construct system will make life choices that validate his or her professional role rather than his or her personal role in life.

In the study there were several different ways of developing a specific form of Professional Identity: Patient Orientation Achievement Orientation, Social Justice Orientation and a balanced-integrated Professional Identity (that included aspects of work, other people and self) that each nurse would consider worked for them.

FAILURE IN RE-CONSTRUING THE PROFESSIONAL IDENTITY

Many people are closed to different or new constructions. This is probably not rare. It could occur when a role has to undergo changes or when a person is faced with invalidation, but keeps the old construction systems anyway. For example, for academics, universities are being run like private businesses. They are expected to change their constructs about their professional worlds. For nurses, they are faced with huge financial cuts to the health system, and are therefore, expected to do things differently. New events, experiences or people should be able to be described by a person's existing constructs. If their superordinate constructs are impermeable, they will be unable to subsume new constructs, and in the case of invalidation of predictions/anticipations they will be unable to modify those predictions or reconstrue the experience. So if nurses construe nursing as a caring activity, with plenty of time for patients, then they may not be able to reconstrue the hospital environment of today, that is focussed on short hospital stays, and technical care.

LACK OF CONSTRUING OF A PROFESSIONAL IDENTITY

Some nurses in the study did not seem to have developed a definite Professional Identity construction. This is a more difficult group to understand. How could they have survived on average 20 years in this professional role with an immature Professional Identity? It is possible that these nurses were faced with anxious moments as students and responded by tightening their construing to protect themselves from further anxiety. Some people tighten their superordinate constructs in the face of imminent anxiety, and "thus maintain a greater measure of organisation at the lower levels of his system" (Kelly, 1991, p. 367). The problem with this strategy is that the person "blocks the readjustive changes which might follow from being anxious for a while. He does not 'face his problems' hence he does not find new solutions for them" (Kelly, 1991, p. 367). Maybe the immaturity protects against stress and strain (as a form of denial) – or maybe some people stay naive and immature all their lives.

SOURCES OF CRISIS AND CONFLICT IN A PROFESSIONAL IDENTITY CONSTRUCTION

The following section describes some of the possible sources of crisis and conflict for the nurses who participated in the study.

THE SOCIAL CONTEXT

It is important and necessary for persons working in the same professional role to construe certain experiences, events and other people in similar ways. This commonality of construing ensures successful and similar outcomes for many professional activities, where people have to either work together or produce the same outcomes. At the same time, it is also possible for people to construe their professional role differently in some ways from their work colleagues. They might interpret experiences or events differently, allocate importance and view implications of their actions differently from their colleagues. Obviously, this can result in many difficulties and lack of understanding between workers, including bosses and subordinates. This interaction with others is very important in the work place. Each person needs to be able to construe the constructions of others to help them understand the other person's perspective. If workers cannot construe their work colleagues' constructions then there are problems between peoples' interpersonal relationships. This is especially so when superiors make no attempt to construe the constructions of the workers for whom they are responsible. Many misunderstandings occur in work situations due to this lack of interaction. It can also occur between colleagues and from workers towards bosses. In circumstances when bosses have moved up through the system they are more likely to understand their workers' constructions, than bosses who have been brought in from outside a particular system. However, bosses who move up from the ranks may change their constructs, too, and become alienated from their former pals. And as workers have not worked as bosses, they can find it difficult to understand the constructions of their bosses.

"SLOT-RATTLING"

As constructs are bipolar, workers use constructs that have most meaning for them in discriminating pertinent aspects of their professional roles. The bipolar constructs provide information about the "whole" meaning people have about their professional role. The emergent pole is the aspect that discriminates or provides the meaning of their choices or anticipations, but it is always in the context of the inclusion of the contrast or opposite pole, which provides for the person an opposite choice that can be made under certain circumstances. Like the construct *nice/nasty*, both poles can be used with different people in the workplace. However, whatever pole of the construct is played out in the workplace, people have a well organised, hierarchical plan of anticipations in a construct system which is organised in a way that will minimise contradictions for them. Therefore, they can be either nice or nasty to different people, and there will be higher order constructs or superordinate constructs that give meaning to this apparently contradicting behaviour. New constructs are not developed, but the person moves along the one construct, from one pole to the other.

CORE CONSTRUCTS AND PROFESSIONAL IDENTITY

It is also possible that the main superordinate or core constructs the person holds are not particularly suited to the professional role they have chosen. It is also possible that there is a contradiction between people's core constructs and their personal superordinate constructs; or that their personal core constructs do not match up with the Professional Identity constructions as portrayed by their professional bodies or more senior managers in their work places. For example, managers are expecting workers to produce more and more. For many people, they cannot increase their work output, except by working longer hours, rather than working faster. Unfortunately, this contradicts with their core constructs about family life. Workers whose core constructs are about achievement are likely to put work before family. The construct system does allow for inconsistencies. In a new situation, such as in the work place, new constructs may not be compatible with existing constructions. However, these inconsistencies can be tolerated as long as the superordinate constructs are permeable enough to subsume the inconsistent constructions. But what is the result for workers whose superordinate constructs are not permeable enough to subsume the inconsistent constructs? Is this what happens to the nurses who want to be "caring" in the old sense of the word, and because of the time pressures of the job, they do not have time to give this extra support to the patients? They end up stressed and disillusioned about their jobs, rather than attempting to reconstrue the situation. This reconstruction could be on "what a good job I am doing under such difficult circumstances" or "I am still making a very valuable contribution to the care of my patients". This reconstruction must also acknowledge the difficulty of change, and the ability to be flexible in the face of change. All constructs have a range of situations to which they can be applied. Many constructs used in the professional role will be useful for that role only, while others will be useful outside the work situation. For example, for nurses, constructs of nursing and self as a nurse may have a limited range of convenience, while constructs of caring will have a much wider range of convenience.

CONSTRUING THE CONSTRUCTIONS OF THE NURSES WHO ARE IN CRISIS AND CONFLICT

In the study there were ten nurses allocated to the Crisis and Conflict group. The conflicts these nurses were experiencing were on issues such as professional versus personal roles, undertaking a caring role that conflicts with the resultant domination of others, the expected demands of the role, confidence in the role equates with aggressiveness, lack of trust of others in the work place, lack of competence and fear of job loss and the need to be flexible to be able to survive in the role and lack of confidence in the role.

I suggest that these nurses could be suffering from the emotion guilt, as defined by Kelly (1991) as: "Perception of one's apparent dislodgment from one's core role structure constitutes the experience of guilt" (p. 370). On the other hand they could also be suffering from the emotion threat. It is defined by Kelly (1991) as: "Threat is the awareness of imminent comprehensive change in one's core structures" (p. 361). The prospective change must be substantial. "One is threatened when that which he thought all along might happen to his core structure at last looks as if it were about to arrive" (Kelly, 1991, p. 361).

Overall, these ten nurses appear to be threatened by a fear of the opposite poles of their Self as a Nurse and Ideal Self as a Nurse constructs. It would appear that they are saying: "I want to be nice, but the opposite pole is not nice", and I am in conflict about the possibility that I am probably more "not nice" than "nice"; or "I need to be competent or confident or flexible in this role, but instead, I am lacking in competence, confidence or flexibility".

CONCLUSIONS

It is possible that nursing students enter their academic education mainly with two different construct systems with regard to Professional Identity: One group has a patient oriented focus that complies with the general notion of nurses as carers. This may be helpful for the adoption of a professional role but may also produce conflicts with reality as it is here and now. The other group appears as a kind of "open slate" which may mean that the role models and non-roles models they encounter during their education and clinical practice experiences will help them form their Professional Identities.

With expert nurses, there seems to be a tendency to develop different Professional Identities that probably match core constructs of the individuals. At first glance, it may appear surprising to find a large number of the expert nurses in the conflict group. However, there had been a very turbulent time in nursing in the five years before the data were collected. Many nurses were made redundant and this resulted in a shortage of nurses. Those who remained become disillusioned with their role in the Health Care system.

The results imply that it would not be adequate to look at nurses as a homogeneous group with respect to their understanding of their professional selves–their Professional Identities. Some manage to allocate themselves to professional contexts where they can survive; others do not. Still others may not have coped at all and left the profession altogether. Unfortunately, they were not part of this study.

More importantly, it is probable that the six types of Professional Identity found in this professional group, could also be found in other health professional groups. Four of the groups (Immature, Achievement-oriented, Crisis and conflict and Balanced) could also be found in any professional or non-professional work group. The challenge is in helping people re-construe their professional identity in such a way as to ensure that they are satisfied with self in the work situation, satisfied with their constructions of their professional identity.

REFERENCES

Ellis, J. (2000). The professional identity of nurses: an empirical investigation of personal constructions using the Repertory Grid Technique. Unpublished PhD thesis. La Trobe University.

Kelly, G. A. (1955, 1991). *The psychology of personal constructs*. London: Routledge.

Shaughnessy, J. J. & Zechmeister, E. B. (1994). *Research methods in psychology* 3rd Edition. New York: McGraw-Hill, International Editions.

SECTION III
Problems of Living

13

Trust and Dependency in Younger and Older People

NICOLE G. ROSSOTTI

DAVID A. WINTER

MARY H. WATTS

INTRODUCTION

The academic interest in trust started over 15 years ago upon hearing clients state that they did not trust anyone. Influenced by Kelly's (1955, 1991) and Walker, Ramsey and Bell's (1988) work on dependency, the first author of this chapter sought to explore the clients' reasons for granting trust and with-holding trust from other people.

Then, 10 years ago, when starting to work with older people, 1 client's story shaped one's interest in looking at trust and dependency, as well as the relationship between these 2 areas of construing and mental health. It involved visiting a woman in her 80's whose husband and older siblings had died. Having never been a "joiner", she had no desire for clubs and groups. She would stay at home with memories of her husband, but she still felt very lonely and depressed. She had trusted her husband but very few other people and there was no longer anyone in her life whom she trusted. Her dependencies were very few and impermeable, consisting of 1 neighbour whom she met occasionally and reluctantly for tea, and another who helped from time to time with shopping.

Trust is fundamental and central to human relationships. Two quotations encapsulate its importance and the need to place trust discriminately. In

Personal Construct Psychology: New Ideas. Edited by Peter Caputi, Heather Foster and Linda L. Viney. Copyright © 2006 John Wiley & Sons, Ltd.

Middlemarch, George Eliot (1871–1872/1965, p. 480) wrote: "what loneliness is more lonely than distrust?" Yet, indiscriminate granting of trust is seen as being ill-advised by Seneca (1917), who wrote "it is equally unsound to trust everyone or to trust no one".

Before proceeding any further, the relationship between trust and dependency will be briefly considered. Dependency requires an action, or a level of construing which involves some degree of contact with another person, whereas trust involves a more abstract form of construing: one may trust somebody with respect to some or many things without needing to turn to them for these things. However, when trust is accompanied by action, trust and dependency converge.

Walker et al.'s study (1988) seems to provide some indication that dependency and trust are different and that trust might be considered to be superordinate to dependency. In one of their studies they made use of a unipolar version of Hinkle's (1965) laddering technique to ask respondents their reasons for depending upon particular individuals. One of the responses they obtained was that these were the people who were trusted.

Even though Kelly (1955) appeared to pay scant attention to trust, which does not receive one entry in *The Psychology of Personal Constructs*, it does not seem that he considered trust and dependency as synonymous. One reference was found in his paper "In whom confide: On whom depend for what?" in which he stated his hope that "psychological theories of the future [would] have significance for all human beings, their longings, and the way they trust and depend upon each other" (Kelly, 1969, p. 204). A quotation from the same article led one to speculate whether he may have thought of trust as "security in [a] dependency relationship" (Kelly, 1969, p. 204).

> Even if one person did not get what he wanted from the other, the fact that his outlook was understood by the other and that the other could see what it was like to have such wants, and that the other can agree that, from the same point of view, he, too would experience a similar yearning – all this is likely to provide greater security in the dependency relationship than getting literally what was asked for (p. 204).

Some evidence for the need to differentiate between trust and dependency is provided by Butt, Burr and Bell (1997) in a research project aimed at investigating people's construal of themselves within different relationships. They found that trust was an important factor in "differentiating between relationships" (p. 10) but what mattered most was not trusting someone with a secret or "allowing the other into some inner sanctum of the true self . . .

[r]ather it was about trusting the other to accept and validate whatever version of our self should emerge in that relationship" (p. 10). Trust was construed as an ontological process. Butt et al., (1997) wrote: "Allowing a social situation to unproblematically conjure up a particular self seems to be what people most enjoy. Having to manage and reflect on an interaction produces unease" (p. 10).

One definition of trust is suggested: trust might be defined as the expectation of validation of one's core construing and distrust as the expectation of invalidation of one's core construing. Butt et al. (1997) considered that trust is about being-in-relationship, which is viewed by the current authors as compatible with an understanding of trust as allowing another to know oneself. How much can we let others know us, be it in terms of secrets, or aspects of self, or being oneself in relationship? It is proposed that whether trust is granted or not might be dependent upon three separate sets of factors (Messie-Rossotti, 1995): (i) intrapersonal factors (such as sociality, pre-emptiveness versus propositionality of construing, previous experience of validation and invalidation as well as subsequent reconstruing); (ii) the presumed construing of the other person (such as assumed sociality, assumed pre-emptiveness versus propositionality of construing, presumed discretion or indiscretion); (iii) relational factors (such as transference, and length and quality of the relationship).

Trust and dependency are deemed to be important psychological processes for people of any age. The bereavements faced by older people deprive them of some (or all) of the people whom they have trusted and/or have depended upon. Although some of their subordinate dependencies might be filled by new acquaintances, trust and validation of core construing take longer to develop and are therefore more difficult to replace. Even though the bond to the deceased might provide much sustenance at some level, for instance, in terms of memories of love, it does not help with the loss of the presence of the person. Great comfort can be obtained from "communication" with a deceased loved one, as reflected by a client, but it did not eradicate for her the sadness that the loss had created. One cannot reach out physically to a deceased person, nor can one share a meal or one's favourite piece of music. So, trust does not need to change unless one reconstrues the relationship and one's construing of the other person. But the nature of the dependency changes. Perhaps this difference can be further illustrated by a philosopher's view of the difference between trust and dependency with respect to reliability. Admittedly, reliability is only one aspect of trust or dependency. For Baier (1986), trust represents "reliance on [other people's] good will", whereas dependency involves reliance on their "dependable habits". One can keep alive memories of good will, but one cannot depend on someone now if they are deceased, just by virtue of their having displayed "dependable habits" in the past.

Some of the aims of the study were (i) to design a measuring instrument for trust and (ii) to consider the relationship that trusting and depending have with mental health.

DEVISING THE TRUST GRID

A list of trust situations was piloted on 3 successive occasions and rated by a number of "judges" (both under and over 65 years of age) on the basis of how much trust would be required in others to disclose the content of the situations. The instructions asked the "judges" to think of important people in their lives and rate the extent to which confiding in these people with regard to 22 situations would require trust. The range of the rating was between 1 (no trust would be required to confide about this) and 5 (complete trust would be needed). Two of the situations were: "Feeling very guilty about something you have done" and "Telling a joke against yourself". Then, a second list was produced, which included a further 11 situations provided by the "judges". This was very helpful in broadening the range of convenience of trusting situations, such as "Your feelings about your own death and dying". Of this list of 33, 15 were retained by virtue of their having received an average rating of 3.5 (or as near as possible to this rating from both age groups of "judges"). A third list was produced, adding to these 15 items, 15 others from Kelly's Situational Resources Repertory Test. The 11 situations that were deemed by the "judges" to focus most on trust were included in the trust grid (Appendix 13.1); another was incorporated as it dealt with whether elements were seen as trustworthy for the respondent. It read: "I would trust this person not to behave knowingly through actions or words in ways which would be hurtful to me". Items borrowed from Kelly's Situational Resources Repertory Test are denoted with (K).

HYPOTHESES

It was predicted that there are significant differences in psychological distress between people with regard to three main factors: (i) the number of trusted people whom they can also depend on, (ii) the subjective ease or difficulty that people experience in trusting others and (iii) participants' perceived accuracy in placing their trust. Specifically, it was hypothesised that people who have very few people whom they trust and whom they can also depend on suffer more psychological distress. It was predicted that people who have great difficulty in deciding whom to trust experience more dissatisfaction in the interpersonal sphere than people who find it easy to decide whom to trust. It was further hypothesised that people who do not feel confident in their judgement of whom they can or cannot trust experience more dissatisfaction in the interpersonal sphere than people who feel confident in their judgement of whom they can or cannot trust.

METHOD

PARTICIPANTS

Forty people participated in the research. Half of them were aged between 30 and 45 (mean age = 37.15, *SD* = 4.64) whilst the other half was aged between 65 and 79 (mean = 70.80, *SD* = 4.53). Within each age group, half were men and half were women. All participants had been referred to a British National Health Service Clinical Psychology Department. Younger people were awaiting psychotherapy and older people were either awaiting therapy or already were being seen.

MEASURES AND PROCEDURES

All participants completed a dependency grid (Kelly, 1955) and a trust grid (Rossotti, 1999). In addition, they filled out two questionnaires that were needed to test the hypotheses. Psychological distress was assessed with the Brief Symptom Inventory (Derogatis, 1993) as it measures "self-report[ed] . . . psychopathology" (Cohran & Hale, 1985, p. 777), alongside nine symptoms dimensions, including depression, anxiety and interpersonal sensitivity. The Inventory of Interpersonal Problems – Short Form (Soldz, Budman, Demby & Merry, 1995) was used to assess psychological distress and interpersonal dissatisfaction, as it has been shown to measure "interpersonal sources of distress" (Horowitz et al., 1988, p. 885).

The grids comprised 11 elements: mother, father, self now, partner or close friend corresponding to sexual orientation, someone I trust very much, someone I have depended on over the last year, someone I would not want to depend on, someone I don't really trust, someone I like, someone I am not close to and ex-partner or former friend.

Trust grids were rated on a 6-point scale from +3 to −3, with the positive ratings indicating that someone was trusted (the higher the number, the higher the trust), and the negative ratings indicating that someone was not trusted (the higher the number, the higher the mistrust). Respondents were asked how much they would trust each element with regards to each situation. It was stressed that they were asked to rate whether he/she would trust someone with the depth of his/her feelings and understanding and not whether he/she has disclosed his/her feelings. A copy of the instructions and the rating scale given to the participants is included in Appendix 13.2.

The dependency grid comprised 12 situations (listed in Appendix 13.3), 6 concerning physical dependency and 6 psychological dependencies. The first 6 situations were chosen with the aim of excluding or minimising trust (e.g., "Being ill at home and needing someone to post a stamped gas or electricity bill payment"); the last 6 dependency situations, which focused on psychological dependency were the 6 highest trust situations which did not include physical dependency on someone else, hence the exclusion, for instance, of "Allowing someone to look after your child or grandchild". Dependency grids were rated on a 7-point scale from +3 to −3, with a zero rating being exclusively used for deceased elements. The zero rating was only available in the dependency grid, based on the premise that dependency, unlike trust or love, ceases (albeit progressively) with the death of the other person. A copy of the instructions and the rating scale for the dependency grid is provided in Appendix 13.4.

In addition to the standardised measures, participants rated two questions regarding their experience of interpersonal trust. The first question read: "How easy or how difficult is it for you to decide whether to trust or not to trust somebody?" This was rated on a scale from one to seven, whereby one was very easy and seven very difficult. The second question was: "How often do you find that you have reached an incorrect judgment about someone (i.e., that you trusted somebody when he/she turned out not so trustworthy or when you did not trust somebody who later was found to be trustworthy)"? Participants' subjective appraisal of the correctness of their judgment was on a one to seven scale, with one being "very often" incorrect and seven "never" incorrect.

RESULTS AND DISCUSSION

It was predicted that regardless of age people who have very few people whom they trust and whom they also depend on suffer more psychological distress. Elements who were trusted and depended upon were operationalised in two ways: (i) by considering the number of elements whom each participant trusted and depended upon on all situations, and (ii) by considering the number of elements whom each participant trusted and depended upon with regard to the six common trust and dependency situations. As mentioned previously, the Brief Symptom Inventory (BSI) and the Inventory for

Interpersonal Problems (IIP) were considered to test some aspects of psychological distress.

Within each of the four subsamples, the number of elements trusted and depended upon by each participant was correlated with the score each participant obtained on three measures using the Pearson product-moment correlation: (i) on the Global Severity Index (GSI) of the BSI, (ii) on the IIP, and (iii) on the Depression (Dep) dimension of the BSI. The results are presented in Table 13.1. The number of people trusted and depended upon was obtained by a simple count of the elements who were trusted and depended upon by each participant (i) on the twelve situations and (ii) on the six common situations.

Most correlations are significant for younger women, and two of them are significant for older men. As predicted, all of these correlations are negative.

Even though the prediction had not differentiated between the different subgroups, the analyses revealed important differences between the 4 groups. The gender difference between the 2 younger groups might be explained in terms of men and women gaining satisfaction from different sources. Arieti and Bemporad (1980) stated that men and women aspire to different dominant goals. Many women seek the pursuit of romantic love, whereas many men's dominant aim is their career. Although this research did not focus on either of these dominant goals, its focus is much closer to the reported preoccupation of women, with its emphasis on close relationship, than it is to the putative goal of men. Furthermore, Caldwell and Peplau (1982) found that men and women differed in the ways they preferred to pass time with their friends. Fifty-seven per cent of women preferred "just talking" rather than "doing some activity" in contrast to only 16% of

Table 13.1 Pearson correlations between number of people depended upon and trusted based on all situations, on situations common to trust and dependency, and IIP, GSI, and the Depression (Dep) dimension of the BSI for each subsample

IIP/GSI/ DEP	No. of situations	Younger men	Younger women	Older men	Older women
IIP	12	−0.17	−0.52	−0.14	0.07
IIP	6	−0.35	−0.64*	−0.67*	0.18
GSI	12	0.00	−0.69*	−0.57*	0.44
GSI	6	0.08	−0.68*	−0.54	0.44
Dep	12	−0.38	−0.81**	−0.40	0.54
Dep	6	−0.29	−0.73*	−0.48	0.60(*)

(*)$p < 0.10$ (two-tailed). *$p < 0.05$ (one-tailed). **$p < 0.01$ (one-tailed).

the men expressing the same preference. However, 84% of men rather than only 43% of women favoured doing some activity. Therefore, if men's core constructs are less predicated upon relationships and more upon activities, it would seem to follow that the number of people they trust and depend upon is less relevant to them and therefore less closely related to psychological or interpersonal distress. Even though this assumption might be convincing for a representative population of men, it might not seem persuasive for this sub-group of younger men who chose to attend this research as some of them stated an interest in trust as their reason for participating in the research. Yet, an interest in this topic, and even an acknowledgment that they do not trust others, might not necessarily imply that they would suffer distress because of it.

Though it was not the case for younger men, there were two significant correlations for older men. The difference between the two subsamples of men might be explained by the change in life orientation in men as they grow older, from the prominence of their career to developing warm nurturing relationships (Lowenthal, Thurnher & Chiriboga, 1975).

There is also a striking difference amongst younger women and older women in the quantity of significant correlations between the number of people trusted and depended upon and psychological distress. A possible explanation may be that, when younger women knew few people whom they depended on and trusted, they might have attributed this low number of confiding relationships to an internalised failure in establishing and maintaining such relationships. In contrast, a number of older women might have externalised this as being attributable to circumstances and the harshness of the increasing number of bereavements associated with ageing, whereas others in the older samples might have internalised this failure in the same way as younger women might have done. Qualitative examination of some of the individual older women's data suggests that further research might fruitfully investigate this hypothesis.

The prediction that people who experience greater difficulty in deciding whom to trust also experience more dissatisfaction in the interpersonal sphere than people who find it easy to decide whom to trust was not borne out in the research. Calculation of the Pearson product-moment correlation between participants' rating of their ease/difficulty in trusting other people and their scores on the IIP yielded a r value of 0.22 ($p > 0.05$, with a one-tailed test). In the course of carrying out the research, a methodological flaw was brought to light. The question answered by the participants was unwittingly ambiguous: one respondent replied that she found it easy to decide whom to trust as she did not trust anybody, whereas the question had been intended to explore the length and the meta-decisions of the CPC cycle. It may be either that the process of deciding whom and when to trust is unrelated to interpersonal satisfaction/dissatisfaction, or that a multifactorial understanding, including ease and difficulty in trusting people, frequency of invalidation, and superordinacy of the events/feelings that people feel invalidated by, is needed to account for a relationship.

The hypothesis that an inverse relationship exists between participants' own perceived accuracy in trusting others and the degree of dissatisfaction they experience in the interpersonal sphere received support for the younger women's sample only ($r = -0.67$, <0.05, one-tailed test). Interpersonal satisfaction was measured by participants' score on the IIP. Table 13.2 gives the r value for the four samples.

One of the weaknesses of the research is that the correlational results are based upon a small number of participants within each subsample and thus are not able to provide strong evidence of relationships between variables.

CLINICAL IMPLICATIONS

Even though the data analyses provide equivocal findings for some of the subsamples, they do suggest some guidelines, such as the importance of trust and dependency for younger women and older men. The results for younger women are consistent with the literature and research findings on younger women. It is suggested that, for younger women and for other clients who experience difficulties with trust and/or dependency, the trust grid be used as another diagnostic instrument. Either on its own or in combination with the dependency grid, it may indicate the areas within trust (and dependency) on which therapist and client could fruitfully work. Both grids can form the basis for qualitative interviews either whilst the grids are filled out or afterwards in order to understand the subtleties of the client's construing. Mismatch between trust and dependency invites further exploration of construing. A good match between the two is not a sufficient condition for

Table 13.2 Pearson correlations between frequency of perceived inaccuracy of assigning trust, and interpersonal satisfaction/dissatisfaction (IIP)

IIP	Younger people	Older people	Younger men	Younger women	Older men	Older women
IIP	Question 2 −0.45*	Question 2 −0.08	Question 2 −0.21	Question 2 −0.67*	Question 2 0.25	Question 2 −0.37

*$p < 0.05$ (one-tailed).

optimal functioning in this regard as very low trust and very low dependency can cause psychological isolation and suffering. Some of the construing which might be usefully explored when difficulties with trust and dependency arise include the following: core construing in terms of trust and dependency and their implications as well as the origins of the construing; construing of others including in the areas of transference; possible areas of anxiety, fear and threat, or terror as defined by Leitner and Guthrie (1992); exploration of tightness and looseness regarding trust and dependency; as well as the clients' journeys through CPC cycles in terms of these areas of construing.

The results of this research warrant further investigation, which could fruitfully concentrate on the construing of older people, with a much greater number of participants.

APPENDIX 13.1

TRUST SITUATION LIST

1. Experiencing an important problem within a close relationship.
2. Allowing someone to look after your child or grandchild.**
3. Feeling very jealous (K).
4. Opening up in depth the positive and negative influences which have made you the person you are.
5. Lending a belonging which is very precious to you.
6. I would trust this person not to behave knowingly through actions or words in ways that would be hurtful to me.
7. Feeling very ashamed about something you have done.
8. Feelings of sexual inadequacy or sexual habits.
9. Having been involved with something illegal (excluding minor traffic offences and breaking copyright).
10. Having made one of the most serious mistakes of your life (K).
11. Sharing your darkest secret.
12. Obtaining a large lottery win.

APPENDIX 13.2

INSTRUCTIONS AND RATING SCALE FOR TRUST GRID

Turning to the first situation: if you experienced an important problem within a close relationship, how much would you trust or not trust each person?

** If you do not have a child or a grandchild, you may wish to imagin having one. Alternatively, you can choose a pet or imagine having a pet.

Starting with your mother, how much would you **trust** your mother **with the depth of your feelings and understanding in this regard?** Then what about your father, how much would you trust or not trust your father in this situation? and so on.

SUMMARY OF RATINGS

+3 = I would **trust** this person **a lot** with my feelings/this situation

+2 = I would **trust** this person **moderately** with my feelings/this situation

+1 = I would **trust** this person **a little** with my feelings/this situation

−1 = I would **distrust** this person **a little** with my feelings/this situation

−2 = I would **moderately not trust** this person with my feelings/this situation

−3 = I would **not trust at all** this person with my feelings/this situation

APPENDIX 13.3

DEPENDENCY SITUATION LIST

1. Being ill at home and needing someone to post a stamped gas or electricity bill payment.
2. Not wanting to go alone to the cinema, or bingo, or a show or a football match OR wanting to engage in your hobby with somebody else (such as sport, card playing, walking) (choose an activity relevant to you).
3. Wishing to have a meal or a cup of coffee/tea with someone.
4. Wanting someone to accompany you or to take you to and from hospital for a minor operation.
5. Having a broken leg and needing someone to help you up the stairs.
6. Needing someone to take your photograph to send to a friend.
7. Feeling very ashamed about something you have done.
8. Discussing feelings of sexual inadequacy or sexual habits.
9. Having been involved with something illegal (excluding minor traffic offences, and breaking copyright).
10. Having made one of the most serious mistakes of your life.
11. Sharing your darkest secret.
12. Disclosing a large lottery win.

APPENDIX 13.4

INSTRUCTIONS AND RATING SCALE FOR DEPENDENCY GRID

This time you are to consider the people in your list with regards to **whether or not you would turn to them** if you were faced with particular situations or problems now.

+3 = **I would definitely turn to** this person if faced with this situation now

+2 = **I would probably turn to** this person if faced with this situation now

+1 = **I would possibly turn to** this person if faced with this situation now

0 = people are deceased

−1 = **I possibly would not turn to** this person if faced with this situation now

−2 = **I probably would not turn to** this person if faced with this situation now

−3 = **I definitely would not turn to** this person if faced with this situation now

REFERENCES

Arieti, S. & Bemporad, J. (1980). *Severe and mild depression.* London: Tavistock.

Butt, T., Burr, V. & Bell, R. (1997). Fragmentation and the sense of self. *Constructivism in the Human Sciences, 2,* 12–29.

Cadwell, M. A. & Peplau, L. (1982). Sex differences in same-sex friendship. *Sex Roles, 8,* 721–732.

Cohran, C. D. & Hale, W. D. (1985). College students norms of the brief symptom inventory. *Journal of Clinical Psychology, 41,* 777–779.

Derogatis, L. R. (1993). *Brief symptom Inventory (BSI): Administration, scoring, and procedures manual.* Minneapolis: National Computer Systems, Inc.

Eliot, G. (1871–1872; 1965) *Middlemarch.* W. J. Harvey (Ed.). London: Penguin Books Ltd.

Hinkle, D. (1965). The change of personal constructs from the viewpoint of a theory of construct implications. Unpublished doctoral dissertation, Ohio State University, Columbus.

Horowitz, L. M., Rosenberg, S. E., Baer, B. A et al., (1988). Inventory of interpersonal problems: Psychometric properties and clinical applications. *Journal of Consulting and Clinical Psychology, 56,* 885–892.

Kelly, G. A. (1955). *The psychology of personal constructs: Vol. 2. Clinical diagnosis and psychotherapy*. New York: W. W. Norton.

Kelly, G. A. (1969). In whom confide: On whom depend for what? In B. Maher (Ed.) *Clinical psychology and personality: The selected papers of George Kelly* (pp. 189–206). New York: Krieger Publishing Company.

Kelly, G. A. (1991). *The psychology of personal constructs: Vol. 1. A theory of personality*. London: Routledge. Original publication: New York: W. W. Norton, 1955.

Leitner, L. M. & Guthrie, A. F. (1992). The awful, awful nature of role relationships: The Gavin Dunnett memorial lecture. In A. Thomson & P. Cummins (Eds), *European perspectives in personal construct psychology*. Lincoln: EPCA.

Lowenthal, M. F., Thurnher, M. & Chiriboga, D. (1975). *Four stages of life*. San Francisco: Jossey-Bass.

Messie-Rossotti, N. G. (1995). An elaboration on the theme of trust. Paper presented at the XI International Congress on Personal Construct Psychology, Barcelona, July 1995.

Rossotti, N. G. (1999). A portfolio of research, practice and study. Unpublished D Psych Thesis. City University, London.

Seneca, L. A. (1917). *Ad Lucilium epistulae morales, III*, 4. Translation: R. M. Gunmere. London: William Heineman.

Soldz, S., Budman, S., Demby, A et al. (1995) A short form of the inventory of interpersonal problems circumplex scales. *Psychological Assessment, 2*, 53–63.

Walker, B. M., Ramsey, F. L. & Bell, R. C. (1988). Dispersed and undispersed dependency. *International Journal of Personal Construct Psychology, 1*, 63–80.

14

THC and PCP: Factors Maintaining Cannabis Use in People With and Without Psychosis

BOB GREEN

In his major work, the *Psychology of Personal Constructs*, George Kelly (1955) only made a few references to alcohol use. For Kelly alcohol use was essentially but one of many human behaviours that could be examined by his approach and therefore did not require specialised explanatory constructs. For example, Kelly discussed the return to drinking in terms of role dislodgment. Both in terms of not being able to comprehensively anticipate what it will be like when confronted with events where drinking might occur and in terms of group identification and role relationships (Kelly, 1955). Kelly also cited alcohol as one means to exert personal control, "Some people find that when they are intoxicated they are able to simplify the issues which appear to confront them and act decisively" (Kelly, 1955). The idea that individuals learn and value certain effects of a substance will be subsequently discussed in more detail when expectancies are considered.

A subsequent small body of empirical (Bailey & Sims, 1991; Lynch, 1995; Viney, 1985) and theoretical work (Dawes, 1985; Klion, 1993; Klion & Pfenninger, 1997; Rivers & Landfield, 1985) have more specifically examined substance use, while Burrell and Jaffe (1999) have elaborated a constructivist perspective on substance use that incorporates Personal Construct Psychology (PCP). The PCP literature, however, generally does not reflect

Personal Construct Psychology: New Ideas. Edited by Peter Caputi, Heather Foster and Linda L. Viney. Copyright © 2006 John Wiley & Sons, Ltd.

the growth in research on substance use, nor theoretical developments, nor the prevalence of substance use in society and the extent of problematic use.

The use of illegal drugs is of particular interest because the use of such substances remains widespread despite legal sanctions and public health messages regarding adverse effects. Of existing illegal drugs, cannabis is the most widely used with an estimated 2.5% of the world's population using cannabis (Costa e Silva, 2002). The 1998 Australian household survey reported that approximately 40% of respondents reported lifetime use, 17% had used cannabis in the last 12 months, while 31.7% of cannabis users met criteria for dependence or abuse (Swift et al., 1999).

Higher prevalence rates have been associated with males, the young and people with mental disorders, such as psychosis (Mueser et al., 2000; Regier et al., 1990). Although psychotic disorders are relatively low prevalence their impact can be profound and wide ranging on individuals, their families and society. Currently there is limited research that examines the factors that maintain cannabis use and less research that directly compares the cannabis experiences of individuals with and without psychosis. In addition to considering how other approaches may enhance PCP oriented research, this chapter also illustrates the potential for PCP oriented research to generate hypotheses and suggest directions for future research.

PCP AND PSYCHOSOCIAL EXPLANATIONS FOR CANNABIS USE

When introducing a paper he was asked to give on motivation, Kelly commented on the irony of his being asked to give the paper, stating, "There is something you should all know at the outset of this paper: I have no use for the concept of motivation". (Kelly, 1996). The Kellian abandonment of motivation has not been without criticism (Mackay, 1997). Mackay has argued that beliefs or constructs (including superordinate constructs) without an accompanying need, motive or desire, provide no basis for choice and as an explanation are incomplete (a "nonexplanation").

The fundamental premise of motivational models of substance use have been described by Cooper (1994) who stated people drink to allow certain valued outcomes and drinking is motivated by certain needs or serves certain functions. This premise has been operationalised in terms of reasons for use (also referred to as motives). Reasons for use have been found to be predictive of alcohol (Cooper, 1994; Newcomb et al., 1988), and cannabis use (Newcomb et al., 1988; Simons et al., 1998) and associated with substance use problems (Mueser et al., 1995).

Expectancies regarding the outcome of using cannabis are another concept that has been extensively utilised to study substance use. Willner (2001) in a study of 11–16 year olds, reported a 3-fold increase in positive expectancies and a 30% decrease in negative expectancies in daily users compared to never users, while a 2-year prospective study of adolescents (Aarons et al., 2001) reported that frequent cannabis users had lower expectancies regarding impairment than non-users or individuals who had ceased use. Expectancies have been found to predict patterns of drug use across a diverse range of groups, including people with schizophrenia (Mueser et al., 1995) and college students (Schafer & Brown, 1991).

Newcomb and colleagues (1988), however, have noted that the distinction between reasons for use and expectancies is "not perfectly clear" and that many reasons for use appear similar to expectancies. An alternative perspective to distinguish expectancies from reasons is to consider reasons as post hoc attributions (Davies, 1996) and expectancies as anticipations about the future based on previous experience. Kelly's (1955) example of expecting to reduce life's complexity through drinking is one example of expectancy.

Despite Kelly's rejection of motivation, outcome expectancies would appear to have much in common with the Kellian notion of anticipation. The essentially anticipatory process of construing that an individual engages in as they seek to control and make sense of their experience is through the individual's system of constructs. Rather than being driven by motivational forces such as emotion, Mancuso and colleagues (Mancuso & Adams-Webber, 1982; Mancuso & Hunter, 1983) have proposed that people as active construers seek to maintain a construction of self through the anticipation of events. This process of anticipation involves the integration of incoming information and sensory input that may confirm or disconfirm prior anticipations, in turn leading to extension or change to the person's construct system. For example, Klion (1993) has discussed that as the role of "addict" becomes central to an individual's definition of self, other roles, sources of social validation and experience diminish as contact with other drug users increases and the individual's attention focuses on personal drug-related experiences.

Given the importance of anticipation by an active construer to PCP an important question that has to be considered is how to account for the role of habit, i.e., "automatic" behaviour which seemingly occurs without thought or reflection. Mills (2001) has suggested that to be habitual in Kellian terms is to expect the duplication of events rather than anticipating the replication of events. In other words, rather than hypothesis testing, an action is initiated in the expectation (conscious or unconscious) that a certain effect will occur. Kelly (1955) also described a range of situations unfavourable to personal experimentation such as seeking to avoid the invalidation of constructs and constellatory thinking (e.g., if I am using cannabis I must be relaxed). Dependency in the Kellian sense (Burr & Butt, 1992) and elaboration of substance use as a core role (Klion, 1993) may also contribute to a lack of self-reflection. This is, however, an area where further theoretical and empirical work is required.

METHODOLOGICAL ISSUES

An underlying assumption of PCP is that individuals can give meaningful accounts of their subjective experiences, including their personal constructs. In contrast, Nisbett and Ross (1980) have reported inferential errors associated with human judgment, while Miller and Fine (1993) have cited research that has found individuals perceive their reasons for use and the effects of alcohol differently when alcohol free. Further the validity of self-report may also be complicated by the presence of factors such as psychosis. Langenbucher and Merrill (2001) have suggested the pertinent question is not whether substance users give accurate self-reports but rather under what circumstances and in regard to what events are accurate self-reports given, and what can be done to enhance self-reports. The review by Langenbucher and Merrill (2001) also makes a number of practical suggestions on this topic such as the importance of assurances of confidentiality, use of trained researchers rather than familiar clinicians and the use of prompts to enhance memory.

Support for the validity of self-report comes from a number of sources. For example, self-report has played a significant role in the development of approaches to measure the differential effects of various substances and their abuse potential (Fischman & Foltin, 1991) while previously cited studies found reasons for use and expectancies predictive of use and different patterns of use. Davies has also distinguished between reasons as causal data and reasons as attributions, which are contextually bound functional explanations, akin to some sociological approaches (Weinstein, 1976). The conceptualisation of reasons as attributions rather than truth statements is a perspective not inconsistent with constructivist approaches.

Another consideration of particular concern which arises out of the literature examining the subjectively perceived effects of cannabis and reasons for use concerns language and personal meaning. To illustrate this point research by Addington and Duchak (1997) will be considered. In this study a group of people with schizophrenia were asked if they experienced a range of effects as a result of cannabis use, including: "anxious", "without purpose", "empty feeling", "friendly" and "depressed". Differences in what these terms might mean were highlighted during the process of developing a coding scheme to categorise the effects of cannabis. Following an initial trial of the coding scheme, 7 mental health professionals were asked to code the cannabis effects included in 11 studies.

In relation to an "empty feeling" there was considerable disagreement among coders as to how this effect should be coded, with at most, only three of the seven coders agreeing on categorisation. The limitation of approaches, which ask participants to endorse items from a list of standard items, is suggested by Kelly's (1955) discussion of the personal use of constructs. Kelly considered not only that words may not adequately reflect what a construct means, but that words mean different things to different people. Words may also not capture the bipolarity of meaning. For example, is being relaxed always the opposite of anxiety? Additionally, there is the question of the implicative relationships between effects or reasons for use, which is the subject of Kelly's (1955) organisation corollary. Consideration of how effects are interrelated has relevance to the current conceptualisation of expectancies as nodes in an information network stored in long-term memory (Goldman, 1999).

The study by Addington and Duchak (1997) is similar to many others that provide a list of effects without examining the inter-relationships between them. An exception to this approach has been a study by Linkovich-Kyle and Dunn (2001) which developed an expectancy questionnaire based on responses to an open-ended questionnaire. A multi-dimensional scaling (MDS) analysis of participants' questionnaire responses revealed interesting differences in the frequently reported effects of four groups that had varying levels of cannabis use. The various effects were identified as being located within two dimensions, labelled "detached-aware" and "relaxed-agitated". The analysis allowed examination of how various effects are located in relation to each other in the resulting spatial plot, much as elements are plotted in a factor analysis of repertory grid data (Slater, 1977). Other limitations of the existing research on cannabis use includes limited attention to the importance of effects and reasons for use, and the use of broad categories of reasons or effects to code open-ended responses thereby obscuring important individual differences.

EXAMINING FACTORS ASSOCIATED WITH CANNABIS USE

To illustrate how cannabis use could be examined from a PCP perspective a subset of data from a study utilising a two-group prospective design will be reported. In the study which is reported more fully elsewhere (Green, Kavanagh & Young, 2004), a set of measures completed at baseline were used to predict cannabis use over a four-week period, in a sample of individuals with psychosis and a control group matched for age. Participants with psychosis were recruited from public mental health services whereas the control group participants were recruited via media advertisements.

Data were collected on substance use over the previous three months, hazardous drinking, problems with cannabis, cannabis dependence, quality of life, as well as demographic and treatment history information. Participants completed a cannabis expectancy and refusal self-efficacy questionnaire that respectively required endorsement of whether certain effects were experienced or whether cannabis could be refused in certain situations. In addition to the expectancy questionnaires participants' self-generated expectancies were collected via a structured interview. Frequency of use and the amount of cannabis used each week over a four week follow-up was collected using the time-line follow-back method (Sobell & Sobell, 1992).

A feature of this structured interview was that participants were shown two photographs (a group of people smoking cannabis and a photograph with two cannabis images). In relation to the group photograph, participants were asked to recall the last time they used cannabis with other people, and in response to the cannabis photograph participants were asked about the last time they had used cannabis alone. The order in which images were shown was varied across participants. The purpose of using these images was to prompt recall and to focus attention on a specific incident.

For both situations, participants were asked: (1) their reasons for using cannabis in the situation; (2) the likelihood of this feeling/situation occurring over the next month; (3) why the reason was important; (4) the opposite of the reason; (5) the respective importance of the most important reason; (6) whether there were any other important reasons for using cannabis; (7) good things that happened after smoking cannabis in this situation; (8) bad things that happened after smoking cannabis in this situation; (9) whether these effects occurred within five minutes of smoking; (10) the likelihood that the most important good and bad effect would be experienced again; and (11) respectively how good or bad the effect was.

Due to difficulties in recruiting women with psychosis the major statistical analysis was restricted to males (see Green, Kavanagh & Young, 2004). However, rather than simply exclude the data obtained from women (three with psychosis and seven controls) these data were used to illustrate some applications of PCP approaches (e.g., laddering and bipolar construct elicitation) to the field of studying cannabis use. The small numbers of participants precluded use of inferential statistics, however, the data from the female participants have been supplemented with some selected case example data from the male participants with psychosis.

To analyse the self-generated data a coding scheme was developed to perform content analysis. The initial coding scheme was trialed on reasons for use and effect data reported in the literature. Following refinement of this coding scheme a larger pool of reasons and effects reported in the literature was categorised by 7 coders. Following this analysis, an expanded 23 item coding scheme was used by 4 independent coders and the author to analyse data collected in the structured interview. Intercoder agreement was calculated using the Alpha program (Krippendorf, 2003). Krippendorf alpha reliability coefficients (Krippendorf, 2004) ranged from 0.70 to 0.75 (for reasons for use and positive effects) and from 0.72 to 0.75 (for reasons for not using cannabis or negative effects), prior to coding disagreements being resolved.

A dictionary of reasons and effects was developed from the coding scheme to allow a computerised content analysis. The major coding scheme consisted of 20 sub-categories which collapsed into 5 major categories (e.g., enhancement, self-regulation, addiction, perceptual change and self-medication). This coding scheme was used to code reasons and positive effects. A modified coding scheme was used to code reasons for not using cannabis and negative effects. The VB-Pro program (Miller, 1995) was used to assign codes to the various reasons or effects (see Appendix for excerpts from the coding scheme). The unit of analysis was words or phrases and while an individual's response might be tagged with more than 1 code (e.g., "relaxed" and "high" would be tagged as $RELAXED relaxed and $FEEL-GOOD high), individual words or phrases would only be assigned a single code.

RESULTS

The average age of the women with psychosis ($n = 3$) was 32.3 years ($SD = 2.0$) compared with 30.3 years ($SD = 9.1$) for the control group ($n = 7$). Cannabis use was first reported by the psychosis group at age 18 years ($SD = 3.6$) whereas the control group reported first cannabis use at age 16 years ($SD = 2.3$). First daily or problem use was respectively reported at 19.3 years ($SD = 2.3$) and 22.1 years ($SD = 5.9$). The women with psychosis reported using an average of 5.8 ($SD = 3.4$) cones per day on an average 5.4 ($SD = 2.1$) days per week, whereas the control group reported use of 9.1 ($SD = 5.2$) cones per day on an average 5.4 ($SD = 1.5$) days per week.

Table 14.1 depicts the percentage of participants reporting a particular reason for use at baseline and at the time of most use over the four-weeks

Table 14.1   Reasons for cannabis use at baseline and reasons for most use at follow-up

Reason	Baseline		Follow-up	
	Psychosis group	Control group	Psychosis group	Control group
Addiction	...	...	33.3%	14.3%
Anxiety/ depression	...	28.6%	33.3%	14.3%
Availability	...	28.6%	...	71.4%
Boredom	33.3%	...	...	28.6%
Cognitive enhancement	...	...	33.3%	14.3%
Cope other neg. mood	...	...	33.3%	...
Entertainment	33.3%	...	66.7%	14.3%
Habit	...	14.3%	33.3%	14.3%
Interaction	66.7%	...	...	...
Mood alteration	33.3%	14.3%	33.3%	14.3%
Perceptual change	33.3%	...	...	...
Physical enhancement	33.3%	28.6%	...	28.6%
Preferred alternative	...	14.3%	33.3%	...
Relaxation	66.7%	42.9%	33.3%	71.4%
Social activity/ offered	66.7%	71.4%	100.0%	42.9%
Wanted to	...	...	33.3%	14.3%

of the follow-up. The percentages are the percentage of participants reporting the reason at least once during the follow-up (e.g., only one participant from each group reported use because of "addiction" at any of the four follow-up contacts).

In addition to asking about reasons for using cannabis, participants were also asked "why is it important or why do you prefer to use cannabis for . . .". This question was asked to identify underlying superordinate constructs and to obtain an elaboration of individual's reasons for cannabis use. Unlike the reasons for use in Table 14.1, in which only two women reported using cannabis as an alternative to other substances, when asked why cannabis use was preferred/important, six women compared cannabis with other substances, e.g., "put's me at ease without loss of control", "a calmer environment than people who just drink alcohol", "it's not violent like alcohol", "drinkers are often not happy people", "don't want to take medical drug relief" and "because have children and don't drink". These responses suggest the choice is not between cannabis and abstinence but between cannabis and various other substances, primarily alcohol. The remaining responses reported by more than two participants were, in order of frequency: social ($n = 4$), mood alteration ($n = 4$), relaxation ($n = 3$), availability ($n = 3$).

Participants were also asked the opposite of their reason for use and the opposite of why cannabis was important/preferred to achieve this reason so as to elicit contrasts to the reasons for use and importance/preference. Across the 2 scenarios, in 9 out of 20 instances, participants did not to give an opposite to their reason for use and in 10 instances an opposite was not given to the question regarding importance/preference for cannabis. In some instances, this was because the initial reason or preference already contained an opposite, whereas in other instances participants found it difficult to think of an opposite, e.g., of habit. In most instances the opposites could be considered logical or expected opposites, whereas for one woman with psychosis the opposite of being stoned and experiencing perceptual change was being paranoid. Another interesting contrast was between the need to calm down after work and "adrenalin–creative energy" (see Table 14.2).

The data from male participants also generated some surprising or instructive contrasts, particularly among individuals with psychosis. One participant reported "passing boredom" as a reason for cannabis use, while being paranoid and scared was the contrast. Paranoia was, however, also a negative effect of cannabis use for this person. For another participant being stoned was important because it was relaxing (the opposite of which was anxiety). This participant distinguished between cannabis induced relaxation and non-cannabis induced relaxation, though could not elaborate on the difference. This participant reported no impact of cannabis on bizarre thoughts or hallucinations on the expectancy questionnaire, though endorsed cannabis as increasing paranoid thinking. Later this participant informally remarked that he "always" had strange thoughts. The meaning of altered consciousness in a person who reports always experiencing strange thoughts is worth consideration, in terms not only of what it means to perceive one's thoughts as always strange, but also in terms of exerting some control over these thought processes through substance use.

In terms of the connection between reasons and the importance/preference of cannabis for this purpose, Table 14.2 depicts responses from a selection of the men and women regarding their reason for use and the opposite of this reason, the importance/preference regarding the use of cannabis and an opposite. The first four rows were from women, two without psychosis and two with psychosis. All four women reported reasons for use related to

Table 14.2 Reasons for use and importance/preference and opposites

Reason	Opposite	Importance/preference	Opposite
Help me calm down after work, otherwise takes time to calm down	adrenalin – creative energy	otherwise up for hours – would get short lived sleep	up for a while – take longer to sleep
To relax	Nil	don't drink – puts me at ease, without loss of control	nil
Relaxes you	alcohol	like the sensation of being stoned – floating outside of self, colours brighter, everything seems more interesting	paranoid
Just to relax	stressed	I'm a very angry person & I need counselling. Calms me down	anger out of control
Addictive – love feeling/ heat in the chest	tranquil – in harmony	Love to kick back/relaxing	Total Stress
Because it was there	boredom	Takes the edge off things	If I don't have cannabis, I think about how shitty my life is. Get depressed. Takes off edge.
Cause I was bored	Doing stuff – normal stuff (golf, fishing)	Takes up so much time – ritual of getting on, chopping up. Fills hours.	In a rush and don't have time. Have other things to think about

relaxing. Why this was important/preferred varied considerably. The last three rows in Table 14.2 contain reasons generated by male participants reflecting use because of addiction, availability and boredom. Social reasons (not presented) also displayed diversity, being important/preferred because of relaxation, it being rude to not use if offered, enhanced communication and something simply not thought about.

Table 14.3 reports the single most important effect reported at baseline for each scenario and the expected effects at follow-up on the day most cannabis was used. With reference to negative effects, only four women reported negative effects in relation to use at the time of the two scenarios. Two women reported paranoia (the woman without psychosis described this as a mild feeling when leaving home in a car) and a woman from each group reported headaches.

DISCUSSION

The expectancy instrument proved to have several advantages over the more idiographic structured interview. These advantages included short time taken, more comprehensive range of items covered and the format was

Table 14.3 Most positive effect at baseline and expected effect of most use at follow-up

Effect	Baseline		Follow-up	
	Psychosis group	Control group	Psychosis group	Control group
Anxiety/ depression	. . .	28.6%	. . .	42.9%
Cognitive enhancement	33.3%	28.6%	. . .	14.3%
Cope other neg. mood	33.3%	14.3%	33.3%	. . .
Entertainment	66.7%	. . .	33.3%	28.6%
Interaction	. . .	28.6%	33.3%	. . .
Mood alteration	. . .	. . .	33.3%	42.9%
Physical enhancement	. . .	28.6%	. . .	28.6%
Preferred alternative	. . .	. . .	. . .	14.3%
Relaxation	33.3%	71.4%	100.0%	85.7%

familiar to participants. Given these advantages, the question has to be considered as to whether the idiographic format had any advantages.

A primary advantage of the idiographic approach was the more fine-grained insight that it afforded into understanding the participants' cannabis use. A secondary advantage was that the interview required participants to reflect on their cannabis use and to engage in an interpersonal process before being asked to respond to the more impersonal questionnaire approach. The main focus of the following discussion will be upon the insights that the idiographic approach afforded into the construing of individual participants and how these insights might contribute to understanding issues raised in the existing literature.

The prominence of relaxation as a cannabis effect in this small sample of women was consistent with effects reported in other studies (Green, Kavanagh & Young, 2003). In relation to individuals with psychosis, a central question concerns why individuals use cannabis when it can increase the symptoms of psychosis and result in relapse or rehospitalisation. There has been limited support for the view that individuals are self-medicating symptoms of psychosis. Rather, studies (Addington & Duchak 1997; Dixon et al., 1991) have reported individuals with psychosis are more likely to use cannabis to relieve anxiety and depression than psychotic symptoms. While few of the women with psychosis in this study reported cannabis use to relieve anxiety, depression or other negative mood this was prevalent among males (Green et al., 2004). However, in the available literature, there are also conflicting findings regarding anxiety and depression. For example, Addington & Duchak, (1997) reported 81% of a group of 21 people with schizophrenia endorsed using cannabis to relax. However, while 71% reported relaxation as being increased, 52% reported increased anxiety and only 24% reported decreased anxiety.

One of the male participants in the current research who generally limited the amount that he smoked on any one occasion reported becoming more anxious if he smoked excessively. However, at the same time he reported that he would be physically relaxed. Data, not reported above that were subsequently obtained from participants regarding how relaxation obtained from cannabis differed from non-cannabis induced relaxation highlighted individual differences in whether relaxation was experienced as a physical or cognitive experience. In these terms physical relaxation could be accompanied by unchanged anxiety or even increased anxiety, or the opposite effect with cognitive relaxation being dominant. This account also suggests why it is problematic to assume that anxiety and relaxation are mutually exclusive and opposing poles of a continuum or that people experience anxiety as a unitary phenomena.

Goode (1970), in a study of 191 marijuana smokers, noted that different individuals experienced opposite effects (e.g., mind wanders versus more concentration) and were affected in different ways at different times. Comments by male participants in the current research afford insight into some of this variation. In relation to the effect cannabis has upon conversation and socialisation one participant described an initial period of increased socialisation before becoming quiet. For another participant the effect upon concentration was reported to be dependent on the amount of cannabis used, while a long time user reported the experience of euphoria as being "long gone", replaced by a general sense of well-being (a phenomena reflected in the Multi Dimensional Scaling analysis of heavy users and experimental users (Linkovich-Kyle & Dunn, 2001). These examples suggest the importance of considering stage of intoxication, dose effects and tolerance as possible sources of variation in self-reported effects. Clearly a model which describes cannabis effects as invariant across situations, stages of use or individuals does not reflect the experience of cannabis users. Further, 2 participants who report using the same amount of cannabis daily, might use cannabis quite differently (e.g., titrated throughout the day versus smoked all in one session) and seek different forms of altered consciousness and effects.

There are likely to be multifactorial reasons for differences between individuals. Kelly has proposed one explanation in terms of the constructs that are used by individuals and how these constructs are organised with subordinate and superordinate relationships within each system of constructs. For one individual, being talkative may be a positively regarded and anticipated effect because of its relationship to the higher order construct of being social and popular, which is the perceived opposite of being an outcast. However, for someone else being talkative might be related to loosened control and creativity.

The small sample size of the above study does not permit generalisation to other populations. However, a strength of the idiographic component of the current research is that it allowed exploration of personal meaning and individual differences, as well as highlighting inter-relations between identified reasons for use and expectancies. The idiographic approach also elicited data regarding social processes and social roles and identity (for many participants "cannabis smoking" is not just "smoking cannabis") associated with cannabis use. Additionally, insight was afforded into some of the anticipatory processes associated with cannabis use (e.g., the ritual of preparing cannabis to be smoked). The research approach adopted has generated some interesting hypotheses, particularly with regards to the differential experience of cannabis upon anxiety and differences in how euphoria is experienced. The findings also highlight how other theoretical approaches can extend the utility of PCP oriented research and the capacity of idiographic approaches, such as PCP oriented research, to examine individual differences in a more fine grained manner and to suggest directions for future research.

APPENDIX

EXCERPTS FROM CONTENT ANALYSIS DICTIONARY

ENTERTAINMENT
appreciation of movie
appreciation of music
appreciation of tv
birthday

PHYSICAL FUNCTION
appetite
back pain
back problem
eat
energy

COG-FUNCTION
alert
alter consciousness
alters mind
alter my mind
awareness

INTERACTION
able to express self
all at one
bond
bonded

GROUP
all smokers
distribution point
enjoy socially
everybody else was
everyone else was
from friend

RELAX
at peace
calmative
calm
calm me

BORED
alleviate boredom
alleviate routine

FEEL-GOOD
become stoned
being stoned
better mood
buzz

COPE
aloofness
aloof
angry
bring out of that state

DISTRESS
agitated
antianxiolytic
anxiety
anxious
antidepressant

HABIT
always do
because do
because we do

WANTED
because want to
didn't feel like it
feel like
felt like having

AVAILABLE
accessibility
afford
appropriate
availability
available

PREFERRED
addicted to nicotine
alternative to alcohol
alternative to drinking

ADDICTION
addicted
addictive
anxiety to smoke

ENHANCER
coming down from speed

PERCEPTION
brighter
can take everything in

PSYCHOSIS
delusions worse
psychosis
paranoia

MEDICATION
take lethargic feeling away

No THOUGHT
didn't really
didn't really think

ACKNOWLEDGMENTS

D. Kavanagh and R.Young assisted with study design and development of the coding scheme, K. Krippendorf provided advice on use of Alpha and reliability analysis, M. Miller provided advice on the use of VB-Pro, R. Levesque assisted with SPSS syntax and S. Mahdasia wrote a parsing program.

REFERENCES

Aarons, G. A., Brown, S. A., Stice, E. et al., (2001). Psychometric evaluation of the marijuana and stimulant effect expectancy questionnaires for adolescents. *Addictive Behaviors*, 26(2), 219–236.
Addington, J. & Duchak, V. (1997). Reasons for substance use in schizophrenia. *Acta Psychiatrica Scandinavica*, 96(5), 329–333.
Bailey, P. E. & Sims, A. C. (1991). The repertory grid as a measure of change and predictor of outcome in the treatment of alcoholism. *British Journal of Medical Psychology*, 64(3), 285–293.

Burr, V. & Butt, T. (1992). *Invitation to personal construct psychology.* London: Whurr Publishers.

Burrell, M. J. & Jaffe, A. J. (1999). Personal meaning drug use and addiction: an evolutionary constructivist perspective. *Journal of Constructivist Psychology, 12(1),* 41–63.

Cooper, M. L. (1994). Motivations for alcohol use among adolescents: development and validation of a four factor model. *Psychological Assessment, 6(2),* 117–128.

Costa e Silva, J. A. (2002). Evidence-based analysis of the worldwide abuse of licit and illicit drugs. *Human Psychopharmacology, 17(3),* 131–140.

Davies, J. B. (1996). Reasons and causes: understanding substance users' explanations for their behaviour. *Human Psychopharmacology, 11(Supp 1),* s39–s48.

Dawes, A. (1985). Construing drug dependence. In E. Button (Ed.), *Personal Construct Theory and Mental Health.* London: Croom Helm.

Dixon, L., Haas, G., Wieden, P. J. et al. (1991). Drug abuse in schizophrenic patients: clinical correlates and reasons for use. *American Journal of Psychiatry, 148(2),* 224–230.

Fischman, M. W. & Foltin, R. W. (1991). Utility of subjective-effects measurements in assessing abuse liability of drugs in humans. *British Journal of Addiction, 86(12),* 1563–1570.

Goode, E. (1970) *The marijuana smokers.* New York: Basic Books.

Goldman, M. S. & Darkes, J. (2004). Alcohol expectancy multiaxial assessment: a memory network-based approach. *Psychological Assessment, 16(1),* 4–15.

Green, B., Kavanagh, D. & Young, R. (2003). On being stoned: the self-reported effects of cannabis. *Drug And Alcohol Review, 22(4),* 453–460.

Green, B., Kavanagh, D. & Young, R. (2004). Reasons for cannabis use in men with and without psychosis. *Drug and Alcohol Review, 23(4),* 445–453.

Kelly, G. (1955). *The psychology of personal constructs.* New York: Norton.

Kelly, G. A. (1996). Europe's matrix of decision. In D. Kalekin-Fishman & B. M. Walker (Eds), *The construction of group realities: Culture society and personal construct theory* Malabar, FL: Robert E. Krieger Publishing Co Inc.

Klion, R. E. (1993). Chemical dependency: a personal construct theory approach. In L. M. Leitner & N. G. Dunnett (Eds), *Critical issues in personal construct psychotherapy.* Malabar, FL: Krueger Publishing Company.

Klion, R. E. & Pfenninger, D. T. (1997). *Personal construct psychotherapy of addictions. Journal of Substance Abuse Treatment, 14(1),* 37–43.

Krippendorf, K. (2003). *Alpha: A computer program for reliability analysis.* Philadelphia: University of Pennsylvania.

Krippendorf, K. (2004). *Content analysis: An introduction to its methodology.* 2nd edition. Thousand Oaks: Sage.

Langenbucher, J. W. & Merrill. (2001). The validity of self-reported cost events by substance abusers. *Evaluation Review, 25(2),* 184–210.

Linkovich-Kyle, T. L. & Dunn, M. E. (2001). Consumption-related differences in the organization and activation of marijuana expectancies in memory. *Experimental and Clinical Psychpharmacology, 9(3),* 334–342.

Lynch, P. (1995). Adolescent smoking: an alternative perspective using personal construct theory. *Health Education Research, 10(1),* 95–106.

Mackay, N. (1997). Constructivism and the logic of explanation. *Journal of Constructivist Psychology, 10(4),* 339–361.

Mancuso, J. C. & Adams-Webber, J. R. (1982). Anticipation as a constructive process: the fundamental postulate. In J. R. Adams-Webber & J. C. Mancuso (Eds), *The Construing Person.* New York: Praeger Press.

Mancuso, J. C. & Hunter, K. V. (1983). Anticipation motivation or emotion: the fundamental postulate after twenty-five years. In J. R. Adams-Webber & J. C. Mancuso (Eds), *Application of Personal Construct Theory.* Toronto: Academic Press.

Miller, M. (1995). *VB-Pro: A program for analyzing verbatim text.* Knoxville: University of Tennessee.

Miller, N. S. & Fine, J. (1993). Current epidemiology of comorbidity of psychiatric and addictive disorders. *Psychiatric Clinics of North America, 16(1),* 1–10.

Mills, D. (2001). *The posture of anticipation: Kelly and Alexander.* 14th International Congress of Personal Psychology Wollongong.

Mueser, K. T., Pallavi, N., Tracy, J. I., et al. (1995). Expectations and motives for substance use in schizophrenia. *Schizophrenia Bulletin, 21(3),* 367–378.

Mueser, K. T., Yarnold, P. R., Rosenberg, S. D. et al. (2000). Substance use disorder in hospitalized severely mentally ill psychiatric patients: prevalence correlates and subgroups. *Schizophrenia Bulletin, 26(1),* 179–192.

Newcomb, M. D., Chou, C-P., Bentler, P. M., et al. (1988). Cognitive motivations for drug use among adolescents: longitudinal tests of gender differences and predictors of change in drug use. *Journal of Counseling Psychology, 35(4),* 426–438.

Regier, D. A., Farmer, M. E., Rae, D. S., et al. (1990). Comorbidity of mental disorders with alcohol and other drug abuse results from the Epidemiologic Catchment Area (ECA) Study. *JAMA, 264(19),* 2511–2518.

Rivers, C. & Landfield, A. (1985). Personal construct theory and alcohol dependence In E. Button (Ed.), *Personal Construct Theory and Mental Health.* London: Croom Helm.

Schafer, J. & Brown, S. A. (1991). Marijuana and cocaine effect expectancies and drug use patterns. *Journal of Consulting and Clinical Psychology, 59(4),* 558–565.

Simons, J., Correia, C. J., Carey, K. B., et al. (1998). Validating a five factor marijuana motives measure: Relations with use problems and alcohol motives. *Journal of Counseling Psychology, 45(3),* 265–273.

Slater, P. (1977). *The measurement of intrapersonal space by grid technique.* Vol 2 Dimensions of Intrapersonal Space. Chichester: John Wiley & Sons, Ltd.

Sobell, L. C. & Sobell, M. B. (1992). Timeline follow-back: a technique for assessing self-reported ethanol consumption. In J. Allen & R. Z. Litten (Eds), *Measuring alcohol consumption: Psychosocial and biological methods.* Totowa: Humana Press.

Swift, W., Hall, W. & Teeson, M. (1999). *Cannabis use disorders among Australian adults: Findings from The national survey of mental health and wellbeing.* Sydney: National Drug and Alcohol Research Centre.

Viney, L. L., Westbrook, M. T. & Preston, C. (1985). The addiction experience as a function of the addict's history. *British Journal of Clinical Psychology, 24(2),* 73–82.

Weinstein, R. M. (1976). The imputation of motives for marijuana behavior. *International Journal of the Addictions. 11(4),* 571–595.

Willner, P. (2001). A view through the gateway: Expectancies as a possible pathway from alcohol to cannabis. *Addiction, 96(5),* 691–703.

15

Counselling After Sexual Assault: A Personal Construct Model of the Impact of Counsellors' Responses to Client Disclosure

CAROLE CARTER

LINDA L. VINEY

People who have been sexually assaulted or abused will later be influenced not so much by the event itself as by their interpretations of the event. In the research described in this chapter, the role of subsequent validation or invalidation of different foci of people's interpretations of the event on their ability to helpfully reconstruct their beliefs was explored. In particular, the impact of people disclosing their experiences to a helping professional was investigated. A personal construct model was developed and revised in the light of the findings to account for the role of different foci of validation and invalidation in enhancing or impeding helpful reconstruction of beliefs. Among the findings was the confirmation that validation of clients' sense of themselves as meaning-makers was integral to enhancing helpful reconstruction of their beliefs.

Personal Construct Psychology: New Ideas. Edited by Peter Caputi, Heather Foster and Linda L. Viney. Copyright © 2006 John Wiley & Sons, Ltd.

INTRODUCTION

It may be assumed that the majority of clients disclosing an experience of sexual assault or abuse to a helping professional are experiencing some difficulty as a result of the interpretations or meanings they have ascribed to their assault or abuse experiences. This is presumably a contributory factor in their needing to consult a helping professional. When people disclose, the resulting validation or invalidation of different aspects of their construing about the assault or abuse will affect the likelihood of their beginning to helpfully revise the meanings they have formed of their experiences of sexual assault or abuse. The study which informs this chapter explored those aspects of clients' construing that are being validated in this exchange with a helping professional, and those that are being invalidated, and the effect of this on the likelihood of constructive revision of clients' unhelpful beliefs.

CONCEPTUAL CONTEXT TO THE STUDY

People disclosing an experience of sexual assault or abuse are a particularly vulnerable client group. Some have suffered very many years of abuse, some from a very young age. For many, disclosing to a helping professional is an act of great courage, sometimes desperation, as in doing so they may be making themselves vulnerable to profound invalidation. This study sought to extend our understanding of the experience of a person disclosing sexual assault or abuse to a helping professional and the extent to which the disclosure experience alters the way she or he then proceeds to manage their abuse experience. How can we better understand what occurred during the disclosure experience, and how, or if, this experience enabled constructive change? How can psychotherapists and counsellors use this knowledge to enhance therapeutic practice?

THE STUDY

The study involved the development and testing of a personal construct model of the effect on clients of counsellors' responses to their disclosures of sexual assault or abuse experiences. While the study was also embedded in sexual assault literature, the chapter is drawn largely from the personal construct literature. A full account of the study is given in Carter (2004).

The roles of validation and invalidation in psychotherapy underpin this exploration. The role of validation and invalidation in revision of construing, described by Kelly as the validational cycle (Kelly, 1955/1991, p. 112), is central to the psychology of personal constructs. It is therefore also central to an understanding of personal construct therapy:

> While the invalidation of a construct does not necessarily produce an appreciable anxiety, it is the normal basis for abandoning the construct. Invalidation is used in therapy to help the client find just where his system breaks down. The psychologist who utilises the psychology of personal constructs intentionally designs his therapeutic programme around a series of practical experiments which will yield validating and invalidating evidence. The invalidating evidence will normally lead to the abandonment of constructs, to anxiety, and thence to revision, with help in reformulation coming either from the therapist or from another source." (Kelly 1955/1991 Vol. 1 p. 368).

Faidley and Leitner (1993) identified the role in therapy of confirmation that is complex and multi-layered, and extends beyond the validation or invalidation of the content of the particular constructs on which the client may be focussing at a given time:

> Great skill on the part of the therapist is required to judge what blend of validation and invalidation will be optimally therapeutic for each client. Clients who have been seriously damaged will be highly threatened by therapist responses that indicate the need for change and extension of their construct system into the unknown. All clients need a broad base of confirmation in order to trust themselves to undertake major revisions of their construct system (p. 87).

What constitutes a broad base of confirmation?

> Persons frequently enter therapy after experiencing core role invalidation (Leitner, 1985). Thus, they are faced with the task of deciding whether the therapist can be trusted with an invalidated core. Will the therapist validate or invalidate this core? This potential threat may lead the client to pay careful attention to the therapist responses to client construals. These responses can be used to decide whether the therapist will validate the client's core (Cummins, 1993, p. 85).

Validation and invalidation are more complex than they may seem. Construing is not one-dimensional. Referring to Kelly's (1951/1991) assertion that validation represents the compatibility (subjectively construed) between a person's prediction and the outcome they observe, and invalidation represents incompatibility (subjectively construed) between a person's prediction and the outcome they observe, Button comments:

This seems straightforward enough, but in practice I'm not sure it's so simple. Unlike the digital computer, which has a simple yes/no and on/off decision to make such "compatibility" is rarely such a black and white matter. As Kelly emphasises, it is very much a *subjective* matter as to whether or not one has been validated or invalidated. I think I'd go further than that and say that it is not just a matter of opinion, but also a matter of *degree* (Button, 2000, p. 142).

We go further still, and say that it is not only a matter of degree, but of *different aspects or foci* of construing being validated or invalidated at any given time. What emerged in this study was the need to understand not only *whether* a person's construing is being validated or invalidated, or the *degree*, but also *what aspect* of a person's construing is being tested and validated or invalidated, and how this relates to the prospects for constructive revision. In this study we suggested that in attempting to understand what is occurring in a therapeutic interaction, for example where a client is disclosing a traumatic experience, there are three primary foci of his or her construing that are being exposed for potential validation or invalidation:

(1) The *content* of their construing about a particular issue or experience (event as object).
(2) Their *beliefs about themselves* (sense of self as object).
(3) Their *construing of their meaning-making processes* (sense of self as subject).

These three foci are elaborated in Carter (2004).

Walker, Oades, Caputi, Stevens and Crittenden (2000) also looked at these issues in relation to validation. They also distinguished three conceptual aspects of construing that are open to validation or invalidation: *content* (similar to 1 above), *structure*, as in the nature of the existing assumed hierarchical system, or "implicative network" referred to by Hinkle (1965), and *process* (similar to (3) above). In looking at structure, the hierarchical nature of people's construct systems, Walker et al. (2000) have identified an aspect of validation that invites further exploration, though not in this context.

Based on our proposed Personal Construct Model, eight potential patterns of the three foci of validation/invalidation (as outlined in (1), (2) and (3) above) are identifiable in any interaction (validation-validation-invalidation, invalidation-validation-invalidation, etc). First, it was anticipated that to enable helpful reconstruction of a client's construing about her abuse experiences, the content of her construing about the abuse would need to be invalidated. Second, it was anticipated that to have the confidence to extend her construct system into the unknown, risking the anxiety which is inherent in potential revision, she would need a broad base of confirmation in the therapeutic situation (Faidley & Leitner, 1993). It was believed this would include validation of her core construing about herself (sense of self), and (thirdly) validation of her construing processes, her sense of herself as capable of attributing meaning.

A Personal Construct Model of the effect of counsellors' responses to client disclosure was developed. This model can be seen in full in Carter & Viney (1999) and is elaborated in detail by Carter (2004). The primary assumptions of the model were that clients would be most likely to reconstruct their unhelpful construing about their sexual assault experiences as a result of the disclosure if they experienced:

(1) Invalidation of their beliefs about their assault experiences (assault as object),
(2) Validation of their beliefs about themselves (self as object), and
(3) Validation of their view of themselves as meaning-makers (self as subject)

METHOD

PARTICIPANTS

Thirty-eight people who had disclosed to a helping professional an experience of having been sexually assaulted or abused were interviewed in the main study. Participants ranged in age from 16 to 59 years. Only 1 male volunteer proceeded to interview. Participants' experiences of sexual assault covered a wide range from repeated, long-term childhood sexual abuse, to a single incident of rape as an adult. Perpetrators were sole or multiple, and ranged from strangers to close relatives. Perpetrators were reported to be "father" in 22% of cases, with "brother" occurring second in frequency (12%).

PROCEDURE

Participants were volunteers who were referred by local counsellors or self-referred as a result of radio interviews, newspaper articles and pamphlets distributed via selected community agencies. All interviewees had, on an earlier occasion, completed a ten-page questionnaire, assessing demographic data and information about their assault or abuse and disclosure experiences. Eleven participants who completed the questionnaire elected not to continue on to interview. Interview locations were selected by the individual particip-ant, and included the participant's home and the premises of community counselling agencies supporting the research.

ASSESSMENT

An interview protocol was developed, piloted and revised. The interview schedule included 15 questions designed to elicit descriptions of participants' experiences of disclosing the sexual assault to a helping professional, an open-ended question about their lives in general, and questions relating to validation and the extent of construct revision following the disclosure ex-perience. The interviews were audiotaped and transcribed.

ANALYSIS

Analysis was largely qualitative, although the devices developed to analyse validation and reconstruction included a visual numerical scale to assist raters' assessments. To assess validation, participants' transcripts were analysed using an assessment device developed for the purpose which we named the Validation Assessment Technique (VAT). A process of double coding was used, involving two independent raters.

Similarly, to assess reconstruction, an assessment device was developed and named the Reconstruction Assessment Technique (RAT), and used to analyse participants' transcripts. Again, the process of double coding was used to assess the extent of revision of their beliefs evident in participants' transcripts.

Additional analysis was undertaken employing qualitative analysis. Them-atic analysis was undertaken of all participants' responses to two interview questions relating to their own perceptions about influential factors in their disclosure experiences. Finally, in-depth analysis of eight participants' stories was undertaken, cases being selected using purposeful sampling and drawn from their questionnaires and transcripts of their interviews.

RESULTS OF ANALYSIS OF VALIDATION AND RECONSTRUCTION

The two most important outcomes of the research were, first, the confirma-tion that validation of their sense of themselves as makers of meaning, Focus (3) in the Model, emerged very clearly from the frequency data and qualitat-ive analyses as central to clients' ability to begin reconstruction.

Second, results of the assessment suggested that while the validation pattern anticipated in our Personal Construct Model occurred very fre-

quently, it ranked second in frequency to a pattern that comprised one important difference. The clients most likely to begin constructive revision
appeared in fact to be those who experienced:

(1) Invalidation of the content of their construing about their assault
    experience,
(2) Invalidation of their construing about self, and
(3) Validation of their meaning-making processes (self as subject).

In summary, what we had anticipated in (1) and (3) appeared to be confirmed. The difference, however, between the pattern that we had anticipated
and the pattern which actually occurred most frequently was in *construing*
about self (2). Where we had anticipated that *validation of construing about*
self was integral to beginning the process of revising their beliefs about their
assault experiences, in fact for the majority of clients, for reconstruction to
begin, *invalidation* of aspects of their sense of self appeared to be important.

DISCUSSION

The findings in relation to beliefs about self (Focus 2) supported Leitner,
Dunnett, Anderson and Meshot's (1993) observation:

> Validating the client's construct system may lead the client to some very
> painful realisations about himself . . . Likewise, invalidation of the client's
> construct system, when done with therapeutic acumen, may lead to new real-
> isations that allow for growth and the elaboration of one's system. For
> example, a client's construction of herself as "evil" because she had co-
> operated in her father's sexual abuse of her may make coming to terms with
> the abuse very difficult. Validation and invalidation are important aspects used
> in construing the client's construing process – the deeply moving relationship
> with the client (Leitner et al., 1993, p. 8).

On close examination of the transcripts of the participants whose patterns
complied with the dominant one, it became evident that their sense of self
as they entered the disclosure experience invariably reflected damage,
impediments to optimal functioning. Invalidation of unhelpful aspects of
their construing about themselves, then, appears to have become important
to their ability to begin the process of reconstruction. For these clients, the
need for extension of their construct system involved revising their beliefs
about themselves as much as revising their interpretation of the assault or
abuse.

Validation of meaning making processes emerged as consistently influential in the ability of participants to begin reconstruction. Even if the meaning that was being confirmed was that they were confused, this still was empowering, as exemplified in the words of one participant:

> . . . all of a sudden I understood why I was so confused, and why I couldn't make any sense of it. It was right for me to be confused and that was enormously powerful. Most powerfully, what was being confirmed was . . . it was OK for me to be so unhappy because there was a reason for it, and that I should have hope because if there was a reason for it and it was logical to feel that way you can do something with that. You can fix it, hopefully, make it better at least.

The results suggested that if their constructions of themselves as makers of meaning are validated, people are able to withstand the threat inherent in experiencing invalidation of their beliefs about traumatic events and in their existing unhelpful beliefs about themselves. Not only that, they are able to use this invalidation constructively to begin revising their beliefs.

CONCLUSIONS

The importance to clients of the therapeutic interaction at the time of disclosure, usually occurring in the early stages of contact, cannot be overstated.

> . . . fundamental decisions about the relationship are made early in the initial sessions of therapy. The success or failure of the entire therapeutic interaction may be determined in the first two or three sessions. While possibly viewed as radical, this position can be explained in a manner consistent with PCP (Cummins, in Leitner & Dunnett, p. 85).

The overall purpose in undertaking this research was to extend existing understandings of the experiences of people disclosing sexual assault to helping professionals, to elaborate understandings of the extent to which clients' experiences, when disclosing, affected their ability to make sense of their sexual assault experiences, and move in the direction of optimal functioning. In particular the intention was to extend understanding of the factors involved in enhancing or impeding this process. This research has been an exploratory process. The extent to which it will make a contribution to enhancing therapeutic practice for this particularly courageous population of clients remains to be seen. The findings challenged some of our assumptions about the therapeutic precursors to reconstruction of clients' beliefs, and confirmed others. What is most likely to enable change is what personal construct therapists do: credulous listening, provision of invalidating evidence for beliefs that are unhelpful, and validation of clients' meaning making processes.

REFERENCES

Button, E. (2000). Validation and invalidation. In J. W. Scheer & A. Catina (Eds), *Empirical constructivism in Europe: The personal construct approach.* Geissen: Psychosozial-Verlag.

Carter, C. (2004). Validation in the reconstruction, with counsellors, of beliefs that clients hold about their sexual assault experiences: A personal construct model. Unpublished PhD Thesis. University of Wollongong.

Carter, C. & Viney, L. (1999). Counselling after sexual assault, Conference Paper. Australasian Personal Construct Conference, Bendigo, Australia.

Cummins, P. (1993). Engagement in Psychotherapy. In L. M. Leitner & N. G. M. Dunnett (Eds), *Critical issues in personal construct psychotherapy.* Malabar, FL: Krieger Publishing Co.

Faidley, A. J. & Leitner, L. M. (1993). *Assessing experience in psychotherapy: Personal construct alternatives.* Westport, CT: Praeger.

Hinkle, D. (1965). The change of personal constructs from the viewpoint of a theory of construct implications. Unpublished PhD thesis. Ohio State University.

Kelly, G. (1955/1991). *The psychology of personal constructs. Vol. 1: A theory of personality.* London: Routledge.

Leitner, L. M., Dunnett, N. G. M., Anderson, T. M. & Meshot, C. M. (1993). Unique aspects of personal construct psychotherapy. In L. M. Leitner & N. G. M. Dunnett (Eds), *Critical issues in personal construct psychotherapy.* Malabar, Florida: Krieger.

Leitner, L. M., Faidley, A. J. & Celentana, M. A. (2000). Diagnosing human meaning making: An experiential constructivist approach. In R. A. Neimeyer & J. D Raskin (Eds), *Constructions of disorder: Meaning-making frameworks for psychotherapy.* Washington, DC: American Psychological Association.

Patton, M. Q. P. (1990). Qualitative evaluation and research methods, 2nd Edition, Sage Publications Inc.

Walker, B. M., Oades, L. G., Caputi, P., Stevens, C. & Crittenden, N. (2000). Going beyond the scientist metaphor: From validation to experience cycles. In J. W. Scheer (Ed.), *The person in society: Challenges to a constructivist theory.* Giessen: Psychosozial-Verlag.

Walker, B. M. (2001). Nonvalidation vs. (In)validation: Implications for theory and practice. In J. D. Raskin & S. K. Bridges (Eds), *Studies in meaning.* Pace University Press.

16

Role Relationships and the Restoration of Coherence in the Stories of Women Diagnosed with Breast Cancer

LISBETH G. LANE

LINDA L. VINEY

Within personal construct theory, relationships with others, based on a mutual intention to understand each other's construction processes, are considered to be a primary source of validation and invalidation of meaning-making. A major task of psychotherapeutic work with people facing the ongoing threat of breast cancer, therefore, is to facilitate interpersonal opportunities in which individuals can formulate, test and elaborate their ongoing stories about themselves. Personal construct ideas relating to meaning-making; including the experience cycle, role relationships and support are presented in this chapter. These concepts provide the framework for personal construct group work aimed at restoring a sense of coherence in women living with breast cancer's ongoing stories of survival.

INTRODUCTION

Until quite recently the psychological "health" of breast cancer patients was not widely considered. Fortuitously, as medical advances have enabled breast

Personal Construct Psychology: New Ideas. Edited by Peter Caputi, Heather Foster and Linda L. Viney. Copyright © 2006 John Wiley & Sons, Ltd.

cancer patients to live longer, increasing attention now focuses on breast cancer survivors' emotional state and quality of life. This has resulted in the development of a number of psychological interventions aimed at helping patients better "cope" with the emotional aspects of living with a cancer diagnosis.

When mortality is "rendered visible" (Little, Jordens, Paul, et al., 1998) by a cancer diagnosis, denial of one's own mortality is gone forever and taken for granted assumptions, the personal and social life goals previously constructed, may now need to be reconstructed. When we need to revise core constructs, those constructs concerned with our existence and place in the scheme of things, personal construct psychology suggests that we turn to our relationships with others to test and elaborate new meanings and restore coherence to our ongoing life stories. A review of the research literature shows that support from the interpersonal environment is an important factor in adaptation to a cancer diagnosis (Allbrook, 1997; Bloom, 1982; Bultz, Speca, Brasher et al., 2000; Dunkel-Schetter, 1984; Dunkel-Schetter & Wortman, 1982; Ell, Mantell, Hamovitch et al., 1989; Lane & Viney, 2005; Mor, Malin, Allen et al., 1994), yet, many women report feeling isolated by their diagnosis (Lane, 2002; Welch-McCaffrey, Hoffman, Leigh et al., 1989). Women living with cancer run the risk of driving away potential support if they exhibit high levels of distress, but frequently fail to receive much needed support if they do not display that distress (Silver, Wortman, Crofton et al., 1990). As a result, at the very time when the world and events within it may seem unpredictable, many women find their anticipation that "others" will understand is disconfirmed and they find themselves bereft of the interpersonal context in which to elaborate a construct system that enables them to interpret their experiences and hypothesise, test and revise new meanings (Lane & Viney, 2000b). Personal construct ideas relating to meaning-making are now presented. They provide the framework for our understanding of how best to facilitate the elaboration of new and more helpful meanings that restore a sense of coherence in women living with breast cancer's ongoing stories of survival.

MEANING-MAKING

Kelly (1991) states that people's understanding of their worlds is a direct function of the organisation and content of their "personal" construct systems (the Construction Corollary). These complex and often idiosyncratic systems of constructs, developed over a lifetime, are the "matrix of meaning" through which they filter their experiences, define their personal realities, and act in the world (Neimeyer, Epting & Krieger, 1983, p. 90). These systems are organised hierarchically (the Organisation Corollary), with relationships of superordination and subordination among their interconnected constructs. Superordinate (abstract and central) constructs subsume subordinate (specific and peripheral) constructs (Hinkle, 1965). Constructs about self are termed core constructs, and the most superordinate of these constructs concern people's values and beliefs, their assumptions about the world and their places within it. These assumptions are fundamental to meaning-making, in that they help to make events appear predictable (Kelly, 1991).

While the attempt to live predictably is a quest for stability, constructs are constantly subject to change (Kelly, 1991). Experience is conceptualised, therefore, as a cycle embracing five phases: anticipation, investment, encounter, confirmation or disconfirmation and constructive revision. The subjective assessment of the outcome of the anticipation in the Confirmation/Disconfirmation stage will determine the degree of revision deemed necessary, preparing for fresh anticipations and further Experience Cycles (Winter, 1992). Epting and Amerikaner (1980) describe this crucial phase as follows:

> On the one hand is the possibility that some areas of the person's life are more compatible than before, aspects that were discrete or in opposition may move towards integration. Previously inaccessible material (not clearly understood experiences) may become more fully synchronised with the rest of the person's life. It is in constructive revision that all of the greater moments of life, which are often recognised and labelled as "growth experiences", take place. From these we are enlivened and invigorated, and feel more fully-grown. On the other hand, the person may now realize that certain beliefs or life stances cannot be maintained, and drastic, painful changes are needed. . . . The recognition of the need to change, to relinquish old constructions, and the subsequent actuality of revision are, of course, what were risked at the outset of the cycle (pp. 58–59).

The completion of the full Experience Cycle is essential for optimal functioning (Winter, 1992). This completion is characterised by openness to interaction with the environment, and an orientation towards movement into the future (Epting & Amerikaner, 1980).

ROLE RELATIONSHIPS

Kelly (1991) argues that people define their constructs about themselves in relation to others. He referred to these important self-images as "core role" constructs, describing these constructs as dimensions that operate to define people's personal identities, their complex and unique senses of phenomeno- logical continuance (Kelly, 1991). Relationships with others, based on an intention to *understand* their meanings, and engaging in interpersonal actions based on these attempts are termed role relationships. Personal construct theory suggests that role relationships provide the context for the elabora- tion of meaning. First, they provide for the validation/invalidation of core construing, leading potentially to definition, and to internal consistency that makes the construct systems clearer and more explicit (Winter, 1992). Second, role relationships allow for extension of core construing. Extension serves to make constructs more comprehensive, by "making more of life's experiences meaningful" (Kelly, 1991, p. 47).

The personal construct concept of understanding in role relationships goes beyond understanding the content of another's construct system to encompass understanding the other person's processes of construing. Understanding another's processes of construing involves understanding their core role constructs: "our sense of who we are, who we would like to be, and who we feel we are becoming" (Leitner & Dill-Standiford, 1993, p. 137).

SUPPORTIVE ROLE RELATIONSHIPS

Kelly states that when people cannot take an unexpected event in their stride, or when they cannot handle all modes of their reality, support minimises the negative results of their experimentations (Kelly, 1991, Vol. II, p. 74). Support is defined as a broad-based response pattern that permits receivers to experiment widely and successfully. Kelly elaborates this definition of support by saying that support, unlike reassurance, does not trap people in their own construct systems. Support is about confirming the others' processes of construing. Supporters, in attempting to see things from the others' points of view, are not responding in terms of certainties or outcomes, but are accepting and acknowledging their processes of construing, and their exploratory attempt to communicate their meanings. This definition of support implies that the mechanism of support lies in validation of people as construers of meaning.

Supportive role relationships are a subset of role relationships that have particular characteristics that may differ from other role relationships in which people are engaged. The intention in role relationships will always be, primarily, in terms of moving people's own construing processes towards optimum anticipation of future events, with a possible secondary intention to move the other's construing processes forward. Supportive role relationships, on the other hand, have the primary intention of moving the other's processes further. The intended direction of movement in supportive relationships will be towards optimal functioning in terms of the receivers' successive engagement in elaborating helpful ongoing cycles of experience.

Support can be derived from sharing common constructs for interpreting experiences (Duck, 1973, 1979), and meanings (Neimeyer & Hudson, 1985; Neimeyer & Neimeyer, 1983). Duck (1973) suggests that when people find others share a similar view, they may subjectively construe this similarity as evidence for the merit of their own construct systems. The more constructs are shared with others, the more the constructs will seem to be well formed and justified. Similarity helps, therefore, to define people's meanings, by confirming the viability of their existing constructs. It follows from this that the success of supportive relationships will be determined, in part, by the extent to which people are able to help others define their existing meanings.

Although some level of similarity in construing may be necessary to conduct supportive role relationships, from Kelly's account of role relationships, understanding is also necessary. So important to him was the notion of understanding, as acknowledgment of another person's construction processes, and engaging in a role based on that understanding, that he suggested that Social Psychology should be the psychology of interpersonal understandings rather than common understandings (Kelly, 1991). Role relationships require people to acknowledge others' ways of seeing the world (Leitner & Faidley, 1995). Supportive role relationships imply, therefore, "understanding" of others' processes of construing and their exploratory attempts to communicate their meanings. As Fran, a breast cancer sufferer, said of the women she met at her local support group: "We've walked in each other's shoes. In different ways we've all been touched and that's our bond".

SUPPORT AND A BREAST CANCER DIAGNOSIS

An essential aspect of relationships is that they are dynamic. Partners and close friends must, therefore, be willing and able to revise their constructs about each other (Duck, 1979). Neimeyer and Neimeyer (1985) suggest that a failure to do so denies the dynamic reality of the relational process and of each partner as a construer of meaning. For example, when women are confronted with a breast cancer diagnosis, constructs of themselves in relation to breast cancer, and breast cancer in relation to themselves, are likely to be new. The new constructs that women are now forced to include in their systems of meanings are also likely to be outside the range of convenience of their relational others. In supporting them, partners, relatives and friends must encompass their new construing within their own. If they are unable to do this, original levels of similarity and support may not be maintained (Duck, 1979). As Gwen, 54 years of age and 2 years from her diagnosis said "I get very frustrated with my husband, and I realise it is because he doesn't always understand. Sometimes I can talk to him and sometimes I can't. It's them not understanding or not knowing, so they don't want to talk about it". According to Neimeyer and Neimeyer (1985), the inability to maintain levels of similarity can: ". . . set the stage for the *disruption* of a once satisfactory relationship that previously offered validation and extension to both partners" (Neimeyer & Neimeyer, 1985, p. 199). This need not imply that these relationships are no longer supporting other systems of construing. Women's existing relationships may be inadequate only in supporting them to elaborate new meanings in relation to themselves as recipients of a diagnosis of breast cancer. However, the implications of this absence of support may have ramifications throughout their entire systems of meaning (Hinkle, 1965). The following woman expresses her inability to obtain support of herself as a construer of meaning from her husband: "I'm not that sort of person (to keep thinking about death), it's not that I dwell on it, but I find these unwanted thoughts. If I said that to my husband he'd have a fit".

THE IMPLICATION OF THESE CONCEPTS

From our description of the relevant personal construct concepts, it should be clear that personal construct theorists view human beings as construers of meaning, striving to organise and anticipate their engagement with the world. People's idiosyncratically structured meanings will be organised around a set of superordinate core constructs that encompass their core assumptions, which both govern their perceptions of events and channel their behaviour in relation to them. Personal construct concepts can help us make sense of women's experiences of breast cancer diagnosis and survival. Central to women's sense of "being in the world" are their assumptions, beliefs and values, their superordinate core constructs. The enormous potential of a breast cancer diagnosis to create emotional turmoil in their lives, despite the evidence that it is not, necessarily, a deadly disease, is understandable when their superordinate core constructs are invalidated and placed under threat. How then, in the face of threat to their sense of being in the world, can these women elaborate new meanings? Personal construct theory suggests that this will take place in the context of their role relationships. But the breast cancer diagnosis is likely to disrupt their relationships, as evidenced in the literature.

As completion of the Experience Cycle is necessary for optimal functioning, women must revise their current meanings in the light of their breast cancer diagnosis. Unless they can do this, they remain dislocated from their meanings about the world of events, and stuck in unhelpful cycles of experience. This understanding helps to explain the ongoing emotional distress many breast cancer survivors experience.

Support, and this includes therapeutic support, according to personal construct theory, requires both acknowledgement of women living with breast cancer's current meanings and their attempts to express them. When they communicate their fears, these must be acknowledged. To pacify or reassure them that what they fear is unlikely to happen serves only to invalidate them as construers of meaning. In the face of this invalidation, some women may feel unable to express their fears again, so they have no opportunity to define their current meanings. Supportive role relationships provide opportunities to experiment with new meanings. Only by allowing women to clarify their current meanings and experiment with new meanings can women be supported in the challenges they face and in the task of restoring a sense of coherence to their ongoing stories of survival. "Being a survivor for me didn't feel like there was a guarantee that you were not going to die. I felt like a survivor when I decided that I was going to live. So that even if I die from the breast cancer, I intend to LIVE till then".

REFERENCES

Allbrook, M. (Ed.). (1997). *Songs of strength.* Women's Cancer Group. Sydney: Macmillan.

Bloom, J. R. (1982). Social support, accommodation to stress and adjustment to breast cancer. *Social Science and Medicine, 16,* 1329–1338.

Bultz, B. D., Speca, M., Brasher, P. M., Geggie, P. H. & Page, A. (2000). A randomized controlled trial of a brief psychoeducational support group for partners of early stage breast cancer patients. *Psycho-Oncology, 9(4),* 303–313.

Duck, S. (1973). *Personal relationships and personal constructs: A study of friendship formation.* Chichester: John Wiley & Sons, Ltd.

Duck, S. W. (1979). The personal and the interpersonal in construct theory: Social and individual aspects of relationships. In P. Stringer & D. Bannister (Eds), *Constructs of sociality and individuality* (pp. 279–297). London: Academic Press.

Dunkel-Schetter, C. (1984). Social support and cancer. Findings based on patient interviews and their implications. *Journal of Social Issues, 40,* 77–98.

Dunkel-Schetter, C. & Wortman, C. (1982). The interpersonal dynamics of cancer: Problems in social relationships and their impact on the patient. In H. S. Friedman & M. R. Matteo (Eds), *Interpersonal Issues in Healthcare* (pp. 69–100). New York: Academic Press.

Ell, K. O., Mantell, J. E., Hamovitch, M. B. & Nishimoto, R. H. (1989). Social support, sense of control, and coping among patients with breast, lung, or colorectal cancer. *Journal of Psychsocial Oncology, 19(2),* 3–27.

Epting, F. R. & Amerikaner, M. (1980). Optimal functioning: A personal construct approach. In A. W. Landfield & L. M. Leitner (Eds), *Personal construct psychology: Psychotherapy and personality* (pp. 55–73). New York: John Wiley & Sons, Inc.

Hinkle, D. (1965). The change of personal constructs from the viewpoint of a theory of construct implications. Unpublished doctoral dissertation, Ohio State University.

Kelly, G. A. (1991/1955). *The psychology of personal constructs.* Vols. 1 and 2: 2nd Edition. London: Routledge.

Lane, L. G. (2002). Living in the Shadow: A personal construct model of adjustment to breast cancer survival and tests of its clinical usefulness. Unpublished PhD thesis: University of Wollongong.

Lane, L. G. & Viney, L. L. (2000a). The meanings of a breast cancer diagnosis: The role of others in validating helpful constructions of the cancer experience. Ninth Australasian Personal Construct Pychology Conference, Bendigo.

Lane, L.G. & Viney, L. L. (2000b). The meanings of a breast cancer diagnosis: A model of women's construing. In J. M. Fisher & N. Cornelius (Eds), *Challenging the boundaries: PCP Perspectives for the new millennium* (pp. 121–131). Farnborough: EPCA Publications.

Lane, L. G. & Viney, L. L. (2005). The effects of personal construct group therapy on breast cancer survivors. *Journal of Consulting and Clinical Psychology, 73,* 284–292.

Leitner, L. M. & Dill-Staniford, T. (1993). Resistance in experiential personal construct psychotherapy: Theoretical and technical struggles. In L. M. Leitner & N. G. M. Dunnett (Eds), *Critical issues in personal construct psychotherapy* (pp. 135–155). Malabar, Florida: Krieger.

Leitner, L. M. & Faidley, A. (1995). The awful, aweful nature of role relationships. In R. A. Neimeyer & G. J. Neimeyer (Eds), *Advances in personal construct psychology* (Vol. 3: pp. 291–314). Greenwich, CT: JAI Press.

Little, M., Jordens, C. F. C., Paul, K., Montgomery, K. & Philipson, B. (1998). Liminality: A major category of the experience of cancer illness. *Social Science and Medicine, 47,* 1485–1494.

Mor, V., Malin, M. & Allen, S. (1994). Age differences in the psychosocial problems encountered by breast cancer patients. *Journal of the National Cancer Institute Monographs, 16,* 191–197.

Neimeyer, R. A., Epting, F. R. & Krieger, S. R. (1983). Personal constructs in thanatology: An introduction and research bibliography. *Death Education, 7,* 87–96.

Neimeyer, G. J. and Hudson, J. E. (1985). Couple's constructs: Personal systems in marital satisfaction. In D. Bannister (Ed.), *Issues and approaches in personal construct theory* (pp. 127–141). London: Academic Press.

Neimeyer, R. A. & Neimeyer, G. J. (1983). Structural similarity in the acquaintance process. *Journal of Social and Clinical Psychology, 1,* 146–154.

Neimeyer, R. A. & Neimeyer, G. J. (1985). Disturbed relationships: A personal construct view. In Eric Button (Ed.), *Personal Construct Theory and Health: Theory, Research and Practice* (pp. 195–223). London: Crook Helm.

Silver, R. C., Wortman, C. B. & Crofton, C. (1990). The role of coping in support provision: The self-presentational dilemma of victims of life crises. In B. S. Sarason, I. G. Sarason & G. R. Pierce (Eds), *Social support: An Interactional View* (pp. 397–426). New York: John Wiley & Sons, Inc.

Welch-McCaffrey, D., Hoffman, B., Leigh, S., Loescher, L. J. & Meyskens, F. L. (1989). Surviving adult cancers. II. Psychosocial implications. *Annals of Internal Medicine, 111,* 517–524.

Winter, D. A. (1992). *Personal construct psychology in clinical practice: Theory, practice and application.* London: Routledge.

17

An Hygienic Process? Researcher and Participants Construing Each Other's Worlds

ALESSANDRA IANTAFFI

PERSONALISING THE POLITICAL OR POLITICISING THE PERSONAL?

Researching personal experiences in relation to disability and within a feminist context has been accused of de-politicising the struggle of the disability movement (Sheldon, 1999). Feminism is, in fact, often seen as a fragmented reality, too often focused on the experiences of privileged women, and both feminism and the women's movement have usually ignored or marginalised the experiences of disabled women in the past. It is nevertheless apparent that disability and feminism meet when discussing disabled women's lives (Blackwell-Stratton et al., 1988), as Morris (1996, p. 5) points out in the following quotation:

> Like women, disabled people's politicisation has its roots in the assertion that "the personal is political", that our personal experiences of being denied opportunities are not to be explained by our bodily limitations (our impairments) but by the social, environmental and attitudinal barriers which are daily part of our lives.

Personal Construct Psychology: New Ideas. Edited by Peter Caputi, Heather Foster and Linda L. Viney. Copyright © 2006 John Wiley & Sons, Ltd.

However, the feminist and the disability movements have usually ignored the lives of disabled women (Asch & Fine, 1988; Fine & Asch, 1985; Lloyd, 1992; Morris, 1996). When these have been addressed, they have usually been relegated in a corner as a "special interest" and have not been seen as integral to the understanding of oppression. They are represented as an oppressed minority, a special case, which does not touch non-disabled women and their lives (Asch & Fine, 1988; Morris, 1993, 1995). In spite of much interest in the sociology of the "body", non-disabled feminists have indeed avoided addressing disability (Begum, 1992, p. 82). Feminist academics have implicitly construed disabled women as other: strangers whose experiences do not touch us, unwilling to accept that "all of us live in bodies that do not always function the way we wish they would" (Stone, 1995, p. 422). Disabled feminists such as Morris have, on the other hand, actively pursued an encounter between disability and feminism in order to find a space and a voice as disabled women, and, although many barriers are still to be overcome, dialogues are starting to flourish. Feminism could become as advocated by Begum (1992), Matthews (1994), Morris (1996) and other disabled feminists, the place within academic discourse where disabled women meet, make strategic alliances with non-disabled researchers (Morris, 1993, 1995) and lead the research on disability.

In this context a feminist epistemology becomes inextricably linked to a feminist ontology, a way of being as well as a way of knowing. The concept of what is knowledge is challenged, as is the status of the academic as expert. In fact, if we refuse the cartesian split between mind and body as false, then we can only reject the divide between knowledge and experience. Individual accounts are placed in the context of the personal as political, creating spaces for disabled women's voices which have been often absent from the public and political discourses (Morris, 1993, 1995, 1996). The research described in the next section strove to create one of these spaces by exploring the tales of some disabled women students in Higher Education (HE) in England and Wales within a constructivist framework.

DISABLED WOMEN IN HIGHER EDUCATION

Disabled women in HE are often invisible. Women have only quite recently gained entrance to HE in Britain, and just over a century ago heated debates focused on how damaging university admission would be to women, men and society at large. Even the medical professions highlighted how such an event might provoke brain fever, sterility, hysteria, disability and even death (Blackwell-Stratton et al., 1988; Delamont, 1996). Men were also concerned at the shifting role between the sexes, which would be reinforced by women's entrance in HE. Educating women at a higher level entailed the risk that demands for equality would soon follow, while also blurring the division between the domestic, private, feminine sphere and the public, masculine one (Gordon, 1990). As the struggle conquered various bastions, more and more women entered HE. A variety of role models emerged, and nowadays British Universities can count women and men almost as equal consumers of HE, although the numbers at the "top" are still far from encouraging with only about 7% of professors being women (Evans, 1995; Ince et al., 1996). It has also been argued by various authors, such as Evans (1995, p. 76), that women inside academia have "internalised, both to their own disadvantage and ultimately to the disadvantage of understanding *per se*, certain key assumptions of male academics". They have subscribed to a masculine culture, which nurtures the split between mind and body, public and private. Within this context a number of women have been constructed as other than academics, have been made strangers to the ivory tower and excluded from the construction of knowledge (Gray, 1994).

Disabled women are amongst those who have been excluded and constructed as other, rendered invisible and forgotten, in most cases, even by feminism, as pointed out in the previous section. Their absence is conspicuous and, although understandable, not easily justifiable (Matthews, 1994). While non-disabled women were achieving their right to go to colleges and universities, disabled women were barely able to achieve a satisfactory education at primary level. They had no role models in HE, apart from Helen Keller's success story, no support and, usually, no physical or sensory access to the learning and teaching environments (Blackwell-Stratton et al., 1988). Even Helen Keller's story, in its uniqueness and isolation, seemed to prove that achievement for a disabled woman in HE was no ordinary event. As pointed out above, disabled women, although gaining access in increasing numbers to HE, are still invisible, and usually not included in a common definition of womanhood. The few voices, which have been raised on the subject, are those of disabled feminist academics and/or writers. Even when and where disabled women are present in HE, the materiality of their bodies is often ignored or perceived as conflictual and uncomfortable in an environment where "well functioning" bodies are taken for granted and are often seen as a prerequisite for academic endeavours (Potts & Price, 1995). The presence of disability, and even more so of gendered disability, becomes, therefore, threatening and exceptional, as it challenges "academic, professional and scientific ethics, parts of our cultural heritage, our attitudes often require additional resources or direct affirmative action" (Cornwall, 1995, p. 397).

This picture was mirrored by some of the themes that emerged from my dialogues with 15 disabled women students. Negative attitudes and prejudices seemed to be the biggest barrier still facing them in HE, as exemplified by Participant F in the following quote:

> Everyday you come up against something, an obstacle, which reminds you that you are not like everyone else.

The women interviewed made up a group that included a variety of ages, background, disabilities and educational choices. Direct questions on their age, choice of degree, type of study (i.e., part or full time), and disability were not asked, but such information emerged naturally either in the correspondence preceding the encounters or during the interviews. This was a riskier approach, since such information might not have emerged and it did require some very gentle probing at times. However, creating a relaxed atmosphere of trust and confidence was deemed to be more important than obtaining complete personal details. If the participants were to be seen as co-researchers, it was not, in fact, appropriate to dissect their personal lives by asking them to reveal their personal data, such as age, marital status, where they lived, what disability they had. Therefore it was decided that most of this information would naturally emerge during the interviews if they were approached as dialogues rather than one-way conversations. In spite of the success of the chosen strategy in this instance, it must be highlighted that this type of path was paved with uncertainties and risks, and that the potential costs to the researcher and the research process had to be weighed carefully during the planning phase. Even the success of such strategy cannot be fully evaluated, since so much depended on the relationships that I, as the researcher, had established with the participants, and which might therefore differ for different researchers in similar situations. Moore et al., (1998, p. 95) express the view that:

> . . . Commendable though the aim of forging alliances between disabled and non-disabled researchers may appear, we have to admit that it is a woolly and often time-consuming business, based on large amounts of nebulous factors such as "goodwill" and "give and take". Steps taken towards evolving participatory ways of working are consequently difficult to evaluate effectively.

It was, however, a positive, if subjective, step towards an emancipatory approach to disability research which was appreciated by the participants, and which proved to be successful in the context of this project.

All the participants were asked to either draw or imagine, depending on their mobility, a river of experience, a modified version of the "snake" technique developed by Denicolo and Pope (1990), to show me the path that led them to become a student in HE. After they talked me through their river and I asked some more questions to clarify how they construed their journey, they were asked to choose an event, person or object to represent what it meant to them to be a disabled woman student in HE. They then described and explained these metaphors to me. An overview of the accounts collected from these dialogues is the focus of the next section.

CHORUS AND SOLOS: WEAVING THE THREADS OF SOCIAL DISCOURSE THROUGH INDIVIDUAL TALES

These individual voices did not stand in isolation, despite the fairly unstructured nature of my dialogues with the participants, but wove intricate patterns where both individuality and commonality found their place. The result was a common story expressed in 15 different, yet similar, ways; a river of experiences with different ramifications, all converging into the same delta of the same river into the same sea. The level of shared experiences, language and strategies of "survival" amongst participants was far greater than it might have appeared at first sight, while their accounts still retained a rich, complex and intriguing individuality. Within this story 12 common themes were identified, as well as 8 threads, which, running through, held the themes together. The themes were:

- normality: "like everybody else"
- disability, disabled
- inclusion/exclusion
- other people's attitude towards disability
- own attitude towards disability
- experiences of schooling related to disability
- past experiences of schooling in general
- reasons for going to university
- own opinion of university
- academic work
- metaphors
- the interview process.

The threads, which emerged across the themes, are listed below.

- "warfare" language
- anger
- apologetic tone
- expectations (family, self, society)
- support networks (formal and informal)
- refusal to be labelled
- desire to be accepted
- perceived non-importance of self, but belief in the importance of project per se.

As well as being one of the themes highlighted, disability also wove in and out of the participants' stories, across many of the other threads and themes. Normality seemed to be placed at the other end of the spectrum, and defined mostly as "like everyone else", as not having a disability. The experiences narrated by the participants illuminated various facets of what being disabled meant to them, and they linked to one another, from one participant to a next, like a thread of pearls: each pearl different and unique, but part of the same string. When the participants talked about their disabilities, they did not usually refer to their medical condition, or their impairment. Instead they discussed how they were affected by it, for example, in relation to access to both the physical and learning environments, or to how they were viewed by non-disabled people. Such accounts fitted within a social, rather than medical model of disability, hence reinforcing a political understanding of these experiences, rather than a fragmented, existentialist one. The participants highlighted through their words a theory of social oppression, rather than personal tragedy. However, they also talked about their experiences of pain and physical limitations, echoing the views expressed. By doing so they reclaimed their individual and embodied experience of impairment, without denying the impact of societal oppression and the existence of a widespread disabling culture (Crow, 1996; Morris, 1991). Therefore, they break free of the view that disability is entirely socially constructed, and, at the opposite end of the spectrum, of the medical discourse which locates disability within the loss and tragedy scenario. Although none of the participants subscribed to the latter theory, they were still influenced by some of the negative images of disability which are so pervasive in our western societies. The desire to be "just like everyone else", the distinctions made between themselves and other "more severely disabled people", and, in some cases, the inability to identify fully with the label "disabled" emerged during the dialogues. These discourses reinforced the view that a positive self image for disabled people is an achievement, when we are surrounded by visual and verbal messages depicting them either as defective, helpless and blameless victims, or as evil fallen angels punished for their sins (Hevey, 1993; Mason, 1990; Morris 1991). The younger participants, especially those who have lived with disability from birth or childhood, seemed to live a paradox caught, as they were, between feeling different from others, and knowing their strength and ability to achieve. This tension was also reflected in Hirst and Baldwin's (1994) research on growing up disabled. The more mature students lived a slightly different paradox, reflecting nevertheless, how damaging the same engraved concept of "normality" could be to the image of disabled people. They found it hard to see themselves as disabled, since, as Participant M reported they can "remember what it's like not to be disabled". Finding themselves suddenly "thrown" into a world which has been constructed as alien, and other than normal by a disabling culture, it was also an experience echoed by those of established disabled women activists and writers, such as Hannaford (1985) and Morris (1991). However, they were also aware that these negative constructions of disability were partial and damaging and they did have a profound understanding of their disabilities and their impact on their lives.

Both the younger and the more mature participants were united in their refusal to be labelled and marginalised because of their disability, as they wanted to be accepted as disabled people, rather than in spite of being disabled people. All the participants expressed a "quiet anger" at being labelled as disabled and other, while their needs were ignored and their rights denied. They wanted to be acknowledged as a person beyond the label. This anger, together with experience of impairment, contributed to the participants using a vocabulary of struggle, which has been defined as "warfare" language in the threads listed above. The experience of "struggling", "bashing away", "battling" and above all "surviving" was certainly shared by other disabled women writers (Keith, 1994; Morris, 1996), although often in the form of anecdotes. Apart from the odd comment, the participants did not talk extensively about being women, and participant G even stated that, in her opinion, this part of her life, namely HE, was a gender free area, although later on she discussed how her supervisor seemed to treat his male students differently. Similarly many comments implied a gender dimension, even when it was not discussed overtly. This was, in fact, a difficult area to unravel, since so many issues interlocked with each other, being a woman, disabled, a student, full or part time, raising a family or being away from home for the first time. Disadvantage, in fact, was not neatly stored in layers. It could not simply be doubled or tripled depending on the circumstances. It was simultaneous, embodied and situated.

Each participant was quite different from the others, but her experiences mirrored and echoed aspects of the others' experiences, becoming together a cause of celebration and pride (Morris, 1991), as well as a tool for political change. Individual accounts, in this context, acquire collective value by creating spaces for those "absent voices" (Morris, 1995) that have been absent from academic discourse for too long. Potts and Price (1995, p. 112) also shared this view. They stated how anti-essentialist critics have contributed towards silencing "the voice of many who have never yet been heard", by disqualifying the legitimacy of individual experiences for the purpose of research. Shildrick and Price (1994, p. 176) also commented on how highlighting the accounts of embodied selves does not need to be seen as an essentialist and dead-end process, but rather as "the refusal to split body and mind, and to the refusal to allow ourselves to be fragmented and pathologised". The participants' experiences create, therefore, a different standpoint from which to view HE and, to a certain extent, society in general.

RESEARCHING REFLECTING: THE DREGS OF THE RESEARCH PROCESS

The participants' active involvement within the research process, and with me as the researcher, was certainly one of the strengths of this piece of research. It also respected the feminist and constructivist framework within which the research was located, but it raised issues of validity because of its supposedly subjective nature. Research has often been seen as an hygienic process, where the researcher disappears in order to be substituted by an objective account. Personal involvement and interest, as well as strong values, such as feminism are seen as pollutants, and as factors contributing to the invalidation of a piece of research. Research, other than feminist, is, in fact, usually "gender-neuter" and therefore allegedly more objective than projects in which the researcher spells out her biases. To illustrate this point, Morley (1996, pp. 127–128) describes a seminar attended with other colleagues:

> As a feminist researcher... I was told that there was danger of collusion and over-identification, even manipulation of my informants. Embedded in this interaction was the hidden discourse of purity and danger, with feminists perceived as pollutants of the otherwise hygienic research process.

Feminist research can be disturbing to the more traditional psychologists, as it is not an hygienic, but a messy process, with a strong political character. Although most research is messy, usually this does not show in the finished product, and the researcher blends into the background, rather than being the active instrument and presenting voice of the research. This prominent position of the researcher in feminist approaches, however, is not an essentialist exercise, carried out to satisfy her female ego, but a tool offered to the reader, so that he or she can judge the validity of the research in context, as well as being an instrument for change.

As stated earlier the research project described in this chapter aimed at uncovering a situated and embodied knowledge within a social and political context, and is consequently value-laden. In order to let the readers themselves judge the validity and authenticity of this research, the process was unravelled and rendered transparent in my thesis (Iantaffi, 1999). There, as much as in this chapter, my voice as the researcher was overtly interjected within the text, rather than hidden behind third person pronouns. By claiming authorship in the first person in my writing, I hope to achieve a high degree of transparency, so that all subjectivities, biases and values, including mine, are clearly visible, rather than hidden behind the false mask of neutrality (Siraj-Blatchford, 1994, p. 18).

The research process is, in fact, a dialogical adventure undertaken by both researcher and participant. When I embarked on this particular project I had my feminist epistemology and Personal Construct Psychology (PCP), as a theoretical and methodological framework, as map and compass but had no clear idea where those might lead me and the participants. Giving a body, beliefs, opinions and a context to my voice as a researcher became then a "method" itself to reclaim a knowledge which is discursive and embodied, and does not exist in a vacuum: it is adding yet another tessera to mosaics which are kept incomplete by apparently "unbiased", "neutral" institutions. As Stanley and Wise (1993, p. 58) argue:

> We feel that it is inevitable that the researcher's own experiences and consciousness will be involved in the research process as much as they are in life, and we shall argue that all research must be concerned with the experiences and consciousness of the researcher as an integral part of the research process.

Claiming social justice for women, such as disabled women, can be done in this way: by making visible categories which are kept hidden behind ungendered and disembodied numbers, and understanding what keeps "them" from "us", placing them under the neutral label of "the disabled", with no gendered, racial, sexual orientation, national and religious identities. Liberation then also becomes a dialogical process of which the researcher is only a part, and not the main agent or the expert.

CONCLUSIONS

In this chapter I strived to highlight the importance of listening to individual voices within research. These voices are not disconnected from each other; each one of them renders our knowledge and understanding of each other and the world more inclusive. This position was illustrated by how the apparently disparate experiences of some disabled women students in HE wove harmonious patterns, which were mirrored in the existing literature and in the experiences of disabled women activists and academics.

I have also highlighted how the research process is not hygienic. The researcher must form relationships with the participants if they are to feel at ease and able to trust her or him with their personal stories and beliefs. In the context of the research discussed in this chapter I saw myself as an ally in the struggle towards liberation but also a facilitator who provided the participants with a space to think and an attentive listener. Acting within a PCP framework allowed me to involve my participants as co-researchers, respecting the belief that they are indeed the experts when it comes to exploring their own lives, and to engage them in a circular research process. From these opportunities and encounters fascinating narratives emerged as the women involved traced the patterns of their paths to HE and sketched the meaning of their experience as disabled women students. The contemplation of, and reflection on, myself, and of other women's contemplation and reflections can, in this framework, be valid, (if messy) research as we attempt to construe and re-construe ourselves and others, reclaiming our stories as part of a wider social, theoretical and political story.

REFERENCES

Asch, A. & Fine, M. (1988). Beyond pedestals. In: M. Fine & A. Asch (Eds), *Women with disabilities. Essays in psychology, culture, and politics* (pp. 1–37). Philadelphia, USA: Temple University Press.

Begum, N. (1992). Disabled women and the feminist agenda. *Feminist Review, 40,* 70–84.

Blackwell-Stratton, M., Breslin, M. L., Mayerson, A. B. & Bailey, S. (1988). Smashing icons: Disabled women and the disability and women's movements. In M. Fine & A. Asch. (1988). (Eds), *Women with disabilities. Essays in psychology, culture, and politics* (pp. 306–332). Philadelphia, USA: Temple University Press.

Cornwall, J. (1995). Psychology, disability and equal opportunity, *The Psychologist, 8,* 396–397.

Crow, L. (1996). Including all of our lives: Renewing the social model of disability. In J. Morris (Ed.), *Encounters with Strangers: Feminism and Disability* (pp. 206–226). London: The Women's Press.

Delamont, S. (1996). *A woman's place in education.* Aldershot: Avebury.

Denicolo, P. & Pope, M. (1990). Adults Learning – Teachers Thinking. In C. Day., M. Pope & P. Denicolo, (Eds), *Insight into teachers thinking and practice* (pp. 155–69). Basingstoke: The Falmer Press.

Evans, M. (1995). Ivory towers: Life in the mind. In L. Morley & V. Walsh (Eds), *Feminist Academics. Creative Agents for Change* (pp. 73–85). London: Taylor & Francis.

Fine, M. & Asch, A. (1985). Disabled women: Sexism without the pedestal. In D. M. Deegan & N. A. Brooks (Eds), *Women and disability. The double Handicap* (pp. 6–22). New Brunswick, USA: Transaction Books.

Gordon, L. D. (1990). Gender and higher education in the progressive era. New Haven, USA: Yale University Press.

Gray, B. (1994). Women in higher education: What are we doing to ourselves? In S. Davies., C. Lubelska & J. Quinn (Eds), *Changing the Subject. Women in Higher Education* (pp. 75–88). London: Taylor & Francis.

Hannaford, S. (1985). Living outside inside: A disabled woman's experience. Berkeley, USA: Canterbury Press.

Hevey, D. (1993). The tragedy principle: strategies for change in the representation of disabled people. In J. Swain., V. Finkelstein., S. French & M. Oliver (Eds), *Disabling barriers – Enabling environments* (pp. 116–121). Buckingham: Open University Press.

Hirst, M. & Baldwin, S. (1994). Unequal opportunities. Growing up disabled. HMSO: Social Policy Research Unit.

Iantaffi, A. (1999). Lost tales? The academic experiences of some disabled women students in higher education in England. PhD Thesis: University of Reading.

Ince, M., Griffiths, S. & Morriss-Kay, J. (1996). Chipping away at the glass ceiling. Times Higher Education Supplement, July 26: 17.

Keith, L. (1994). (Ed.) Mustn't grumble. Writing by disabled women. London: The Women's Press.

Lloyd, M. (1992). Does she boil eggs? Towards a feminist model of disability. *Disability, Handicap & Society, 7(3)*, 207–221.

Mason, M. (1990). Identity. In M. Mason & R. Rieser. *Disability equality in the classroom: A human rights issue* (pp. 22–33). London: Inner London Education Authority.

Matthews, J. (1994). Empowering disabled women in higher education. In S. Davies., C. Lubelska & J. Quinn (Eds), *Changing the Subject. Women in Higher Education* (pp. 138–45). London: Taylor & Francis.

Moore, M., Beazley, S. & Maelzer J. (1998). *Researching disability issues.* Buckingham: Open University Press.

Morley, L. (1996). Interrogating patriarchy: The challenges of feminist research. In L. Morley & V. Walsh (Eds), *Breaking boundaries: women in higher education* (pp. 128–148). London: Taylor & Francis.

Morris, J. (1991). *Pride against prejudice. Transforming Attitudes to Disability.* London: The Women's Press.

Morris, J. (1993). Feminism and disability. *Feminist Review, 43*, 57–70.

Morris, J. (1995). Creating a space for absent voices: Disabled women's experiences of receiving assistance with daily living activities. *Feminist Review, 51*, 68–93.

Morris, J. (1996). (Ed.) Encounters with strangers: Feminism and disability. London: The Women's Press.

Potts, T. & Price, J. (1995). Out of the blood and spirit of our lives: The place of the body in academic feminism. In L. Morley & V. Walsh (Eds), *Feminist Academics. Creative Agents for Change* (pp. 102–115). London: Taylor & Francis.

Sheldon, A. (1999). Personal and perplexing: feminist disability politics evaluated. *Disability & Society, 14(5)*: 643–657.

Shildrick, M. & Price, J. (1994). Splitting the difference: Adventures in the anatomy and embodiment of women. In G. Griffin., M. Hester., S. Rai & S. Roseneil (Eds), *Stirring It: Challenges for feminism* (pp. 156–179). London: Taylor & Francis.

Siraj-Blatchford, I. (1994). *Praxis makes perfect: Critical educational research for social justice.* Ticknall: Education Now Books.

Stanley, L. & Wise, S. (1993) *Breaking out again. Feminist ontology and epistemology.* London: Routledge.

Stone, S. D. (1995). The myth of bodily perfection. *Disability & Society, 10(4)*, 413–424.

SECTION IV

Evidence-Based Interventions

18

Menopause: The Start of Change

HEATHER FOSTER

LINDA L. VINEY

Every woman of sufficient age goes through the transition of menopause. Furthermore, in Western society, at this time, working women in particular feel obliged to make this transition with as little fuss as possible. Yet the common name, "change of life", crystallises and preserves a meaning that is at odds with current expectations.

Our previous research into the meaning of menopause involved interviews with 74 women (Foster & Viney, 2000). In that study some women said that menopause meant nothing to them and most women continued with the routine of their lives at work and at home. Many women, however, reported distressing feelings in relation to menopause. Women said that they were having difficulty in predicting what was happening, that they had feelings of confusion, feelings of loss of control over their bodies and an awareness of the need for change.

We developed a model of menopause based on a personal construct account of change and informed by women's meanings (Foster & Viney, 2000). The model incorporates an intervention pathway to facilitate involvement in a creative change process and reconstruing in relation to the changes of the menopausal transition.

Personal Construct Psychology: New Ideas. Edited by Peter Caputi, Heather Foster and Linda L. Viney. Copyright © 2006 John Wiley & Sons, Ltd.

A MENOPAUSE WORKSHOP

We decided that a group intervention strategy was appropriate in the case of menopausal women who had identified a lack of opportunities for discussion of their experience (Foster & Viney, 2000), with a consequent lack of opportunities for experiencing commonality and validation (Winter, 1992). We developed a menopause workshop designed to be brief and flexible in recognition of the nature and needs of the women, and the requirements of future users of the intervention such as women's health centres. The women were predominantly in the paid workforce and did not construe themselves as ill. They were not in search of "therapy" as such. We recognised that, as mature women, they were likely to have to balance work and family responsibilities. The intervention, although adaptable to more extended delivery, was based on a core of three sessions of 1.5 hours.

Since the workshop was to be a brief intervention, it was important to structure the process (Foster & Viney, 2005) to promote therapeutic movement (Neimeyer & Merluzzi, 1982; Viney & Henry, 2002; Winter, 1992); to avoid the dangers of uncontrolled loosening or tightening (Winter, 1996); and to provide opportunities for group members to provide alternative meanings for each other (Viney, 1996; Winter, 1996). At the same time, we explicitly involved the women as co-researchers throughout the workshop in order to guard against the processes creating a distance between researcher and participants (Leitner, 1985). We trusted the women's ability to choose the degree to which they disclosed their construing and their "good sense" in avoiding "intolerable levels of negative emotions" (Winter, 1996, p. 150), given their knowledge that this was a brief process. We also recognised that women would "approach the first session already anticipating some sort of change" (Fisher, 2000, p. 436).

AIMS AND HYPOTHESES

The major aim of this study was to test whether provision of a brief intervention in the form of a menopause workshop could (1) reduce women's distressing emotions, such as anxiety and feelings of helplessness in relation to menopause, and (2) increase women's feelings of control, hope, and positive feelings in relation to menopause.

In accordance with our aims we tested whether women whose levels of distress are higher than normal are likely to experience a reduction in levels of anxiety, a reduction in levels of helplessness, and an increase in feelings of control, hope and positive affect, when they have opportunities to reconstrue in relation to menopause.

METHOD

THE WORKSHOP

The three workshop sessions were each structured around a major activity. These activities were planned as a series of explorations that moved from reflection about the self to engagement in the Creativity Cycle and engagement and resolution in the Circumspection-Preemption-Control (decision-making) cycle.

In Session 1, the major activity was writing a self-characterisation (Fransella, 1981; Kelly, 1955/1991a, 1955/1991b). This activity provided a safe preparation for experimentation as it was written to be seen only by the writer. Each woman chose what she would reveal from it. The discussion that followed focused on the way a woman could approach menopause, drawing on the positive qualities revealed in the self-characterisation.

In Session 2, the major activity was based on "a drawing and its opposite" (Ravenette, 1999) in relation to a menopausal choice. This activity provided women with a novel situation for experimentation to facilitate engagement in the Creativity Cycle (Kelly, 1955/1991a, 1955/1991b) that consists of a cycle of loosening and tightening constructs. Whole group and triadic discussion about the preferred choice and support for the choice followed.

In Session 3, the major activity was an enactment (Kelly, 1955/1991a, 1955/1991b) in relation to the second choice identified in the Ravenette activity. This provided an opportunity for controlled experimentation in a safe setting as women chose the content and level of enactment. Either verbal or nonverbal enactment was encouraged. The session ended with a discussion about women's choices, new possibilities and predictions, and with a sharing of sources of information and support to promote dispersion of dependency (Kelly, 1955/1991; Walker, 1993).

In recognition of the brief nature of the intervention and the potentially diverse construing styles of participants (Winter, 1988a), activities in the workshop were chosen with the aim of providing different modes for making meaning explicit. These included a verbal activity (self-characterisation); a non-verbal activity using images to draw on the sense of self and personal knowledge "that are not available at high levels of awareness" (Ravenette, 2001, p. 203); an activity potentially drawing on pre-verbal construing, using acting or embodiment: a verbal-imaging-acting (V-I-A) pathway for movement. Women were invited to reflect about the self "now" in the self-characterisation, to anticipate possible courses of action in the drawing activity and to predict probable courses of action following the enactment.

SAMPLING

Thirty-eight women volunteered to take part in the Menopause Workshops. A further 16 women took part in 2 data collections to provide a Contrast Sample. Purposive sampling was directed predominantly to healthy women in mid-life in paid employment. The consequent limitations to generalisation of findings are accepted.

The sample had the following characteristics: women's ages ranged from 37 to 61, with a median age of 47.5; 73.7 % of women were of English speaking background (ESB) and 26.3 % were from a non-ESB; 84.2 % of women were in paid employment and 15.8 % were not employed; women were employed in occupations ranging from *Labourers and Related Workers* to *Managers*, classified according to the Australian Standard Classification of Occupations (ABS, 1998).

MEASURES

Content analysis scales were used in this study to measure negative feelings linked with times of transition, positive feelings that indicate validation of choices, and to predict the women who should benefit most from the opportunity for reconstruction, by screening the women for levels of distress. Two sets of content analysis scales were used: (a) Australian scales developed by Viney and Westbrook, the Cognitive Anxiety Scale, (Viney & Westbrook, 1976) measuring anxiety, the Pawn and Origin Scales (Westbrook & Viney, 1980) measuring helplessness and control, respectively, and the Positive Affect Scale (Westbrook, 1976) measuring positive feelings; and (b) American scales developed by Gottschalk and colleagues, the Hope Scale (Gottschalk & Gleser, 1969) measuring hope; and the Depression Scale (Gottschalk & Hoigaard, 1986) measuring distress.

The usefulness of these measures for assessment of psychological states across the lifespan has been previously demonstrated (Viney, 1980) and they are theoretically appropriate for personal construct psychology researchers (Winter, 1990). The psychometrics for the scales are strong and have been reported elsewhere (Gottschalk & Bechtel, 1990; Gottschalk, Lolas & Viney, 1986; Viney & Caputi, 2005; Viney, Caputi & Webster, 2001). In the case of the Viney and Westbrook scales interjudge reliability was tested on a random sample of 33 % of cases using 2 additional independent raters. Pearson's product-moment correlation coefficients were calculated among judges' rating resulting in coefficients of more than 0.82 for all scales.

The Gottschalk-Hoigaard Depression Scale (Gottschalk & Hoigaard, 1986) was used as a diagnostic and predictive measure. It is based on a psychiatric diagnostic system, but it assesses a range of disruptive and distressing states (Viney, 1983) and was used in this study as a measure of distress.

The key outcome measure in this study was anxiety. In our previous research we had identified uncertainty, and an inability to predict what would happen, as major themes in women's meanings of menopause (Foster & Viney, 2000). Anxiety, in the personal construct sense, was particularly relevant to the women in this study. The Cognitive Anxiety scale (Viney & Westbrook, 1976) measures uncertainty, identical to the personal construct definition of anxiety.

We used additional scales, within a personal construct framework, to measure women's feelings of helplessness and control, hope and positive feelings. The Pawn Scale (Westbrook & Viney, 1980) was used to measure women's feelings of helplessness. It assesses the extent to which people ascribe their actions as shaped by forces beyond their control (Viney, 1993). The Origin Scale, (Westbrook & Viney, 1980) was used to measure women's feelings of control, as an indication of whether they felt able to deal with changes relating to menopause. The scale assesses the personal meanings that people ascribe to their actions as determined by their own choice. These measures therefore served as an indication of whether or not women were having difficulty considering and making choices during a time of menopausal change, that is, engaging in, or completing, the Decision-Making Cycle.

The Westbrook and Viney (1980) Pawn and Origin scales and the Westbrook (1976) Positive Affect scale were used to test workshop aim (2) to increase women's feelings of control in relation to menopause. Feelings of hope and positive feelings were also measured by scales appropriate within a personal construct framework. The Gottschalk-Gleser (1969) Hope scale was used to assess any change in hopefulness. In addition, the Westbrook (1976) Positive Affect Scale was used as an indication of whether women were feeling satisfied with the choices they were making. This scale assesses people's expressions of good feelings such as happiness, pleasure or satisfaction.

PROCEDURE

For the Menopause Workshops, seven groups were formed, guided by women who nominated group membership usually based on existing work groups. This strategy was adopted to provide a context where women would experience minimal anxiety about participation and discussion of difficult issues. The need for group formation and initial anxiety reduction activities was therefore minimised. The number of women in groups ranged from three to eight.

Women chose the location for workshops (most often at workplaces) and nominated their preferred pattern of delivery. Five groups nominated three consecutive sessions and two groups nominated a whole day workshop.

The total research project included a 7-part data collection process in accordance with the criteria established by Viney (1998), however the focus of this Chapter is on data collected in a 2-part process. Women were asked to respond to an open-ended question: "Please would you describe your life at the moment in relation to menopause, the good things and the bad – what it's like for you" prior to the commencement of the workshop to provide baseline data (Time 1), after the workshop (Time 2), and after 5 months (Time 3), to measure changes in the women's construing. The 16 women in the Contrast Sample took part in 2 data collections 5 months apart. This 5 month period between data collections paralleled the 5 month period between pre-workshop and 5 month post-workshop follow-up data collections for the women taking part in the workshops.

ANALYSIS OF DATA

Following the intervention, women's responses were prepared using the standard scoring instructions for each content analysis scale. The American scales were scored by *PCAD 2000*: Psychiatric Content Analysis and Diagnosis (Gottschalk & Bechtel, 1990). The Australian scales were scored using the *Analyse* computerised scoring system (Viney, Caputi & Webster, 2001).

The women were divided into two sub-samples on the basis of their levels of distress, measured by the Gottschalk-Hoigaard Depression Scale, so that responses to the workshop could be compared. Sample A (Above average) ($n = 19$) was composed of women whose scores were above the normal range; and Sample B (Normal) ($n = 18$) was composed of women whose scores were within the normal range.

RESULTS

An evaluation study was conducted, using a repeated measures, contrast group design, to examine whether differences occurred between and within Samples A (Above average), B (Normal), and C (Contrast), pre-workshop, and post-workshop. A series of repeated measures analyses of variance were carried out to investigate differences in the content analysis scale scores between Samples A (Above average), B (Normal), and C (Contrast) and within the samples. Data were collected on three occasions: pre-workshop, post-workshop and after five months. As a number of tests were included in the analyses, $\alpha = 0.01$ was used in order to reduce the risk of Type 1 error (Tabachnick & Fidell, 1989).

The hypothesis, which related to the women in Sample A (above average), was only partially confirmed. At Time 2 there was significant, and close to significant, evidence to confirm the proposition in relation to all measures.

By Time 3 this picture had changed. The women of Sample A (Above average), showed a statistically significant long-term decrease in anxiety scores. Time 1 ($M = 3.67$, $SD = 0.89$), and Time 3 ($M = 2.70$, $SD = 0.93$): $F(1,18) = 16.42$, $p < 0.01$, Wilks' lambda = 0.52, partial eta squared = 0.48, with an observed power of 0.86. The women also showed a long-term decrease in Pawn Scale scores (feelings of helplessness) that approached significance at $p = 0.026$. The significant short-term improvement in relation to positive measures was not sustained after five months. (see Table 18.1)

In an unexpected result, however, participation in the Menopause Workshop also appeared to produce beneficial results for the women in Sample B (Normal), those women whose initial distress was within normal levels. There was a statistically significant reduction in anxiety scores between Time 1

Table 18.1 Summary of significant results for Samples A (Above average), B (Normal)

Scales	Sample	Effect for time	Contrasts Times 1 & 2	Contrasts Times 1 & 3
Cognitive Anxiety	A	$p < 0.001$	$p = 0.001$	$p < 0.01$
	B	$p < 0.01$	$p < 0.015^a$	$p < 0.01$
Origin	A	$p = 0.023^a$	$p < 0.01$	
	B	$p < 0.02^a$		
Pawn	A	$p < 0.01$	$p < 0.01$	$p = 0.026^a$
	B	$p < 0.01$	$p < 0.001$	$p < 0.01$
Hope	A	$p = 0.015^a$	$p < 0.01$	
	B	$p < 0.02^a$	$p < 0.01$	$p = 0.047^a$
Positive Affect	A	$p = 0.014^a$	$p < 0.01$	
	B	$p < 0.01$	$p < 0.01$	

[a] Included to provide full information. Although result is not significant at $\alpha = 0.01$, it approaches significance.

($M = 3.52$, $SD = 1.34$), and Time 3 ($M = 2.58$, $SD = 0.77$): $F(1,17) = 13.42$, $p < 0.01$, Wilks' lambda $= 0.56$, partial eta squared $= 0.44$, with an observed power of 0.77. There was also a statistically significant long-term reduction in Pawn Scale scores (feelings of helplessness) for these women. Time 1 ($M = 2.14$, $SD = 0.58$), and Time 3 ($M = 1.61$, $SD = 0.50$): $F(1,17) = 11.83$, $p < 0.01$, Wilks' lambda $= 0.59$, partial eta squared $= 0.41$, with an observed power of 0.70. There was no statistically significant difference shown between means for Times 1 and 3 in Sample C.

The key measures that distinguished between Workshop Samples A (Above average), and B (Normal), and C (Contrast), were those of anxiety and helplessness. Within-Sample reductions in Cognitive Anxiety Scale scores, in Workshop Samples A (Above average), and B (Normal), were not shown in Contrast Sample C, indicating that significant change occurred in the Workshop Samples, but not in Contrast Sample C. In addition, differences between samples at Time 1, for Cognitive Anxiety Scale scores, were not present five months after the workshop at Time 3, indicating that a significant change occurred for the Workshop Samples. (see Table 18.2).

In relation to the measure of helplessness, a significant reduction was shown in Sample B between Pawn Scale scores pre-workshop at Time 1, and five months after the workshop at Time 3. There was also some evidence of a reduction in Pawn Scale scores over time in Sample A. No such difference was shown for Contrast Sample C. In summary, these results point to workshop participation as a possible effect in reducing anxiety and feelings of helplessness in the Workshop Samples.

DISCUSSION

The choice of design, while appropriate for this study, limits the ability to generalise from the findings. The outcomes must therefore be regarded as

Table 18.2 Summary of significant results for Samples A, B and C

Scales	Significant effects	Between-samples difference	Sample	Within-sample difference
Cognitive	(Sample/Time) and	Time 1	A	$p < 0.01$
Anxiety	Time	$p < 0.001$	B	$p < 0.01$
Pawn	Time	Time 1	A	$p < 0.03$[a]
		$p < 0.01$	B	$p < 0.01$

[a] Although result is not significant at $\alpha = 0.01$, it approaches significance.

applicable only to other women with comparable characteristics. It is encouraging, however, that the workshop appeared to have a beneficial effect for women with normal levels of distress, as well as women with higher than normal levels of distress, which suggests that further research with more representative samples could be undertaken without undue risk.

The Menopause Workshop did appear to achieve some significant results for the participating women. A long-term reduction in anxiety and feelings of helplessness, and a short-term increase in feelings of control, hope and positive emotions occurred for those women with higher initial levels of distress. The changes indicate that these women were more satisfied with their meaning-making choices, and not experiencing the same need for change. In addition, the women with normal initial levels of distress also showed a reduction in feelings of helplessness, and an increase in hope and positive feelings, after the Menopause Workshop. It appears the Menopause Workshops assisted women at a transitional time.

Other examples of the successful use of brief interventions have been reported in the personal construct literature (Harter & Neimeyer, 1995; Ravenette, 1999). The significant results of this brief workshop are in some ways similar to the significant results found by Viney, Clarke, Bunn and Benjamin (1985) in their provision of brief crisis counselling for adults with illnesses. In that research, many patients had only one or two interactions with the counsellor, and few had more than four. The researchers comment that, "the unusually powerful effects of the counselling intervention can be attributed to its provision during a period of crisis for the patients . . . people in crisis are open to change" (p. 63). Although menopause was not commonly experienced as a crisis by women in this study, it was evident that it meant a significant transition for some women. As Viney (1995) says: "transitions give people opportunities to revise their construing" (p. 113). When women experience menopause as significant, it may well present a similar opportunity for change.

Brief interventions are likely to become increasingly important (Neimeyer & Raskin, 2000). This study offers evidence of a brief and novel application of a personal construct approach, which was helpful to women experiencing the menopausal transition, regardless of their levels of distress.

REFERENCES

Australian Bureau of Statistics. (1998). *A guide to major ABS classifications, occupation: Australian Standard Classification of Occupations (ASCO)*. Canberra, Australian Capital Territory.

Fisher, J. (2000) Creating the future? In J. W. Scheer (Ed.) *The person in society: Challenges to a constructivist theory* (pp. 428–437). Giessen: Psychosozial-Verlag.

Foster, H. & Viney, L. L. (2000). Meanings of menopause: Development of a PCP model. In J. M. Fisher & N. Cornelius (Eds), *Challenging the boundaries: PCP perspectives for the new millennium* (pp. 87–108). Farnborough: EPCA Publications.

Foster, H. & Viney, L. L. (2001). Meanings of menopause: Changing lives. 9th Australasian Personal Construct Psychology conference, Bendigo. *Australian Journal of Psychology, 53* (Supplement), 92.

Foster, H. & Viney, L. L. (2005). Personal construct workshops for women experiencing menopause. In D. Winter & L. L. Viney (Eds), *Personal construct psychotherapy: Advances in theory, practice and research* (pp. 320–332). London: Whurr.

Fransella, F. (1970). And then there was one. In D. Bannister (Ed.), *Perspectives in Personal Construct Theory* (pp. 63–89). London: Academic.

Fransella, F. (1981). Nature babbling to herself: the self characterisation as a therapeutic tool. In H. Bonarius, R. Holland & S. Rosenberg (Eds), *Personal construct psychology: Recent advances in theory and practice* (pp. 219–230). London: Macmillan.

Gottschalk, L. A. & Bechtel, R. J. (1990). *PCAD 2000: Psychiatric Content Analysis and Diagnosis*. Corona del Mar, CA: GB Software.

Gottschalk, L. A. & Gleser, G. C. (1969). *The measurement of psychological states through the content analysis of verbal behaviour*. Berkeley: University of California Press.

Gottschalk, L. A. & Hoigaard, J. (1986). A depression scale applicable to verbal samples. In L. A. Gottschalk, F. Lolas & L. L. Viney (Eds), *Content analysis of verbal behavior: Significance in clinical medicine and psychiatry* (pp. 105–122). Berlin: Springer-Verlag.

Gottschalk, L. A., Lolas, F. & Viney, L. L. (1986). *Content analysis of verbal behavior in clinical medicine*. Heidelberg, Germany: Springer.

Harter, S. L. & Neimeyer, R. A. (1995). Long-term effects of child sexual abuse: Towards a constructivist theory of trauma and its treatment. In R. A. Neimeyer & G. J. Neimeyer (Eds), *Advances in Personal Construct Psychology*. Volume 3 (pp. 229–269). Greenwich, CT: JAI.

Kelly, G. A. (1955/1991a). *The psychology of personal constructs: Volume I*. New York: Norton.

Kelly, G. A. (1955/1991b). *The psychology of personal constructs: Volume II*. New York: Norton.

Leitner, L. M. (1985). The terrors of cognition: on the experiential validity of personal construct theory. In D. Bannister (Ed.), *Issues and approaches in personal construct theory* (pp. 83–104). London: Academic.

Neimeyer, G. J. & Merluzzi, T. V. (1982). Group structure and group process: personal construct therapy and group development. *Small Group Behavior, 13(2)*, 150–164.

Neimeyer & Raskin, J. (2000). On practicing postmodern therapy in modern times. In R. A. Neimeyer & J. D. Raskin (Eds), *Construction of Disorder: Meaning-Making Frameworks for Psychotherapy* (pp. 207–242). Washington, DC: American Psychological Association.

Ravenette, T. (1999). *Personal construct theory in educational psychology: A practitioner's view*. London: Whurr Publishers.

Tabachnick, B. G. & Fidell, L. S. (1989). *Using multivariate statistics* (2nd ed.). Northridge, CA: HarperCollins.

Viney, L. L. (1980). *Transitions*. Sydney: Cassell.

Viney, L. L. (1983). The assessment of psychological states through content analysis of verbal communications. *Psychological Bulletin, 94(3)*, 542–563.

Viney, L. L. (1995). A personal construct model of crisis intervention counselling for adult clients. *Journal of Constructivist Psychology, 9,* 109–126.

Viney, L. L. (1996). *Personal construct therapy: A handbook.* Norwood, NJ: Ablex.

Viney, L. L. (1998). Should we use personal construct therapy? A paradigm for outcomes evaluation. *Psychotherapy, 35(3),* pp. 366–380.

Viney, L. L., Clarke, A. M., Bunn, T. A. & Benjamin, Y. N. (1985). An evaluation of three crisis intervention programmes for general hospital patients. *Journal of Counselling Psychology, 32,* 29–39.

Viney, L. L. & Caputi, P. (2005). Using the Origin and Pawn, Positive Affect, CASPM, and Cognitive Anxiety content analysis scales in counseling research. *Measurement and Evaluation in Counseling and Development, 38(2),* 115–126.

Viney, L. L., Caputi, P. & Webster, D. (2001). Computerised content analysis scales: Their use in personal construct research. Ninth Australasian Personal Construct Psychology conference, Bendigo. *Australian Journal of Psychology, 53* (Supplement), 92.

Viney, L. L., Henry, R. M. (2002). evaluating personal construct and psychodynamic group work with adolescents who are offenders and non-offenders. In G. J. & R. A. Neimeyer (Eds), *Advances in personal construct psychology: New directions & perspectives* (pp. 259–94). New York: JAI Press.

Viney, L. L. & Westbrook, M. T. (1976). Cognitive anxiety: A method of content analysis for verbal samples. *Journal of Personality Assessment, 40(2),* 140–150.

Walker, B. (1993). Looking for a whole "mama": Personal construct theory and dependency. In L. M. Leitner & N. G. M. Dunnett (Eds), *Critical issues in personal construct psychotherapy* (pp. 61–81). Malabar, Florida: Krieger.

Westbrook, M. T. (1976). The measurement of positive affect using content analysis scales. *Journal of Consulting and Clinical Psychology, 12,* 85–86.

Westbrook, M. T. & Viney, L. L. (1980). Scales measuring people's perception of themselves as origins and pawns. *Journal of Personality Assessment, 44(2),* 167–174.

Winter, D. A. (1988). Towards a constructive clinical psychology. In G. Dunnett (Ed.), *Working with people: Clinical uses of personal construct psychology* (pp. 24–38). London: Routledge.

Winter, D. A. (1990). Therapeutic alternatives for psychological disorders: Personal construct investigations in a health service setting. In G. J. & R. A. Neimeyer (Eds), *Advances in personal construct psychology* (pp. 89–116). New York: JAI Press.

Winter, D. A. (1992). *Personal construct psychology in clinical practice: Theory, research and applications* (pp. 149–159). London: Routledge.

Winter, D. A. (1996). Psychotherapy's contrast pole. In J. W. Scheer & A. Catina (Eds), *Empirical constructivism in Europe: The personal construct approach* (pp. 149–159). Giessen: Psychosozial-Verlag.

19

When the Unreal Becomes Real: An Evaluation of Personal Construct Group Psychotherapy with Survivors of Breast Cancer

LISBETH G. LANE

LINDA L. VINEY

This chapter reports on the benefits, in terms of decreased levels of negative affect and an increase in positive affect, of a personal construct group therapy developed to work therapeutically with women diagnosed with non-metastatic breast cancer. What follows is a brief description of the therapy, and then the participants are introduced. Accounts of the research design and measures used precede the presentation of the statistical results. This is followed by an account of the participants' evaluation of their experience of the therapy. Together, the findings suggest that personal construct concepts and practices have much to contribute to current understanding of how we, as therapists, may help women adjust to breast cancer survival.

INTRODUCTION

A diagnosis of breast cancer is a major life event for many women. Following diagnosis as many as 80% of breast cancer patients have been found to

Personal Construct Psychology: New Ideas. Edited by Peter Caputi, Heather Foster and Linda L. Viney. Copyright © 2006 John Wiley & Sons, Ltd.

experience emotional distress, most frequently anxiety about recurrence and death (Spiegel, et al., 1999) and psychological morbidity continues to be high for some women for two or more years post-surgery (Bleiker et al., 2000; Ganz et al., 1992; Irvine et al., 1991). Even five years after diagnosis long-term survivors have been found to experience elevated levels of anxiety and depressive symptoms (Lane, 2002; Lane & Viney, 2000, 2005; Saleeba, Weitzner & Meyers, 1996; Vickberg, Bovbjerg, DuHamel et al., 2000).

In recent years increasing attention is being paid to the psychological needs of breast cancer survivors. As a result, a number of outcome studies have examined the benefits of psychotherapy with this population. Meta-analyses of these studies provide strong evidence of the beneficial effect of psychotherapy on emotional adjustment and social functioning (Devine & Westlake, 1995; Meyer & Mark, 1995, Sheard & Maguire, 1996). Outcome studies of group psychotherapies (Fawzy, Cousins, Fawzy et al., 1990; Spiegel & Yalom, 1978; Spiegel, Bloom & Yalom, 1981; Spiegel, Morrow, Classen et al., 1999) have consistently shown promise in improving emotional adjustment, and psychotherapy is now considered to be a necessary part of comprehensive care for women with breast cancer (Burke & Kissane, 1998).

PERSONAL CONSTRUCT CONCEPTS OF DISTRESS

Kelly (1991) integrated emotional experience within his theory by defining negative emotion as people's awareness that their systems of constructs, evolved to anticipate and predict the world of events, are inadequate for construing the events with which they are now confronted (Fransella & Dalton, 1990). In personal construct terms, emotions are people's experience of, or resistance to, change (Bannister & Fransella, 1980). Emotions serve as signals of the state of people's meaning-making attempts, in the wake of challenges to the adequacy of their constructions (Neimeyer, 1998).

One dimension of distress on which this research is formulated is threat. Threat is the process that underlies and sustains the symptoms of distress many breast cancer survivors experience (Lane, 2002). In personal construct terms, threat is defined as: "the awareness of imminent comprehensive change in one's core structures" (Kelly, 1991, p. 391). Threat occurs when these women recognise that their most influential meanings are seriously inconsistent with their cancer diagnosis and they find themselves on the threshold of deep changes that have far-reaching implications. When the unreal becomes real, women diagnosed with breast cancer face threat to both their physical and psychological integrity.

Positive affect is associated with people's recognition that the system of constructs they have evolved to anticipate and predict the world of events successfully allows them to construe the events with which they are now confronted. The positive affect evaluating concept for this study is hope. Hope is characterised by a readiness to engage in encounter, "to affect and be affected" (Epting & Amerikaner, 1980, p. 60). It implies willingness to interact with the environment, and an orientation towards movement into the future.

THE PERSONAL CONSTRUCT GROUP THERAPY

In the cancer literature the term adjustment is often used to imply the absence of "psychological morbidity", or the end point of "coping" with the global threat of cancer; the goal of psychotherapy being to reduce elevated levels of distress and return these to normatively derived levels (Brennan, 2001). Rarely, however, do people return to their pre-cancer diagnosis state of being in the world (Doka, 1997; Ferrell & Dow, 1996; Frank, 1995; Janoff-Bulman, 1992; Taylor, 1983; Wilkinson, 2000). A major task of psychological intervention with women facing the ongoing threat of breast cancer is to help these women's adjustment to a new state of being. This requires the revision of old meanings, and the elaboration of new meanings (Lane, 2002). Based on this model, the overall goal of the group intervention was to encourage interpersonal opportunities for group members to formulate, confirm, revise, elaborate, and test their meanings of living as breast cancer survivors.

The group therapy was conducted over a period of eight weeks with the participants attending eight weekly two-hour sessions (Lane & Viney, 2005). Participants were allocated to either a day or evening group to suit their individual needs. Two therapy groups, with ten participants in each, were run concurrently over a period of eight weeks.

THE PARTICIPANTS

The sample consisted of 42 women. Participants were randomly assigned to either the intervention or wait-list control condition if they met all of the inclusion criteria and none of the exclusion criteria. Inclusion criteria were as follows: availability and willingness to participate in a group therapy trial; first occurrence biopsy-proven breast cancer; less than 70 years of age (to eliminate the confounding effects of age related illness); and being within

10 years of diagnosis. Exclusion criteria were metastases beyond adjacent lymph nodes; recurrence to breast or other tissue; other cancers or illnesses thought to be life-threatening; a history of major psychiatric illness; currently receiving psychotherapeutic support; and having participated in an earlier study conducted by the authors.

THE CONTENT ANALYSIS SCALES

Although cancer may be "the night side of life" (Sontag, 1979), from the personal construct perspective, women living with breast cancer are expected to function psychologically just as healthy individuals do, that is, reacting with distress to that which is distressing because changes in their meanings are needed (Viney, 1985). Beyond their roles as breast cancer survivors, these women continue to perceive themselves in other roles (mother, daughter, friend, colleague, wife etc.), and to have other needs beyond those precipitated by their cancer status (companionship, intimacy, etc.), and other interests (Rainey, 1984). The measures chosen, therefore, needed to ask participants to evaluate their everyday experience of living. The data analysed in this study were the participants' written responses to the following request: "I would like you to write about your life right now, both the good and the bad. Write as much as you like in about fifteen minutes".

An advantage of content analysis over questionnaire type instruments is that it allows for the interpretation of the contributor's meanings (Viney, 1988). Furthermore, application of content analysis scales allows for quantitative summaries of a series of qualitative content analyses, making comparisons of the experiences of one person with another feasible (Viney & Caputi, 2001). The scales have been used in medical settings (Viney, Benjamin, Clarke & Bunn, 1985, and have been shown to be more sensitive to the status of the medically ill, including women with breast cancer, than other self-report affect scales (Lane, 2002; Lebovits & Holland, 1986). Importantly, they are consistent with personal construct assumptions and concepts (Viney, Caputi & Webster, 2000).

Statistical analysis of these personal meanings was achieved through the utilisation of the Total Anxiety Scale (Gottschalk & Gleser, 1969), and Death Anxiety Subscale (Gottschalk & Gleser, 1969) to measure threat to their physical and psychological integrity (Lane & Viney, 2005; Weekes, 1998) and the Hope Content Analysis Scale (Gottschalk, 1974) to measure hope. These measures were taken from both groups at baseline and were repeated immediately after the intervention and 12 weeks later.

THE RELIABILITY AND VALIDITY OF
THE CONTENT ANALYSIS SCALES

Gottschalk and Bechtel (1995) point out that the conversion of the data into scales measuring psychological dimensions affords many points where distortion and random error may occur if scorers make assumptions about contributor's meanings. An example of this is the possible tendency to classify references to cancer as necessarily evidence of death anxiety. Data were scored using the *PCAD 2000* programme (Gottschalk & Bechtel, 1998) to overcome this potential for error. Inter-scorer reliability between automated and human scoring is satisfactory with reported correlations above 0.80 (Gottschalk & Bechtel, 1982, 1995, 1998).

As the meanings expressed are the participant's own, content validity of the Content Analysis Scales is assumed. Reported evidence of the external validity of these scales is plentiful (Gleser, Gottschalk & Springer, 1961; Gottschalk, 1974; Gottschalk & Gleser, 1969; Gottschalk & Hoigaard, 1986; Gottschalk, Lomas & Viney, 1986). Gottschalk, Stein & Shapiro (1997) have examined the validity of the computerised content analysis scales, which confirm previous satisfactory validatory studies.

Each of the sets of scores was analysed using multiple univariate repeated measures analyses of variance. A 2×3 mixed design analysis of variance was utilised with one between subjects group variable with two levels, (intervention or control), and one within subjects variable, three levels, baseline Time 1, Time 2 eight weeks later, and Time 3 twelve weeks following Time 2.

STATISTICAL RESULTS

Means and standard deviations for scores on the dependent variables were calculated for both groups and are presented in Table 19.1.

At Time 1 the intervention group mean indicated moderate threat, as measured by the CAS Total Anxiety Scale, for the group. Gottschalk and Gleser (1969) suggest that a score above 2.2 is indicative of moderate distress and a score of 3.0 or more is indicative of the presence of pathological anxiety. Examination of the individual data revealed that 11 women (55%) in the treatment group had a Total Anxiety Score above 2.2, with 4 women (18%) in the control group having similarly elevated scores. Two women in each group were found to have a score above 3.0, indicating the presence of pathological distress. At Time 3, for the treatment group, no individual scores were now above 2.2. Seven women in the control group expressed moderately

Table 19.1 Means and standard deviation for content analysis scale scores by group for Times 1, 2 and 3

Time	CAS total anxiety		CAS death anxiety		CAS hope	
	M	**SD**	**M**	**SD**	**M**	**SD**
Treatment Group						
Time 1	2.33	(0.54)	0.84	(0.51)	1.72	(2.11)
Time 2	1.72	(0.68)	0.56	(0.19)	2.89	(1.88)
Time 3	1.53	(0.44)	0.57	(0.16)	3.10	(2.35)
Control Group						
Time 1	2.03	(0.63)	0.70	(0.27)	2.05	(2.38)
Time 2	2.08	(0.82)	0.66	(0.23)	1.97	(2.84)
Time 3	1.85	(0.75)	0.78	(0.37)	1.24	(2.41)

elevated distress, as measured on the Total Anxiety Scale, with one score above 3.0.

Examining the interaction effects of the independent variables of time and group on the dependent variable, CAS Total Anxiety, measuring threat, a significant interaction effect, $F[2,39] = 4.944$, $p = 0.01$, ($\eta^2 = 0.20$) suggested that a change in scores occurred over time, and that this change was not the same for both groups. A significant interaction effect of time and group on the dependent variable CAS Death Anxiety Subscale was also revealed, $F[2,39] = 3.155$, $p = 0.05$ ($\eta^2 = 0.14$). A significant interaction effect for the CAS Hope Scale scores ($F(2,39) = 3.912$, $p = 0.028$, ($\eta^2 = 0.17$) was also observed.

The results suggest that the personal construct group therapy was helpful to the women in this study. Levels of threat, as measured by the content analysis scales, were found to have decreased immediately after therapy for the intervention group and not for the control group. Differential decreases were also maintained three months later. Similarly, the therapy group, three months after therapy, were found to express more hopeful meanings.

THE PARTICIPANTS' EVALUATION

Historically, most of what has been written about how clients experience their therapy has been generated out of the perceptions and impressions of practitioners, researchers and theorists (Quinn, 1996). To date, only a few studies have asked intervention participants directly to explore, reflect on, or comment in an open-ended fashion about their experience of psychotherapy (Macormack et al., 2001). Fortunately, within a personal construct framework, there is no assumption that there is an "actual" truth. The theory places the participants in the centre of their own truth. Therefore, if participants change as a result of therapy, their understanding of the processes is very important to personal construct theorists and clinicians.

At the end of the last session, participants received a form on which they could write their contact details to be shared with each group member. On a tear-off section, they were asked to comment on their experience of therapy. The purpose of this invitation was, first, to evaluate the therapy, second, to gain insight into how changes took place for these women, and third, to gain information on how this group therapy might be improved. The participants' responses to this question were not identifiable by name. Such anonymity was hoped to allow the women to respond truthfully, and without a concern for the therapist's feelings. All the women filled in a comment about the group.

From their responses it was evident that the sharing of their stories was a central process of change for them. Of the 20 responses, 18 referred to the interpersonal context in which their therapy took place. Many women commented on the opportunities the therapy had given them to disclose their meanings. "I needed someone to unload on. Everything that I felt, without having to worry about how it might affect others" (Christine). Others commented on the levels of understanding they had received. "It's very important to be able to share with other women who have some understanding of the trauma involved with breast cancer" (Katherine). They spoke of their common bonds " I found this small group of very lovely women very easy to relate to about a lot of issues that we have in common" (Sue); and the understandings they had gained into others' experiences, which strengthened their own understanding. As June wrote: "The insight I obtained into other women's experiences, supported my belief that we, as women, can overcome most problems/concerns and are so very caring and supportive of each other". Another reported: "I found the other women so very inspirational. They showed me their quiet strength and ability to endure".

DISCUSSION

One of the unique aspects of human experience is that people attempt to find meaning, even in incomprehensible events such as life-threatening illness and death (Feifel, 1959). This task can be made harder if the context in which to "try out new meanings" is unavailable. From the responses of the participants, the group intervention provided them with the context in which to define their current meanings and elaborate new and more helpful meanings.

Their perception of the beneficial effects of these opportunities is supported by the statistical findings. Opportunities to talk about their fear of death and dying were found to be especially valuable. Interestingly, it was in these discussions that the women first recognised their new meanings. The following extract from Sandra illustrates this elaboration.

> It's very hard to make sense of, I mean I am only 32, and I have always been fit, I never smoked. And how can you make sense of that. I have three small kids and a husband, and I am just starting my life. I've just moved into a new home – I'm just starting out in my life. I'm thinking no way – I am determined, I want to see my children grow up and graduate. So I have come to peace with whatever happens. I don't want my children to remember me as a miserable old hag. I want to enjoy everything I have with them and be a positive person in their life. I mean I hope I will be here, but if I am not, then they will remember me well. They are probably sick of me, but they see me 24 hours a day. I don't want to regret, and that is a choice that I have made.

The major limitation of this study relates to the size of the sample. With such a small sample, generalisation to the population of breast cancer survivors at large is limited. Future studies, with larger samples, might fruitfully explore the contribution of age on treatment effects. A comparison of personal construct group and individual therapy is also called for.

In conclusion, personal construct group therapy has been shown to be effective in reducing levels of threat and increasing hope in women diagnosed with breast cancer. The study, the first to use personal construct psychology principles in group therapy specifically developed for this population, has further shown that personal construct principles and methodology have much to offer in our understanding of the ongoing issues faced by breast cancer survivors. When women have the opportunity to develop new meanings they are able to envisage a future that accommodates their changed circumstance. They can again anticipate some positive outcomes of their future-oriented predictions. As Yvonne, a 49-year-old woman who has had 2 breast cancer diagnoses in the past 5 years, said 3 months after the intervention: "I suppose now, looking back on it, it's changed my life. You can't say it's better than it was, because you never would want to get sick in the first place. But now, I have a new meaning of life. I think I've come to terms with having cancer."

We acknowledge the invaluable assistance of the many women currently living with breast cancer, who have shared their experiences so generously. The names of participants have been changed to protect their anonymity.

REFERENCES

Bannister, D. & Fransella, F. (1980). *Inquiring man: The psychology of personal constructs.* (2nd ed.). London: Crook Helm.

Bleiker, E. M. A., Pouwer, F., van der Ploeg, H. M., Leer, J. W. H. & Ader, H. J. (2000). Psychological distress two years after diagnosis of breast cancer: Frequency and prediction. *Patient Education & Counseling, 40(3),* 209–217.

Brennan, J. (2001). Adjustment to cancer – coping or personal transition. *Psycho-Oncology, 10,* 1–8.

Burke, S. & Kissane, D. W. (1998). Psychosocial support for breast cancer patients: A review of interventions provided by specialist providers. Sydney: NHMRC National Breast Cancer Centre.

Devine, E. C. & Westlake, S. K. (1995). The effects of psychoeducational care provided to adults with cancer: meta-analysis of 116 studies. *Oncology Nursing Forum, 22,* 1369–1381.

Doka, K. J. (1997). The quest for meaning in illness, dying, death and bereavement. In S. Strack (Ed.), *Death and the quest for meaning: Essays in honor of Herman Feifel* (pp. 241–255). Northvale, NJ: Jason Aronson.

Epting, F. R. & Amerikaner, M. (1980). Optimal functioning: A personal construct approach. In A. W. Landfield & L. M. Leitner (Eds), *Personal construct psychology: Psychotherapy and personality,* (pp. 55–73). New York: John Wiley & Sons, Inc.

Fawzy, F. I., Cousins, N., Fawzy, N. W., Kemeny, M. E., Elashoff, R. & Morton, D. (1990) A structured psychiatric intervention for cancer patients: I. Changes over time in methods of coping and affective disturbance. *Archives of General Psychiatry, 4,* 720–725.

Feifel, H. (1959). *The meaning of death.* New York: McGraw-Hill.

Ferrell, B. R. & Dow, K. H. (1996). Portraits of survivorship: a glimpse through the lens of survivors' eyes. *Cancer Practice, 4(2),* 76–80.

Fransella, F. & Dalton, P. (1990). Personal construct counselling in action. London: Sage.

Frank, A. W. (1995). *The wounded storyteller: Body, illness, and ethics.* Chicago: Chicago University Press.

Ganz, P. A., Schag, A. C., Lee, J. J., Polinsky, M. L. & Tan, S. J. (1992). Breast conservation versus mastectomy. Is there a difference in psychological adjustment or quality of life in the year after surgery? *Cancer, 69(7),* 1729–1738.

Gleser, G. C., Gottschalk, L. A. & Springer, K. J. (1961). An anxiety scale applicable to verbal samples. *Archives of General Psychiatry, 5,* 593–605.

Gottschalk, L. A. (1974). A hope scale applicable to verbal samples. *Archives of General Psychiatry, 30,* 779–785.

Gottschalk, L. A. and Bechtel, R. J. (1982) The measurement of anxiety through the computer analysis of verbal samples. *Comprehensive Psychiatry, 23,* 364–369.

Gottschalk, L. A. & Bechtel, R. J. (1995). Computerized measurement of the content analysis of natural language for use in biomedical research. *Computer Methods and Programs in Biomedicine, 4,* 123–130.

Gottschalk, L. A. & Bechtel, R. J. (1998). *Psychiatric content analysis and diagnosis (PCAD2000).* Corona del Mar, California: GB Software.

Gottschalk, L. A. & Gleser, G. C. (1969) *The Measurement of psychological states through the content analysis of verbal behavior.* Berkeley: University of California Press.

Gottschalk, L. A. & Hoigaard-Martin, J. (1986). A depression scale applicable to verbal samples. *Psychiatry Research, 17(3),* 213–227.

Gottschalk, L. A., Lolas, F. & Viney, L. L. (1986). *Content analysis of verbal behavior.* Heidelberg: Springer Verlag.

Gottschalk, L. A., Stein, M. K. & Shapiro, D. H. (1997). The application of computerized content analysis of speech to the diagnostic process in a psychiatric outpatient clinic. *Journal of Clinical Psychology, 53(5)*, 427–441.

Irvine, D., Brown, B., Crooks, D., Roberts, J. & Browne, G. (1991). Psychosocial adjustment in women with breast cancer. *Cancer 67(4)*, 1097–1117.

Janoff-Bulman, R. (1992). *Shattered assumptions: Towards a new psychology of trauma.* New York: Free Press.

Kelly, G. (1991/1955). The Psychology of Personal Constructs, Vols. 1 and 2, 2nd ed. London: Routledge.

Lane, L. G. (2002). Living in the Shadow: A personal construct model of adjustment to breast cancer survival and tests of its clinical usefulness. Unpublished PhD thesis: University of Wollongong.

Lane, L. G. & Viney, L. L. (2000). The meanings of a breast cancer diagnosis: A model of women's construing. In J. M. Fisher, N. Cornelius (Eds), *Challenging the Boundaries: PCP perspectives for the new millennium,* (pp. 120–131). Farnborough: EPCA Publications.

Lane, L. G. & Viney, L. L. (2005). The effects of personal construct group therapy on breast cancer survivors. *Journal of Consulting and Clinical Psychology, 73*, 284–292.

Lebovits, A. H. & Holland, J. C. (1986). Use of the Gottschalk-Gleser verbal content analysis scales with medically ill patients. In L. A. Gottschalk, F. Lolas & L. L. Viney (Eds), *Content analysis of verbal behavior: Significance in clinical medicine and psychiatry* (pp. 133–148). Heidelberg/Berlin: Springer-Verlag.

MacCormack, T., Simonian, J., Lim, J., Remond, L., Roets, D., Dunn, S. & Butow, P. (2001). "Someone who cares": A qualitative investigation of cancer patients' experiences of psychotherapy. *Psycho-Oncology, 10(1)*, 52–65.

Meyer, T. J. & Mark, M. M. (1995), Effects of psychosocial interventions with adult cancer patients: a meta-analysis of randomised experiments. *Health Psychology, 14*, 101–108.

Neimeyer, R. A. (1998). *Lessons of loss: A guide to coping.* New York: McGraw-Hill.

Quinn, W. H. (1996). The client speaks out: Three domains of meaning. *Journal of Family Psychotherapy, 7*, 71–93.

Saleeba, A. K., Weitzner, M. A. & Meyers, C. A. (1996) Subclinical psychological distress in long-term survivors of breast cancer: A preliminary communication. *Journal of Psychosocial Oncology, 14(1)*, 83–93.

Sheard, T. & Maguire, P. (1999). The effects of psychological interventions on anxiety and depression in oncology: Results of two meta-analyses. *British Journal of Cancer, 80(11)*, 1170–1180.

Sontag, S. (1979). *Illness as metaphor.* London: Allen Lane.

Spiegel, D., Bloom, J. R. & Yalom, I. (1981). Group support for patients with metastatic breast cancer. *Archives of General Psychiatry, 3*, 527–533.

Spiegel, D., Morrow, G. R., Classen, C., Raubertas, R., Stott, P. B., Mudaliar, N., Pierce, H. I., Flynn, P. J., Heard, L. & Riggs, G. (1999). Group psychotherapy for recently diagnosed breast cancer patients: A multicentre feasibility study. *Psycho-Oncology, 8*, 482–493.

Spiegel, D. & Yalom, I. (1978). A support group for dying patients. *International Journal of Group Psychotherapy, 28*, 233–245.

Taylor, S. E. (1983). Adjustment to threatening events: A theory of cognitive adaptation. *American Psychologist, 38P*, 1161–1173.

Vickberg, S. M., Bovbjerg, D. H., DuHamel, K. N., Currie, V. & Redd, W. H. (2000). Intrusive thoughts and psychological distress among breast cancer survivors: Global meaning as a possible protective factor. *Behavioral Medicine, 25(4)*, 152–160.

Viney, L. L. (1985). Physical illness: A guidebook for the kingdom of the sick. In E. Button (Ed.), *Personal construct theory and mental health: Theory, research and practice* (pp. 262–273). London: Croom Helm.

Viney, L. L. (1988). Which data-collection methods are appropriate for a constructivist psychology? *International Journal of Personal Construct Psychology, 1*, 191–203.

Viney, L. L., Benjamin, Y. N., Clarke, A. & Bunn, T. (1985). Sex differences in the psychological reactions of medical and surgical patients to crisis intervention counseling: Sauce for the goose may not be sauce for the gander. *Social Science & Medicine, 20(11)*, 1199–1205.

Viney, L. L. & Caputi, P. (2001). Computer-supported content analysis scales: Their use in psychotherapy research. 14th International Congress of Personal Construct Psychology, Wollongong, Australia.

Viney, L. L., Caputi, P. & Webster, D. (2000). Computerised content analysis scales: Their use in personal construct research. In J. Ellis-Scheer (Ed.), *Proceedings of the ninth Australasian personal construct psychology conference*. Bendigo, Australia.

Viney, L. L., Clarke, A., Bunn, T. & Benjamin, Y. N. (1985). The effect of a hospital-based counseling service on the physical recovery of surgical and medical patients. *General Hospital Psychiatry, 7(4)*, 294–301.

Weekes, P. (1998). Giving birth to and parenting children with developmental disabilities: An application of personal construct psychology. Unpublished PhD Thesis. University of Wollongong.

Wilkinson, S. (2000). Women with breast cancer talking causes: Comparing content, biographical and discursive analyses. *Feminism & Psychology, 10(4)*, 431–460.

20

Personal Construct Group Work with Troubled Adolescents

DEBORAH TRUNECKOVA

LINDA L. VINEY

Research has established the clinical efficacy of personal construct group work as a therapeutic intervention for adults. However, the veracity of such a claim for adolescents is questionable, as currently there has only been a handful of outcome studies. The present research attempts to redress this imbalance. The effectiveness of personal construct group work with troubled adolescents was assessed by following three paths of inquiry. One path of inquiry assessed the effect of personal construct group work on individual construing and behaviour. Another path set out to assess effectiveness of group work as perceived by the adolescent group members, their parents and teachers. The third path investigated personal construct group work processes. The results from the three paths of inquiry provided some evidence that personal construct group work was effective in bringing about individual changes, was perceived as an effective intervention, and was effective through the group processes, by positively changing adolescents' constructions of themselves. These results do suggest that personal construct group work can enhance the understanding and therapists' capacity to share meaning worlds with troubled adolescents. Adolescence is a time of many maturational changes that adolescents need to make sense of and integrate. Strong feelings, both positive and negative are experienced, and often it is the expression of those negative feelings that brings adolescents into hurtful

Personal Construct Psychology: New Ideas. Edited by Peter Caputi, Heather Foster and Linda L. Viney. Copyright © 2006 John Wiley & Sons, Ltd.

and conflictual relationships. Reactions to these negative feelings carry costs for the adolescents, their families, their schools and communities. Adolescents become highly vulnerable to emotional distress leading to mental illness, and to a range of harmful behaviours (Moon, Meyer & Grau, 1999; National Health & Medical Research Council, 1997). The cost to all who are touched by the adolescents can be extremely high and painful, emotionally, socially and economically (Moon et al., 1999).

In this research study we propose that while personal construct psychology has been primarily established as an effective treatment for adults (Viney, 1998; Viney, Metcalfe & Winter, 2005; Winter, 1985a; Winter, 1992a; Winter & Watson, 1999), it could offer a lot for adolescents. The core tenets of the theory (Kelly, 1991a, 1991b) can accommodate the developmental needs of adolescents by enabling an understanding and appreciation of the transitional nature of adolescence and the processes of change involved. Personal construct psychology can make sense of the psychological processes of change in adolescence, and the personal construct approach would enable the group work leader to seek understanding about what the adolescents feel make sense and do not make sense, to examine these meanings and to assist the adolescents in subjecting alternatives to experimental test and revision (Kelly, 1979).

The results from recent accounts of personal construct group work with adolescents (Jackson, 1992; Truneckova & Viney, 2001; Viney & Henry, 2002; Viney, Henry & Campbell, 2001; Viney, Truneckova, Weekes & Oades, 1997; Viney, Truneckova, Weekes & Oades, 1999) have indicated that personal construct group work is an effective therapeutic intervention for troubled adolescents, functional adolescents, and adolescent offenders. The outcomes have been shown to be comparable with other therapeutic models of intervention for adolescents (Viney & Henry, 2002; Viney, Henry & Campbell, 2001).

AIMS AND HYPOTHESES

AIMS (INVESTIGATIONS 1–3)

The aims of these investigations were to research the effects of personal construct group work on troubled adolescents:

- to explore the differences in the content and structure of the construing of troubled and functional adolescents;
- to demonstrate the perceived effectiveness of the group work for troubled adolescents, their parents and their teachers; and

- to inquire into the processes of personal construct group work with adolescents.

HYPOTHESES

Individual Change

- The troubled adolescents, before the group work, will make less use of abstract construing than will the functional adolescents;
- After group work, the troubled adolescents will use more abstract construing than the control group;
- After group work, the troubled adolescents will use more interpersonal themes than the control group; and
- After group work, they will show less disruptive behaviour both at school and home than before it.

Perceived Group Work Effectiveness

- Personal construct group work will be an effective intervention, as assessed by the troubled adolescents themselves, their parents and their teachers.

Group Processes

- During group work, the group members will use more interpersonal themes than at the beginning of the group work;
- During group work, the group members will increasingly evaluate themselves more positively on achieving the goals of group work than at the beginning of the group work;
- During group work, the group leaders will report an increasing attainment of the goals of the group work by the group members;
- During group work, the differences between the ranking by the group members of themselves and the group leaders on the goals of group work will decrease.

METHOD

PARTICIPANTS

Seventy-six adolescents, including 48 troubled adolescents (32 males, 16 females), aged between 12 years and 15 years ($M = 13$ years 9 months, SD

= 0.95) attending 5 government secondary schools in New South Wales, Australia, and representative of adolescents attending comprehensive secondary schools in the region (Department of School Education, 1999; Illawarra Regional Information Services, 1996, 1999), took part in the research, together with their parents and teachers. The demographic data for the participating adolescents reported the following: 65% males, 39% females; 4% Aboriginal Descent; 17% speaking a language other than English; and 35% coming from a Sole Parent Household. Wait-list control groups involving both adolescents experiencing (Control Sample 1) and not experiencing (Control Sample 2) interpersonal difficulties were used as comparisons. The troubled adolescents were randomly assigned to the treatment (Group Work Sample) and control sample (Control Sample 1). There were 5 group work groups with 3 of them having 2 group leaders while the other 2 had only 1. All group leaders were trained psychologists employed as School Counsellors with the Department of School Education.

GROUP WORK

The group work was conducted weekly, for 10 sessions, of 1.5 hours duration, in the schools during school hours. Twenty-six adolescents participated in 5 group work interventions, with each group closed and its size ranged from 4 to 8 adolescents. This personal construct group work used the Interpersonal Transaction Group format (Landfield & Rivers, 1975), a short-term intervention with structured group events which has been successfully tested with adolescents (Viney et al., 1997).

OUTCOME MEASURES

Measures to Assess Individual Change

The first path, *Investigation 1*, set out to assess the effect of personal construct group work on individual construing and behaviour. This phase involved using outcome measures of individual change to assess treatment and control groups before the intervention began, and after the intervention ended, and 12 months follow-up on 1 measure for the treatment group. Responses to the outcome measures of individual change were also sought from parents and teachers of all the adolescents participating. In order to assess individual change, 3 measures were used, the Repertory Grid and the Self-Characterisation, developed by Kelly (1991a, 1991b), and a behaviour measurement, the Conners' Rating Scales, drawn from an alternative, but compatible psychological approach (Conners, 1990, 1997). On the

Conners' Rating Scales, the overall total score was used, high scores indicating more troubled behaviours.

To enable assessment of the adolescents' constructions, a rating scale was developed to measure the amount of change and type of change on the self-construing of the adolescents. Assisted by data gained by a pilot study using personal construct group work, two categories of content analysis were developed. A brief overview of the two categories is presented in Table 20.1.

Each construct provided by the Repertory Grid, and each sentence of the Self-Characterisation, was considered one unit of meaning, and was rated, firstly, according to the criteria for Category A, Self Description, and secondly, according to the criteria for Category B, Level of Abstraction. Inter-rater reliability coefficient, *kappa* (K), ranged from moderate to good, and was consistent across all categories (K ranged from 0.64 to 0.99, $p < 0.01$, one tailed).

Table 20.1 Categories for the assessment of the content and structure of adolescents' responses to the Repertory Grid and Self-Characterisation

---

Category A-self description
    A.1 Construing of Self
    A.2 Construing of Self in Relation to Others
    Category A is designed to accommodate two ways in which adolescents may construe themselves. The first measure, *construing of self*, refers to psychological statements made by adolescents. These are personal statements or descriptions of themselves, their unique characteristics. The second measure, *construing of self in relation to others*, refers to interpersonal construing. This measure assesses the way in which adolescents make sense of themselves in relation to important people in their lives, that is, friends, parents, family.

Category B-level of abstraction
    B1 Concrete Construing
    B2 Abstract Construing
    Category B is designed to measure the level of abstraction of construing. The structural complexity of construing can vary from physicalistic constructions to psychological constructions. The first measure, *concrete construing*, refers to descriptions of physical attributes and behavioural accomplishments such as sports, hobbies and future careers. The second measure, *abstract construing*, refers to attempts by adolescents to not only understand their own systems of personal constructs, but the personal construct system of the person with whom they are relating. There is an attempt by adolescents to establish a role relationship in which they are trying to interpret the psychological behaviour of themselves and others. Establishing a role relationship requires the adolescent to draw on abstract construing, enabling the adolescents to engage in perspective-taking and empathic behaviour.

Measures to Assess the Perceived Effectiveness of the Group Work

For *Investigation 2*, the second pathway, structured interviews and standardised questionnaires were designed and used to evaluate the effectiveness of personal construct group work, as perceived by the adolescent group members, their parents and their teachers. This path of inquiry sought to assess the effectiveness of personal construct group work as perceived by the adolescent group members, their parents and teachers. The primary focus of the different interviews was to encourage the participants to provide their own constructions of effectiveness. The participants' assessments were sought before the group work commenced, and following the termination of the group work. The data were subject to qualitative analyses, the responses were content analysed and three categories, assisted by the pilot study of personal construct group work, were established: Personal Behaviour, Interpersonal Behaviour and School Achievement. Each clause in the participant's response was scored for only one of the categories, and the total number of responses of each category was calculated as a percentage of the total number of responses for each question. Inter-rater reliability coefficient, *kappa* (*K*), showed moderate to good level of agreement across all the data analysed (*K* ranged from 0.67 to 0.96, $p < 0.01$, one tailed).

Measures to Assess Group Processes

The third path of inquiry, *Investigation 3*, the assessments of group processes were drawn from the data of five measures, the Mood Tag, the Group Members' Session Evaluation, the Group Leaders' Session Evaluation, Group Grid 1 and Group Grid 2. Measures for the evaluation of group processes were employed as part of the structure of the sessions, as an overview and review tool at the end of each session, and as a means of collecting data from the group members during the group work.

The Mood Tag was introduced by Landfield and Rivers (1975), as part of the format for the Interpersonal Transaction Group, to elicit emotional constructs at the beginning and ending of the session. It was predicted that the Mood Tag would be able to demonstrate group processes by firstly, showing how the adolescents and the group leaders anticipated each session, and what impact the session had on them. Secondly, it was anticipated that the Mood Tag would identify when intrapersonal constructions of the group members and leaders shifted to themes that were interpersonal. In order to investigate the level of interpersonal construing during the group work, the Mood Tags were content analysed. The criteria used to investigate personal/interpersonal content were drawn from the system of content analysis established to evaluate the Repertory Grid and the Self-Characterisation. The inter-rater reliability ranged from moderate to good (*K* ranged from 0.67 to 0.89), and the level of agreement was found to be significant.

The Group Session Evaluations were completed by the group members and leaders. In the Session Evaluation, the adolescents were asked to say how they felt at that moment, and how they viewed themselves in terms of eight supplied constructs developed from the group work goals (see Table 20.2), on a scale from one to five (five being the positive pole of the construct). The Group Session Evaluation completed by the group leader and co-leader, looked at group processes, by rating each member in terms of the eight supplied constructs, developed from the group work goals (see Table 20.2), on a scale from one to three (three being the positive pole of the construct).

A personal construct technique used in the measurement of therapeutic change has been the Group Grids (for example, Koch, 1983a, 1983b; Winter, 1985b, 1992b). In this investigation into group processes, the constructs of

Table 20.2 Goals for the group work

Stages of group development (Kelly, 1955; 1991)	Therapeutic strategies
	1. To provide validation for the construing of each member
1. Initiation of mutual support	2. To develop a sense of belonging to the group
2. Initiation of primary role relationships	3. To develop a sense that others in the group understand
3. Initiation of mutual primary enterprise	4. To develop sufficient trust within the group to allow for the sharing of constructions
4. Exploration of personal problems	5. To explore personal problems and begin to formulate hypotheses and to design experiments leading to change
5. Exploration of secondary roles	6. To explore the similarities and differences in both the group members and significant others outside the group
6. Exploration of secondary enterprises	7. To reconstrue ways of applying the group experiences to everyday situations
	8. To grow in self-validation and self-regard.

one group grid (Group Grid 1) reflected the goals established for the group work (see Table 20.2), while the constructs for the second group grid (Group Grid 2) were drawn from constructs elicited from the Repertory Grids of the adolescents. The group members and leader were required to rank themselves and other group participants on the supplied constructs, the positive pole on the left and the negative pole on the right. The ranking numbers ranged from the number 1 to the number of elements (members/leader) forming the group, from "most like" to "least like", with low ratings indicating close proximity to the positive pole and high ratings showing close proximity to the negative pole.

DESIGN

Measures to assess individual change were collected on three occasions: before the intervention, pre-group (Time 1), and following the intervention, post-group (Time 2) and twelve months later (Time 3) for the Conners' Rating Scales. Measures to assess the perceived effectiveness of group work were collected from the three participants twice, at Times 1 and 2. These participants were the adolescents in the Group Work Sample, and their parents and teachers. Dependent variable data involving measures to assess group processes were collected for the Group Work Sample. Data from the Mood Tag were collected twice each session, at the beginning and towards the end of the session. Data involving the Group Session Evaluations were completed at the end of each session. Using Group Grid 1 and Group Grid 2, these data were collected during the second, fifth and ninth sessions.

INVESTIGATION 1: INDIVIDUAL OUTCOMES

The Repertory Grid and the Self-Characterisation were used to measure changes in the self-construing of adolescents before the group work (Time 1), and again after the group work (Time 2). It was hypothesised that troubled adolescents before the group work would make less use of abstract construing than would the functional adolescents. The content analyses (the level of abstraction, rated concrete or abstract) of these measures, the Repertory Grid and Self-Characterisation, did offer some support for the hypothesis. Firstly, the analyses of variance established differences between the sample groups at Time 1 on the two levels of abstraction. Significant differences were found in the level of concrete construing as measured by the Repertory Grid ($F[2,75] = 7.52$, $p < 0.001$), and by the Self-Characterisation ($F[2,75] =$

8.670, $p < 0.001$), with troubled adolescents generally using more concrete construing than the functional adolescents. Significant differences between the three groups were found in the number of constructs rated abstract construing measured by the Repertory Grid ($F[2,75] = 7.520$, $p < 0.001$), and by the Self-Characterisation ($F[2,75] = 12.40$, $p < 0.001$). Figure 20.1 shows the functional adolescents were using more abstract construing than the troubled adolescents in the Group Work Sample.

Comparisons were then made at Times 1 and 2, and between the scales, concrete or abstract construing, to test the hypothesis that the troubled adolescents who participated in the group work used more abstract construing than they did before the group work. The constructs elicited from the Repertory Grid and the Self-Characterisation for the two samples of troubled adolescents were content analysed at Time 2 according to the criteria established to determine levels of abstraction. Differences in the number of constructs rated as abstract or concrete from the Group Work Sample and Control Sample 1 on the individual measures were examined by using multivariate analysis of variance (MANOVA). The effect of treatment on the overall rate of abstract constructs by troubled adolescents was found (multivariate $F[1,41] = 3.04$, $p = 0.089$). For the treatment sample, Group Work Sample, there was a significant main effect of treatment on the rate of concrete construing of these adolescents (multivariate $F[1,41] = 4.15$, $p < 0.05$), with

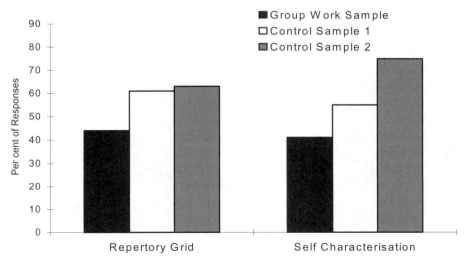

Figure 20.1 The use of abstract constructs on the Repertory Grid and Self-Characterisation by group work sample, Control Sample 1 and Control Sample 2 at Time 1

more of these adolescents decreasing their rate of concrete construing after the group work. A moderate effect size was found for both the Repertory Grid (Time 1, $M = 8.79$, $SD = 3.98$; Time 2, $M = 10.65$, $SD = 4.71$) $d = 0.47$, and the Self-Characterisation (Time 1, $M = 4.71$, $SD = 2.42$; Time 2, $M = 5.92$, $SD = 2.51$) $d = 0.5$, and these increases in abstract construing for Group Work Sample are illustrated in Figure 20.2.

The constructs elicited from the Repertory Grid and the Self-Characterisation for the two samples of troubled adolescents, were also analysed at Time 2 in terms of the level of interpersonal construing compared to personal construing. The analyses of the data provided some support for the hypothesis that the troubled adolescents who participated in the group work used more interpersonal construing after it than they did before it. MANOVA found a significant main effect of treatment on the overall measure of the number of interpersonal constructs (multivariate $F[1,41] = 3.86$, $p = 0.056$), with a significant effect of treatment on the number of interpersonal constructs as measured by the Self-Characterisation of troubled adolescents (multivariate $F[1,41] = 7.64$, $p < 0.01$). On the Repertory Grid, a medium effect size $d = 0.43$ (Time 1, $M = 7.50$, $SD = 3.77$; Time 2, $M = 9.12$, $SD = 3.09$), was found with a small to medium effect size $d = 0.39$ on

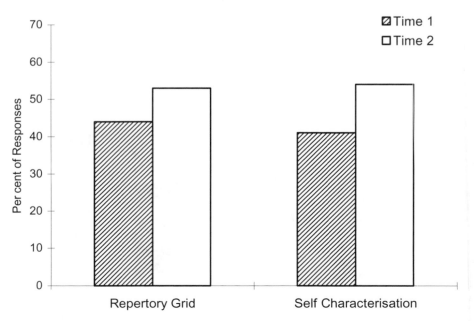

Figure 20.2 The use of abstract constructs on the Repertory Grid and Self-Characterisation by Group Work Sample at Time 1 and Time 2

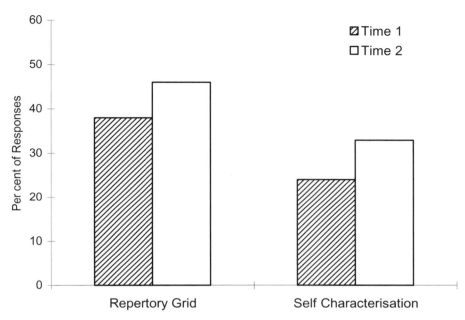

Figure 20.3 The use of interpersonal constructs on the Repertory Grid and Self-Characterisation by Group Work Sample at Time 1 and Time 2

the Self-Characterisation (Time 1, $M = 2.29$, $SD = 1.61$; Time 2, $M = 2.92$, $SD = 2.28$). In the Group Work Sample, more adolescents were providing interpersonal rather than personal constructs on the two measures at Time 2 (see Figure 20.3).

The results of the third measure of individual changes, the Conners' Rating Scales (Conners, 1990, 1997), the Conners' Parent Rating Scale-48 (CPRS-48) and the Conners' Teacher Rating Scale-39 (CTRS-39) were analysed, and the behavioural changes recorded on these scales provided support for the hypothesis that the troubled adolescents who participated in the group work would show less disruptive behaviour. A significant main effect of treatment on the CPRS-48 and the CTRS-39 of troubled adolescents at Time 2 (multivariate $F[1,39] = 4.95$, $p < 0.05$) was found, and approaching medium effect size $d = 0.40$ (CPRS-48) and $d = 0.43$ (CTRS-39). There were decreases in the mean scores of the CPRS-48 and CTRS-39 for the Group Work Sample, disruptive behaviours were greater at Time 1 ($M = 42.46$, $SD = 19.17$ and $M = 83.04$, $SD = 34.58$ respectively) than at Time 3 ($M = 30.80$, $SD = 20.14$ and $M = 65.46$, $SD = 34.86$ respectively) (see Figure 20.4).

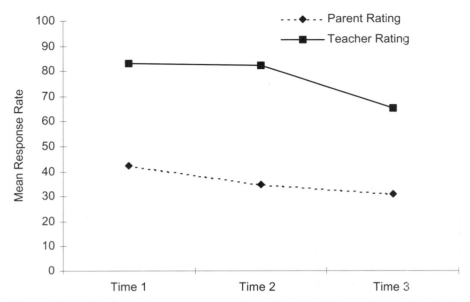

Figure 20.4 The mean response rates of the Conners' Parent Rating Scale-48 and the Conners' Teacher Rating Scale-39 for Group Work Sample at Time 1, Time 2 and Time 3

INVESTIGATION 2: PERCEIVED EFFECTIVENESS OF THE GROUP WORK

The second line of inquiry, the perceived effectiveness of the group work, involved collection of data at Times 1 and 2 from the structured interviews with the adolescents who were taking part in the group work, and their parents, and from the standardised questionnaire completed by the teachers of these adolescents. The instruments developed for the research were content analysed. The results of these analyses qualitatively described the anticipations the participants had of the group work and the evaluations the participants had of the group work. The results provided support for the hypothesis that personal construct group work would be assessed by the adolescents, their parents and their teachers as an effective intervention for troubled adolescents. Personal construct group work was evaluated by more adolescents and their parents as effective in bringing about changes in interpersonal behaviour, and by more teachers, as effective in bringing about changes in the personal behaviour of the troubled adolescent (see Figure 20.5).

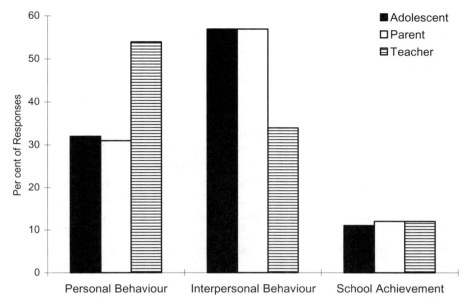

Figure 20.5 Adolescents', parents' and teachers' assessment of behavioural change which occurred after personal construct group work

INVESTIGATION 3: THE GROUP PROCESSES

The third path of inquiry investigated personal construct group work processes. These investigations examined a number of hypotheses, and the data were gathered from tools completed during the group work sessions by the adolescents and the group leaders. It was predicted that during the group work, group members would use more interpersonal themes on their Mood Tags than at the beginning of the group work. The data from the Mood Tags were content analysed. However, the data from the Mood Tags failed to support the hypothesis, with group members using predominantly personal rather than interpersonal construing. Personal construing over the 10 sessions, averaged 81 % ("I feel . . ."), 89 % ("I don't feel . . .") at the beginning of the sessions, and averaged 79 % ("I feel . . ."), 85 % ("I don't feel . . .") at the end of the sessions.

Group processes were also investigated, by measuring how the group members evaluated themselves on the group members' session evaluations at the end of each session. Evaluations were made by the group members on their attainment of the eight goals established for the group work intervention (see Table 20.2). It was hypothesised that the evaluations by the group members would become more positive as the group work progressed. Analysis determined there were significant differences between sessions ($F[1,7] = 530.57$, $p < 0.001$), and the mean evaluations showed there were both interpersonal and personal growth (see Figure 20.6). Group members were increasingly indicating that they felt they belonged more to the group, that the group had a greater understanding and acceptance of them, and that they had a greater understanding and acceptance of themselves.

Support for this positive trend came also from the group leaders' reports on the group members in relation to the group work goals. It was hypothesised that these reports would show progressive attainment of the goals of the group work by the group members. Support for the hypothesis was sought by collecting data using the group leaders' reports, and these reports were compared across the sessions. Significant differences between sessions in the ratings were found ($F[1,7] = 773.68$, $p < 0.001$) (see Figure 20.7). The group members were evaluated as increasingly experiencing validation from the group, as increasingly being understood and trusted by the other members, as questioning more their personal meanings, and trying out new ways of behaving inside and outside the group. The reports also described how the group members, through a process of understanding the similarities and differences amongst group members, had increased self-validation and self-regard.

Assessment of the group processes also involved inquiring into the differences between the ranking on Group Grid 1 and Group Grid 2 by group

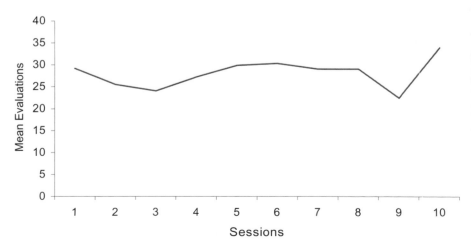

Figure 20.6 The mean evaluation of the 10 sessions by group members of their attainment of the goals of group work

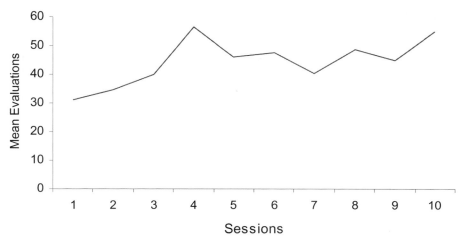

Figure 20.7 The mean evaluations for 10 sessions reported by group leaders of the attainment of the goals of group work by group members

members of themselves and the group leaders on the goals of group work (see Table 20.2). It was hypothesised that the differences between the ranking by group members of themselves and the group leaders on these goals, would decrease. The differences in scores between the group member's ranking of self and of group leader were measured at Times 1, 2 and 3 (Sessions 2, 5 and 9) for the eight constructs of Group Grid 1 and Group Grid 2. The ranking given to each construct for both the group member and leader was determined by awarding the construct with the lowest mean ranking (representing the highest frequency of positive rankings) with a ranking of one, the next lowest a ranking of two and so on until the ranking of eight was given to the construct with the highest mean ranking (representing the lowest frequency of positive rankings).

A repeated measures ANOVA was undertaken to determine if there were any significant differences between Times 1, 2 and 3 of the group members' rankings of self and leader on the eight constructs of Group Grid 1 and of Group Grid 2. The results yielded significant difference across time on the group members' ranking of self ($F[2,14] = 92.16$, $p < 0.001$), and group members' ranking of group leader ($F[2,14] = 22.41, p < 0.001$) on Group Grid 1. ANOVA conducted on Group Grid 2 produced a similar result. There was a significant difference across time of the group members' ranking of self ($F[2,14] = 21.93$, $p < 0.001$), and of the group members' ranking of the group leader ($F[2,14] = 8.81$, $p < 0.01$). The results (see Table 20.3) illustrate that the group members ranked themselves less positively at Time 1 than at Time

Table 20.3 The means and (standard deviations) of the rankings by group members of themselves and the group leaders on Group Grid 1 and Group Grid 2 at Time 1, Time 2 and Time 3

	Time 1	Time 2	Time 3
Group Grid 1			
Self Ranking	3.51	2.67	2.95
	(0.16)	(0.08)	(0.17)
Ranking of Leader	3.61	3.04	3.53
	(0.31)	(0.24)	(0.17)
Group Grid 2			
Self Ranking	3.41	2.84	3.04
	(0.16)	(0.21)	(0.21)
Ranking of Leader	3.62	3.10	3.44
	(0.23)	(0.48)	(0.23)

2 and Time 3 on both the group grids. Similarly, on both grids, the group members ranked their group leaders less positively at Time 1, than at Time 2 and Time 3. Support for the hypothesis is limited, with the differences the group members saw between themselves and the group leader decreasing only on some constructs where the content included the following themes: feeling important, feeling comfortable, feeling understood, feeling the person wants the best for me and feeling valued by the person.

CONCLUSIONS

By following three paths of inquiry, the results from this investigation were able to provide some evidence that personal construct group work was able to bring about some individual changes, was perceived by participants as a worthwhile intervention, and was able through the group processes, to help adolescents to change positively their constructions of themselves. While these research results are encouraging, they need to be tempered in the light of a number of design problems identified elsewhere in greater detail (Truneckova & Viney, 2005), such as, size and representativeness of samples, control groups with no-treatment and tools untested beyond this research. Nonetheless, the results do provide support to previous research that has reported on the clinical efficacy of personal construct group work as a therapeutic intervention for troubled adolescents. The final word in support comes from the adolescents themselves. When they were asked what was good about being in the group, one adolescent said "it helped (me) get along with people when you play games and stuff" and another said "to share me problems in a room with people I get along with" while another adolescent remarked " you could tell personal things knowing that they wouldn't go out the group and say things you wouldn't be usually able to say".

REFERENCES

Conners, C. K. (1990). *Conners' rating scales manual.* New York: Multi-Health Systems.

Conners, C. K. (1997). *Conners' rating scales-revised: Technical manual.* Canada: Multi-Health Systems.

Jackson, S. R. (1992). A PCT therapy group for adolescents. In P. Maitland & D. Brennan (Eds), *Personal construct theory, deviancy and social work.* London: Inner London Probation Service/Centre for Personal Construct Psychology.

Kelly, G. A. (1991a). *The psychology of personal constructs. Volume 1. A Theory of Personality.* London: Routledge. (Original work published 1955).

Kelly, G. A. (1991b). *The psychology of personal constructs. Volume 2. Clinical diagnosis and psychotherapy.* London: Routledge. (Original work published 1955).

Kelly, G. A. (1979). The psychotherapeutic relationship (1969). In B. Maher (Ed.) *Clinical psychology and personality: The selected papers of George Kelly.* New York: Krieger Publication Press.

Koch, H. C. H. (1983a). Changes in personal construing in three psychotherapy groups and a control group. *British Journal of Medical Psychology, 56,* 245–254.

Koch, H. C. H. (1983b). Correlates of changes in personal construing of members of two psychotherapy groups: changes in affective expression. *British Journal of Medical Psychology, 56,* 323–328

Landfield, A. W. & Rivers, P. C. (1975). An introduction to interpersonal transaction and rotating dyads. *Psychotherapy: Theory, Research and Practice, 12,* 365–373.

Moon, L., Meyer, P. & Grau, J. (1999). Australia's young people – Their health and wellbeing 1999. Australian Institute of Health and Welfare, Canberra, Australia: http://www.aihw.gov.au/publications/health/ayp99.html.

National Health and Medical Research Council (1997). Depression in young people: Clinical practice guidelines. Canberra, Australia: Australian Government Publishing Service.

Truneckova, D. & Viney, L. L. (2001). Can personal construct group work be an effective intervention with troubled adolescents? *Australian Journal of Psychology, 53* (2001 Supplement), 106.

Truneckova, D. & Viney, L. L. (2005). Personal construct group work with troubled adolescents: Unhelpful and helpful forces. In: D. A. Winter & L. L. Viney (Eds), *Personal construct psychotherapy: Advances in theory, practice and research* (pp. 271–286). London: Whurr Publishers.

Viney, L. L. (1998). Should we use personal construct therapy? A paradigm for outcome evaluation. *Psychotherapy, 35,* 366–380.

Viney, L. L. & Henry, R. M. (2002). Evaluating personal construct and psychodynamic group work with adolescent offenders and nonoffenders. In G. J. Neimeyer & R. A. Neimeyer (Eds), *Advances in personal construct psychology: New directions and perspectives* (pp. 259–294). Westport, CT: Praeger.

Viney, L. L., Henry, R. M. & Campbell, J. (2001). The impact of group work on offender adolescents. *Journal of Counseling and Development, 79,* 373–381.

Viney, L. L., Metcalfe, C. & Winter, D. A. (2005). The effectiveness of personal construct psychotherapy: a meta-analysis. In: D. A. Winter & L. L. Viney (Eds) *Personal construct psychotherapy: Advances in theory, practice and research* (pp. 347–364). London: Whurr Publishers.

Viney, L. L., Truneckova, D., Weekes, P. & Oades, L. (1997). Personal construct group work with school-based adolescents: Reduction of risk-taking. *Journal of Constructivist Psychology, 10,* 167–186.

Viney, L. L., Truneckova, D., Weekes, P. & Oades, L. (1999). Personal construct group work for adolescent offenders. *Journal of Child and Adolescent Group Therapy, 9(4),* 169–185.

Winter, D. A. (1985a). Personal styles, constructive alternativism and the provision of a therapeutic service. *British Journal of Medical Psychology, 58,* 129–136.

Winter, D. A. (1985b). Group therapy with depressives: A personal construct theory perspective. *International Journal of Mental Health, 13(3–5),* 67–85.

Winter, D. A. (1992a). Personal construct psychology in clinical practice: Theory, research and applications. London: Routledge.

Winter, D. A. (1992b). Repertory Grid technique as a group psychotherapy research instrument. *Group Analysis, 25,* 449–462.

Winter, D. A. & Watson, S. (1999). Personal construct psychotherapy and the cognitive therapies: Different in theory but can they be differentiated in practice? *Journal of Constructivist Psychology, 12,* 1–22.

SECTION V

Other Interventions, Clinical and Educational

21

Tapping into Pre-service Teachers' Perceptions of Successful Language Teachers: A Repertory Grid Approach

PAMELA LEUNG

INTRODUCTION

Studies on learning to teach have indicated that student teachers' pre-existing knowledge, theoretical beliefs and perceptions have a direct influence on their instructional decisions and behaviours (Block & Hazelip, 1995; Campbell, 1985; Conners et al., 1990; Elbaz, 1983; Johnson, 1992; Johnson, 1994; Kagan, 1992; Munby, 1982; Pajares, 1992; Weinstein, 1990). That is, these mental conceptions affect "what" and "how" they learn to become teachers.

Whether positive or negative, findings of all studies on perceptions of teaching and learning cannot neglect the influence of teachers on students' perceptions. Lortie (1975) and Almarza (1996) suggest that early learning experiences and "apprenticeship of observation" are salient to teachers' professional development, even more influential than teacher education. Accordingly, the question of what constitutes good teaching is particularly important to developing teachers, as their answers to the question will influence the kind of teacher they become (Kauchak & Eggen, 1998). To ensure the quality

Personal Construct Psychology: New Ideas. Edited by Peter Caputi, Heather Foster and Linda L. Viney. Copyright © 2006 John Wiley & Sons, Ltd.

of teacher education, it is necessary that both student teachers and teacher educators are aware of student teachers' pre-existing knowledge, theoretical beliefs and perceptions of learning and teaching (Grossman, 1990; Grossman, 1991; Johnson, 1996; Woods, 1996).

As a teacher educator of Chinese Language, this author has adopted the Repertory Grid Technique to inquire into pre-service teachers' perceptions of "successful" teachers of Chinese over the period of their initial teacher education. Effective teachers are perceived as "successful" in traditional Chinese thinking in the sense that they can transmit all their knowledge to students, and their students can perform well according to what they are taught. Data elicited by means of the Repertory Grid Technique yielded illuminating findings for recognising the participants' shared perceptions of teachers of Chinese and provided sound evidence for indicating professional growth in these pre-service teachers.

BACKGROUND

A METHOD WITH THEORETICAL UNDERPINNING

Evolved from Kelly's personal construct theory (1955/1991), the repertory grid is a method which involves highly flexible techniques and has a variety of application (Pope & Denicolo, 2001). The basic assumption of personal construct theory is that what people do is guided by their beliefs, and that the best way to understand people is to understand their beliefs from "within": to understand people from inside looking out, rather than from the outside looking in.

Repertory Grid Technique has a long history in psychological research, especially when the subjective ways in which individuals interpret and explain their perceptions to themselves are the objects of inquiry (Fransella & Bannister, 1977). Burr and Butt (1992) suggest that the technique is so well known because it offers endless computational possibilities and perspectives combined with some sort of "psychic X-ray". Bannister and Mair (1968, p. 136) define a repertory grid as "any form of sorting task which allows for the assessment of relationships between constructs and which yields these primary data in matrix form". Providing a more operational definition, Bell (1988, p. 102) suggests that a repertory grid is "a set of representations of the relationship between the set of things a person construes (the ELEMENTs) and the set of ways that person construes them (the *constructs*)". The convention of writing ELEMENT in capitals and *construct* in italics follows Ryle (1975).

In brief, the repertory grid is a method for representing the way a person thinks about things. The idea is to provide a format through which individuals can express their own view of reality. Although the repertory grid does not measure emotions and feelings in any direct sense, it gives us a clear picture of how the individual's cognitive and affective experiences relate to each other (Fontana, 1995, p. 207). In this study, using Repertory Grid Technique means that the participants were not asked to talk about the abstract notion of learning and teaching Chinese, but were encouraged to think about their perceptions of actual experiences in which they were taught by their teachers. As the technique focuses on "internal" processes, the comparisons the technique required the participants to make were more concrete. Connections generated from comparisons between the ELEMENTs offered insights that represent meaningful perceptions and values (Lambert et al., 1997).

In addition, Repertory Grid Technique has been proven to be an effective tool for understanding how people view the world of events and tracking people's perceptual change in various studies on language teaching (Augstein & Thomas, 1977), teachers' beliefs (Cronin-Jones & Shaw, 1992; Munby, 1983), teacher thinking, (Corporaal, 1991; Hillier, 1998; Pope & Denicolo, 1993; Roberts, 1999; Solas, 1992) and teacher education and development (Artiles & Trent, 1990; Cole, 1990; Corporaal, 1987; Ethell, 1997; Hopper, 2000; McQualter, 1985; Reid & Jones, 1997; Yaxley, 1991; Yeung & Watkins, 2000).

Overall, grid data are proximities or similarities. By helping the participants to compare and contrast the ELEMENTs which are within their experience in their own words, the psychological researcher is in a better position to explore the individual realities of the participants and of intragroup commonalities. As the ultimate aim of this study is to understand how the participants construed learning and teaching Chinese in the process of their initial teacher education, Repertory Grid Technique was considered an appropriate method for eliciting the participants' relevant perceptions from their own perspectives.

THE PARTICIPANTS

The pre-service teachers in this study were participants of a Certificate of Primary Education Course offered by the Hong Kong Institute of Education from 1998–2000. Most of the participants were secondary school leavers and were being trained to become primary school teachers qualified to teach a total of four subjects. In addition to Chinese, Mathematics and General Studies, their fourth elective subject was the key component which determined the different training they received. Within the two-year teacher education, the participants received subject-based training as well as training on Professional Studies. In the second semester of Year One, they had a first chance to attach to primary schools for about four weeks, practising teaching of two to three subjects excluding their fourth elective. In the second semester of Year Two, they were appointed to primary schools for about eight weeks and had to practise teaching all four subjects.

PROCEDURES

Due to practical constraints, it was not possible to conduct the study on an individual basis. As a result, 12 participants were chosen from the whole cohort ($N = 531$) using nominal group technique. In doing so, it was hoped that overviews of the participants' perceptions could apply to understanding the whole cohort in general. Of the 12 participants, 9 of them were female and 3 were male. The ratio of female to male participants reflected the actual ratio of gender difference in the cohort. Table 21.1 illustrates the distribution of gender and the fourth electives of the participants.

As the purpose of the study was to investigate the participants' perceptions of self, good Chinese teachers and poor Chinese teachers in general, and whether these perceptions changed over the period of the teacher education programme, the participants were invited to complete two rounds of repertory grid exercises. The first one was set at the beginning of their second year study after their preliminary teaching experience in primary schools. The second one was organised when the participants returned from the second teaching practice towards the end of the second semester. At each

Table 21.1 Gender distribution and the fourth elective subjects of the participants

4th Elective	Male	Female
Physical Education	3	1
English	0	3
Chinese	0	1
Putonghua (Mandarin Chinese)	0	1
Arts & Design	0	1
Computer Studies	0	1
Mathematics & General Studies	0	1

round of the repertory grid exercises, the participants met the author in groups of two or three at their convenience.

THE GRID DESIGN

The format of the repertory grids used in the two rounds of exercises was basically the same. The ELEMENTs in the repertory grid were supplied and *constructs* elicited were considered representative perceptions of the same cohort. To obtain a minimum number of possible triads for comparison, six ELEMENTs were supplied as follows:

E1   Present You
E2   Ideal self of language teacher of Chinese
E3   A good language teacher of Chinese
E4   A poor language teacher of Chinese
E5   A good language teacher of Chinese
E6   A poor language teacher of Chinese

Completing a repertory grid was a new experience to all the participants. Before briefing the participants about the procedures of completing the repertory grid, the objective of the exercise "to further understand your perceptions of Chinese language teaching" was stated on the blank grids. Three questions were listed to guide the participants:

1. As a would-be teacher, who influenced your Chinese language teaching most?
2. How well are you prepared to become a Chinese language teacher?
3. What kind of Chinese language teacher would you like to become?

In order to establish the participants' *constructs*, they were asked to make comparisons among the six supplied ELEMENTs according to the prescriptive triads marked on the blank grids. As ELEMENTs have to be personally significant to participants, the two good teachers and the two poor teachers must have taught the participants Chinese. The participants were asked to specify, by designating a code to each of them, the two good Chinese teachers and two poor Chinese teachers. These codes were only meant to be reminders to the participants of whom they were referring to. As long as the participants could differentiate the ELEMENTs, they did not have to disclose the identities of the teachers concerned.

Following Zuber-Skerritt's (1988) design, there were a total of eight triads to cover all the six ELEMENTs within a grid for comparison. To form the emergent pole (alike) of a *construct*, the participants were asked what they thought the ELEMENTs marked with an "X" had in common; and to form the implicit pole (different), they were asked in what way the ELEMENT marked with a "Y" was different from the similarity of the "X" ELEMENTs. The ninth *construct* successful-unsuccessful was supplied. After devising the first eight *constructs*, the participants were then asked to rate the ELEMENTs from one to seven for each *construct*. A rating of one meant that the particular ELEMENT was closest in meaning to the emergent construct pole; a rating of seven meant that the ELEMENT was closest to the implicit construct pole; a rating of four meant that the ELEMENT was in the middle between the contrast poles. Finally, the participants were asked to rate each ELEMENT for overall success as a teacher of Chinese Language.

METHOD OF ANALYSIS

A total of 24 repertory grids were elicited, of which half were collected before their comprehensive teaching practice and half were collected afterwards. All participants were given a fictitious name when the data was processed on the computer. The Socio, FOCUS and PrinCom options of the RepGrid2 software (Center for Person-Computer Studies, University of Calgary, 1992) were adopted.

The two batches of grids were processed in RepGrid2 as individual grids. Grids of the same batch were processed through Socio to obtain (i) the most frequently used *constructs* (mode *constructs* and *construct* modes) by all participants at the same stage and (ii) a sequence of diagrammatic socionets showing the extent to which each participant had common construing over ELEMENTs with other participants. Each batch of mode *constructs* were then FOCUS-ed to produce a mode grid and the extent of sharing was revealed in the diagram of cluster analysis. When put through PrinCom, the relative positions of ELEMENTs of a mode grid were shown on a two-dimensional graph. Results from the two stages of data elicitation were then compared and interpreted.

RESULTS

On the whole, participants' perceptions of the ways in which the ELEMENTs' self, good Chinese teachers and poor Chinese teachers differ were very similar. In order to enable construct links to be prominently displayed and the interpretations simplified, both the mathematic threshold (normally 80 %) and the number of matches required (normally set at 50 %) were set at 100. For instance, when the mathematic threshold was set at 100 for the first batch of grids, 10 *construct* modes comprising 25 mode *constructs* from 10 grids were obtained; when the threshold was lowered to 95, 8 *construct* modes comprising 80 mode *constructs* were obtained from all the 12 grids. Given that the total number of *constructs* was only 108 including 12 (successful-unsuccessful) supplied, and only 96 were *constructs* provided by participants at each time, it seemed necessary to set the match value at such a high level. The situation for the second batch was "worse". When the match value was set at 100, 14 *construct* modes comprising 32 mode *constructs* from 11 grids were obtained. When the value was lowered to 95, only 2 *construct* modes remained but 74 mode *constructs* from 11 grids were included. Table 21.2 and Table 21.3 show the *construct* modes and mode *constructs* extracted from the 2 batches of grids.

It is obvious that *constructs* with the same verbal labels, e.g., successful-unsuccessful appeared repeatedly under different *construct* modes. This on the one hand reflects the fact that successful-unsuccessful was the supplied *construct*, which appeared in every grid. On the other hand, the results further reveal the way mode *constructs* were extracted. According to Shaw (1980), most often used *constructs* are considered with respect to the way in which they order the ELEMENTs rather than to the verbal labels given to the poles of the *construct*. In this case, even a mode *construct* shared the same verbal label with others, the way it ordered the ELEMENTs differed. This is why *constructs* with the same label were retained and their linkages to other *constructs* were seen as pre-service teachers' criteria for successful Chinese teaching. The source of mode *constructs* ("G" for grid, "C" for *construct*) is relevant as each *construct* was obtained from one individual participant and was in no way changed when used in the mode. Therefore, when mode *constructs* of the same batch were FOCUS-ed to form a mode grid, the grid was not a consensus grid, which averaged out the individualities to produce a pale imitation. Rather, the mode grid was weighted towards the commonality or intersection of construing within the same batch of participants (Shaw, 1980).

As depicted in Table 21.2 and Table 21.3, while the participants' *constructs* appear to be rather similar in terms of their verbal labels, *constructs* in the second round of exercise were clustered into more modes. This suggests that there were more subtle variations in the perceptions of good Chinese teachers and poor Chinese teachers among pre-service teachers towards the end of their teacher education programme.

Of the 10 *construct* modes in the first batch, Mode 1 and Mode 2 are associated with the content of language teachers' teaching. Whether a lesson is well prepared was construed as directly related to a teacher's attitude towards

Table 21.2 Mode *constructs* extracted from 10 of the 12 grids of the first batch

Mode *constructs* of the first batch of grids at 100.0		
Construct Mode	*Source*	*Mode Construct*
1	G3C8	sufficient preparation – insufficient preparation
1	G11C2	good attitude towards teaching – bad attitude towards teaching
1	G12C8	sufficient preparation – insufficient preparation
2	G1C3	insufficient knowledge of the subject – rich knowledge of Chinese
2	G1C9	unsuccessful–successful
2	G5C4	dis-organised teaching – well-organized teaching
3	G3C2	self-centred–student-centred
3	G11C4	inflexible and dull – flexible and interesting
3	G11C7	dull lessons – lively and effective lessons
4	G6C2	dull and not conscientious – skillful and conscientious
4	G6C4	poor relation with students – good rapport with students
4	G9C5	unwilling to take up responsibilities – willing to share students' difficulties
5	G6C6	ignores students – concerned about students
5	G9C2	only teaches according to the textbook – concerned about students' needs
5	G9C6	aims only at earning money – strives to teach every student
6	G1C6	teaches for the sake of teaching – adores the Chinese subject
6	G2C3	inflexible–flexible
7	G1C7	solves individual student's problems – never pays attention to students' problems
7	G4C8	substantial presentation – vague presentation
8	G2C6	students dare not ask or answer questions – students respond actively to questions
8	G4C5	poor classroom atmosphere – good classroom atmosphere
9	G3C9	unsuccessful–successful
9	G6C7	seldom provides extra knowledge – provides much extra knowledge
10	G9C1	many activities – mainly traditional teaching
10	G10C9	successful–unsuccessful

teaching. Knowledge of the subject was linked to a teacher's success in teaching Chinese and his or her ability in organising teaching. Mode 3 through Mode 5 relate to teacher-student relationships. A student-centred teacher was perceived as "likely to be flexible and interesting" and "likely to conduct lively and effective lessons", whereas teachers who have a poor relation with students were construed as not conscientious and unwilling to take up responsibilities. The ways in which teachers of Chinese neglected students were labeled as "ignores students", "only teaches according to the textbooks" and "aims at earning money" under Mode 5. This of course left

Table 21.3 Mode *constructs* extracted from 11 of the 12 grids of the second batch

		Mode *constructs* of the second batch of grids at 100.0

Construct Mode	Source	Mode Construct
1	G1C1	takes care of individual student – concerned about overall students
1	G6C7	teaches Chinese well – doesn't know how to teach Chinese
1	G9C4	popular among students – unpopular among students
1	G9C5	caring – lack of tenderness
2	G4C9	unsuccessful–successful
2	G5C2	not sure about the scope of teaching Chinese – knows the scope of teaching Chinese well
2	G6C4	dull lessons – enthusiastic and reflective
2	G6C9	unsuccessful–successful
3	G1C2	designs flexible scheme of work – follows the set scheme of progress only
3	G6C8	different varieties of teaching – dull lessons
4	G1C3	designs different teaching activities – talks through most of the lessons
4	G12C4	knowledgeable about the language – insufficient knowledge of the language
5	G1C6	not prepared – fully prepared
5	G11C5	detached to students – warm and friendly to students
6	G1C9	unsuccessful–successful
6	G11C1	empathetic to students' situation and ability – solves students' difficulties effectively
7	G2C2	willing to spend extra effort on improving students' learning – doesn't follow up students' learning progress
7	G11C8	adjusts teaching according to students' learning progress – pays no attention to students' learning progress
8	G3C4	insufficient preparation – sufficient preparation
8	G6C2	poor relation with students – good rapport with students
9	G3C8	unable to use texts effectively – uses texts effectively
9	G11C4	not trusted by students – students totally convinced
10	G6C6	doesn't know what students need – cares about students' learning needs
10	G9C7	lazy – not lazy
11	G7C2	sufficient preparation for each lesson – insufficient preparation
11	G11C7	sets different goals for teaching different topics – absent minded teaching
12	G7C5	leaves school right after the bell rings – cares about every student's needs
12	G11C2	doesn't teach conscientiously – strives to teach each lesson as best as he can
13	G10C5	can't meet students' needs of learning – meets students' needs of learning
13	G12C8	good classroom discipline – pays no attention to classroom discipline
14	G10C7	can't motivate students – motivates students to learn
14	G12C2	dis-organised teaching – well-organised teaching

the participants with a very bad impression. Mode 6 is associated with a teacher's attitude towards the subject. A teacher who adores Chinese as a subject was perceived as likely to teach it flexibly. Mode 7 addresses students' problems of learning. If a teacher pays attention to students' problems, his or her presentation was construed to be more substantial. Mode 8 consists of *constructs* related to classroom climate. The atmosphere of a classroom was construed as good if students respond actively to questions. If students dare not ask or answer questions, the classroom atmosphere was regarded as poor. Lastly, both Mode 9 and Mode 10 were associated with the overall success of a Chinese teacher. Extra-curricular knowledge and activities in class were also considered as indicators of success in teaching Chinese. All in all, *teachers' commitment to teaching* and *their knowledge of the subject* appeared to be the pre-service teachers' key perceptions of the ways in which self, good Chinese teachers and poor Chinese teachers differed before they attended their last teaching practice.

Among the 14 *construct* modes extracted from the second batch of grids, Mode 1 can be considered most representative. Since two of the mode *constructs* under Mode 2 are exactly the same, successful-unsuccessful, Mode 1 consists the largest number of mode *constructs*. The four mode *constructs* under Mode 1 form a broader view of Chinese teachers. Apart from transmitting subject knowledge, the participants were more attentive to whether enough care had been provided for students and whether teachers were accepted by students. Detailed linkages among the mode *constructs* are better depicted in the FOCUS-ed displays of the mode grids in Figures 21.1 and 21.2. In short, although some of the *construct* modes form perceptions of Chinese teachers on similar aspects, e.g., Mode 3 and Mode 4, the rest of the modes appear to stand on their own as independent perceptions. From Mode 3 and Mode 4, flexibility and varieties of teaching were concerned. Participants at the second stage appeared to care more about students' learning rather than their own teaching.

Figures 21.1 and 21.2 were produced by using the FOCUS program in RepGrid2. The original ratings of each mode *construct* for the ELEMENTs are displayed. The "trees" on the right provide visual representations of the degree of similarity of adjacent *constructs* or ELEMENTs and their clusters. The higher the matching score between two *constructs* or elements, the higher the degree of association between them.

Figures 21.1 and 21.2 show that the participants' perceptions of the ELEMENTs were rather similar at the same stage. All the *constructs* match at the level of 88.9 in the first round and at 86.1 in the second. Their perceptions of good Chinese teachers and poor Chinese teachers clustered in the same pattern respectively. How these general agreements emerged among

FOCUS: modegrid1
Elements: 6, Constructs: 25, Range: 1 to 7, Context: Preservice teachers' perceptions

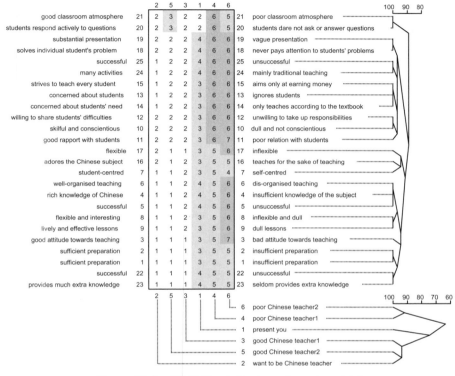

Figure 21.1 FOCUS-ed display of mode grid 1

the participants can be revealed by a sequence of diagrammatic socionets. The socionets produced by the Socio programme in Figures 21.3 through 21.6 and Figures 21.4 through 21.8 indicate the extent each participant had common construing over ELEMENTs with other participants at each stage.

These 2 sequences of socionets were obtained by varying the match level of the grids involved in a descending order until finally every possible link was made. Within each socionet, links between individual participants are shown by arrows indicating that their *constructs* are highly matched with each other under the pre-selected criteria. When the match level was set at 95 in Figure 21.3, all participants remained isolated. No link appeared until the level was set at 90. As shown in Figure 21.4, arrows in the socionet form 3 main targets. The first target was formed by arrows pointing from Cathy, Charles, Elaine, Nancy and Tom to Gloria. The second was formed by arrows pointing from Elaine, Gloria, Keith, Lucy and Nancy to

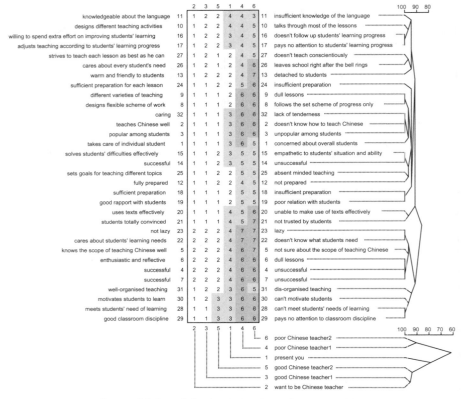

Figure 21.2 FOCUS-ed display of mode grid 2

Tammy. The third was formed by arrows pointing from Keith, Mandy, Nancy and Tammy to Tom. With the exception of Joyce and Karen, all participants shared some common construing over the ELEMENTs with others. When the match level was lowered to 85 in Figure 21.5, Karen could be included and was found to share common construing with Lucy, Mandy, Nancy and Tom. At this level, the *construct* links among participants were mainly 1 way except that the link between Gloria and Charles, and the link between Tom and Tammy were reciprocal. Joyce, however, still remained isolated. This means that Joyce had no common construing with any other participants to this point. When the match level was lowered to 80, Joyce finally was included and many other reciprocal links were formed. As shown in Figure 21.8, except the link between Keith and Lucy, all *construct* links among the participants were reciprocal at the level of 70.

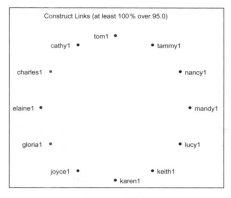

Figure 21.3

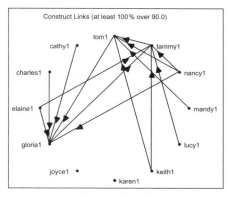

Figure 21.4

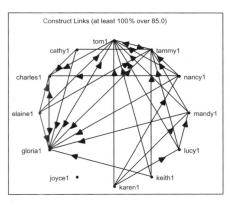

Figure 21.5

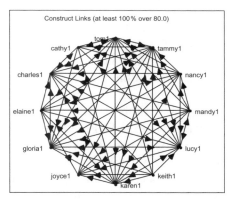

Figure 21.6

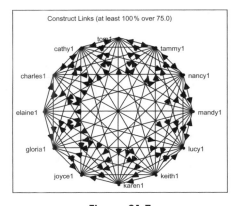

Figure 21.7

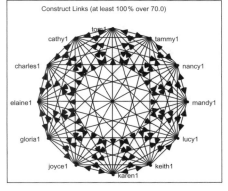

Figure 21.8

The second sequence of socionets, Figures 21.9 through 21.16, appears to be more delicate in terms of the variations among the match levels. *Construct* links were first found at the level of 93 and Joyce was not as isolated as in the first sequence. Her construing was shared by Mandy. As shown in Figure 21.10, the *constructs* link to each other in a more dispersed way than those in Figure 21.4 indicating that towards the end of their teacher education programme the participants possessed more diversified personal views over the ELEMENTs. On the other hand, even at the high match level of 90, no participant was isolated. This suggests a great commonality among the participants' perceptions. From Figures 21.4 through 21.16, the socionets reveal only the subtle differences between *construct* links until every reciprocal link emerged at the level of 60.

Another way of making use of the repertory grid data in revealing the participants' perceptual change is by using the PrinCom program of RepGrid2. The PrinCom algorithm spatially clusters the ELEMENTs and *constructs* in a repertory grid based on principal components analysis. According to Easterby-Smith (1981, p. 22), the main difference between principal components analysis and cluster analysis is that the former searches out the greatest variation in the grid and imposes mathematical axes on these; the latter relies on building up a series of hierarchical groups based on the strongest associations in the matrix. In order to investigate whether the participants' perceptions of the ELEMENTs changed over the period of their teacher education programme, the two mode grids were put through the PrinCom program. The output first showed the relationships between the constructs, expressed as correlations; then those between the ELEMENTs, the percentage of variance for each Component, *construct* loadings and ELEMENT

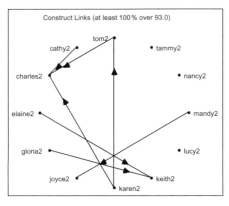

Figure 21.9

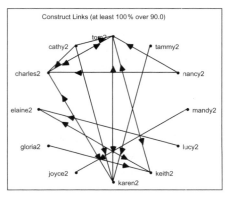

Figure 21.10

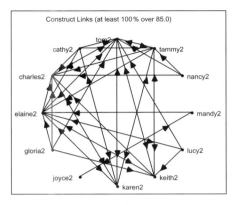

Figure 21.11

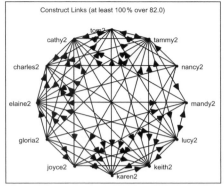

Figure 21.12

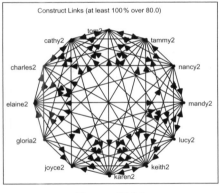

Figure 21.13

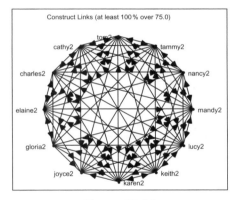

Figure 21.14

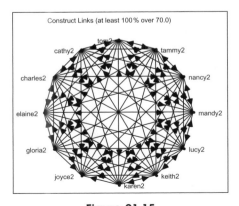

Figure 21.15

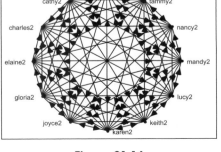

Figure 21.16

loadings on each Component. *Construct* loadings on each Component provided an identification of the manner in which a participant ordered the ELEMENTs. The ELEMENTs were then mapped onto a diagrammatic representation of the major Components. In doing so, not only the way in which the domain under investigation was given meaning, but also the way in which persons, roles, etc., relevant to the construals of that domain was made clear (McQualter, 1986).

Normally, coordinates can be provided for all the *constructs* and ELEMENTs, indicating where they are located in relation to the first two Components (as indicated by the broken axes in Figures 21.17 and 21.18). The Components are linked to the *constructs* and ELEMENTs with the greatest variance (most extreme ratings) and it is assumed that they indicate the main dimensions in which the participants differentiate between the ELEMENTs (Easterby-Smith, 1981).

In order to enable the positions of ELEMENTs to be prominently displayed, dimensions of *constructs* were hidden deliberately in the following figures. Figure 21.17 shows a brief result of the Principal Components Analysis of mode grid 1. Component 1, which accounts for 94.99 % of the total variance, is the vertical axis. Component 2, which accounted for 2.89 % of the variance, is the horizontal axis.

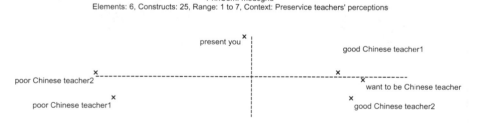

Figure 21.17 PrinCom display of mode grid 1

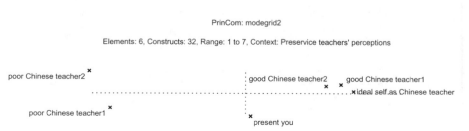

Figure 21.18 PrinCom display of mode grid 2

Although some of the participants had not had the experience in teaching the subject in their first teaching practice, they drew a clear distinction between good Chinese teachers and poor Chinese teachers. In general, they saw themselves as in between the good teachers and the poor teachers of Chinese and relatively closer to the poor ones. Regarding the good Chinese teachers and the Chinese teacher they wanted to become, the distance between "present you" and the latter was further apart than the distance between "present you" and the former. In other words, the participants seemed to be rather idealistic at this stage and intended to become teachers of Chinese even better than the good Chinese teachers who had taught them.

Figure 21.18 presents a slightly different picture of the pre-service teachers' perceptions of the ELEMENTs. Towards the end of their teacher education programme when every participant at least had had a chance to practise teaching Chinese in primary school, they saw themselves as "present you" in the same domain with the good Chinese teachers and the Chinese teacher they aspired to become.

At the second stage of the study, while the participants' perceptions of poor Chinese teachers were quite similar to those identified at the first stage, there were subtle changes of their perceptions of the ELEMENTs. As shown in Figure 21.18, the "present you" has moved to the right across the vertical axis, which appears to be further differentiating the good Chinese teachers from the poor ones. Additionally, the "good Chinese teachers" and the "want to be Chinese teacher" cluster above the horizontal axis, which separates them from the "present you". This seems to suggest that although the participants saw their own professional growth towards the ideal and good teachers, they also perceived that there was still a long distance to go before they could achieve ideal teaching of Chinese Language.

DISCUSSION

The findings outlined above have shown how Repertory Grid Technique functioned to achieve the purposes of this study. Coming from different educational backgrounds, the pre-service teachers were found sharing common perceptions of self, good Chinese teachers and poor Chinese teachers at different stages. Their perceptions of good Chinese teachers referred not only to the teachers' subject knowledge, teaching methods and attitude towards teaching the subject, but also to other aspects related to teacher–student relationship and classroom climate. While skills and methods (5 out of 10 *construct* modes) and subject knowledge (3 out of 10) appeared to be key concerns when the participants were in the middle of their teacher education programme, they seemed to be more concerned with students' learning and needs (6 out of 14 *construct* modes) towards the end of the programme. This seems to suggest that these pre-service teachers finally started to see the essence of learning and teaching. Regardless of how knowledgeable and skilful a teacher is, the success of teaching seems to depend on whether it meets students' learning needs. Therefore, among the second batch mode *constructs*, "takes care of individual student", "empathetic to students' situation and ability", "willing to spend extra effort on improving students' learning", "cares about students' learning needs" and "meets students' needs of learning" etc., were found. In fact, these can be considered different terminologies for the same *construct*. On the other hand, the distinction between the pre-service teachers' construing of "subject knowledge" and "skills and methods of teaching Chinese" became less explicit. For instance, as shown in Table 21.3, knowledge of the subject was less emphasised by the end of the programme. When "knowledge about the language" did appear, it was seen as similar to "designs different teaching activities" under mode 4. This will not be surprising if one goes through the list of mode *constructs* carefully. At this stage, the importance of preparation for lessons was re-iterated under modes 5, 8 and 11. The scope of teachers' preparation was expected to extend beyond "setting different goals for teaching different topics" to "being warm and friendly to students" and "establishing good rapport with students". Again, the pre-service teachers' focus of concern had moved from "what" teachers of Chinese were to teach to "how" these teachers facilitated student learning.

The FOCUS-ed display of the two mode grids in Figures 21.1 and 21.2 provide detailed ratings of each mode *construct* over the ELEMENTs. As mode *constructs* are most often used *constructs*, they tend to be highly clustered in the mode grids. According to Shaw (1980, p. 92), these clusters generally display a high degree of both literal and conceptual similarity in the *construct* labels. In this case, the *constructs* at each stage matching at a level of over 85 offered sound evidence for supporting the "consensus" among the pre-service teachers' perceptions.

The two sequences of socionets were intended to illustrate how each consensus was reached. By looking at the repertory grid data from this perspective, how an individual's constructs linked with others' was revealed. Consistent with the findings of the mode *constructs*, the participants' constructs were found linking closely with each other. Arrows in each socionet never appeared alone. That is, similar constructs links among the participants always appeared simultaneously. Although how each participant's constructs were linked step by step to others is not clear from the socionets, the socionets still provide a useful source of information. For instance, Joyce's constructs were found particularly outstanding as she was isolated in the first sequence of socionets. Not until the match level was lowered to 80 was Joyce linked with other participants. When Joyce's original grid was revisited, it was found that she did not set goals for the Chinese teacher she wanted to become as high as others at the first stage. Obviously at the later stage, this was no longer valid and Joyce's constructs were among the earliest shared by Mandy. Still, it is not clear from the socionets whether Joyce had changed her construing to meet with those of others or Mandy had changed hers and shared with Joyce. The sequences of socionets helped identify special cases among the participants in the process of investigating their perceptions. From Figures 21.9 through 21.16, the increase in the number of diagrams indicates a higher delicacy of the second sequence of socionets. The participants at this stage appeared to have developed a more personal view of the ELEMENTs, which differed subtly from others. Whether this was a sign of these pre-service teachers' professional growth could be further investigated.

Last but not least is the PrinCom analysis of the grid data. The PrinCom displays of the two mode grids offer straightforward snapshots of the pre-service teachers' construing of their positions in relation to the good and the poor Chinese teachers at each stage. Figures 21.17 and 21.18 can be seen as overviews of their perceptions of the ELEMENTs. The move of the ELEMENT "present you" towards the cluster of "good Chinese teachers" and the "want to be Chinese teacher" reflects their growth in confidence and professional commitment throughout the teacher education programme. The distance between "present you" and the cluster of "good Chinese teachers" in Figure 21.18 indicates that these pre-service teachers were quite realistic at this stage. Although they were aware of what constitutes a successful teacher of Chinese, they also realised that it is not easy to become a successful Chinese teacher. If this is a general perception, future research should continue to explore: (a) how long it normally takes for pre-service teachers to shorten this psychological distance before becoming competent teachers and, (b) what should be done to facilitate more effectively their becoming competent teachers.

CONCLUSION

This study has shown how Repertory Grid Technique can contribute to revealing pre-service teachers' perceptions of self, good Chinese teachers and poor Chinese teachers. Data elicited suggests that the participants' perceptions of "self" in relation to successful Chinese teachers evolved from idealistic to realistic. By using the RepGrid2 computer software, efficient analyses were made easier. Both textual and diagrammatic analyses were produced in minutes and the differences and commonalities between *constructs* were cross-examined from different perspectives. Nevertheless, there are still information gaps to fill. It is evident from the repertory grid analyses that changes of perceptions did occur throughout the teacher education process. But what had caused these changes remains unclear. More information must be obtained to reveal a fuller picture of the learning-to-teach Chinese Language process. Finally, this study has provided solid evidence for supporting the claim that Repertory Grid Technique is a powerful means through which we can have an "authentic" view of people's perceptions. The potentialities of the technique rely on user creativity and should never be underestimated.

REFERENCES

Almarza, G. G. (1996). Student foreign language teacher's knowledge growth. In D. A. Freeman & J. C. Richards (Eds), *Teacher learning in language teaching*. New York: Cambridge University Press.

Artiles, A. J. & Trent, S. C. (1990). Characteristics and constructs: Prospective teachers' descriptions of effective teachers (ERIC Document No. ED340 691).

Augstein, E. S. & Thomas, L. F. (1977). *The Kelly repertory grid as a vehicle for eliciting a personal taxonomy of purposes for reading*. Uxbridge (England): Centre for the Study of Human Learning, Brunel University.

Bannister, D. & Mair, J. M. M. (1968). *The evaluation of personal constructs*, London/New York: Academic Press.

Bell, R. C. (1988). Theory appropriate analysis of reporting grid data. *International Journal of Personal Construct Psychology. 1*, 101–118.

Block, J. H. & Hazelip, K. (1995). Teachers' beliefs and belief systems. In L. W. Anderson (Ed.), *International encyclopedia of teaching and teacher education*. 2nd ed. Cambridge, UK: Pergamon Press.

Burr, V. & Butt, T. (1992). *Invitation to personal construct psychology*. London: Whurr.

Campbell, C. E. (1985). Variables which influence student teacher behaviour: Implications for teacher education. *Alberta Journal of Educational Research, 31*, 258–269.

Cole, A. L. (1990). Personal theories of teaching: Development in the formative years. *Alberta Journal of Educational Research, 36*, 203–222.

Conners, R., Nettle, E. & Placing, K. (1990). Learning to become a teacher: An analysis of student teachers' perspectives on teaching and their developing craft knowledge. In M. Bezzina & J. Butcher (Eds), *Annual Conference of Australian Association for Research in Education*. Sydney, Australian Association for Research in Education.

Corporaal, A. H. (1987). Six shared dimensions concerning "Good Teaching". *European Journal of Teacher Education, 10*, 57–66.

Corporaal, A. H. (1991). Repertory grid research into cognitions of prospective primary school teachers. *Teaching and Teacher Education, 7*, 315–329.

Cronin-Jones, L. & Shaw, E. L. J. (1992). The influence of methods instruction on the beliefs of preservice elementary and secondary science teachers: Preliminary comparative analyses. *School Science and Mathematics, 92,* 14–22.

Easterby-Smith, M. (1981). The design, analysis and interpretation of repertory grids. In M. L. G. Shaw, (Ed.), *Recent advances in personal construct technology.* London: Academic Press.

Elbaz, F. (1983). *Teacher thinking: A study of practical knowledge,* New York: Nichols.

Ethell, R. G. (1997). *Reconciling propositional and procedural knowledge: Beginning teachers' knowledge in action.* Brisbane, QLD: Griffith University.

Fontana, D. (1995). *Psychology for teachers.* Basingstoke: Macmillan in association with BPS Books.

Fransella, F. & Bannister, D. (1977). *A manual for repertory grid technique.* London: Academic Press.

Grossman, P. L. (1990). *The making of a teacher: Teacher knowledge and teacher education.* New York/London: Teachers College Press.

Grossman, P. L. (1991). Overcoming the apprenticeship of observation in teacher education coursework. *Teaching & Teacher Education, 7,* 345–357.

Hillier, Y. (1998). Informal practitioner theory: Eliciting the implicit. Studies in the *Education of Adults, 30,* 35–52.

Hopper, T. F. (2000). Student teachers' transcending the limits of their past: Repertory grid framing narratives for learning to teach. Annual Meeting of the American Educational Research Association. New Orleans, LA.

Johnson, K. E. (1992). The relationship between teachers' beliefs and practices during literacy instruction for non-native speakers of English. *Journal of Reading Behavior, 24,* 83–108.

Johnson, K. E. (1994). The emerging beliefs and instructional practices of preservice English as a second language teachers. *Teaching and Teacher Education, 10,* 39–52.

Johnson, K. E. (1996). Cognitive apprenticeship in second language teacher education. In G. T. Sachs & M. N. Brock, (Eds) *Directions in second language teacher education.* Hong Kong: City University of Hong Kong.

Kagan, D. M. (1992). Professional growth among preservice and beginning teachers. *Review of Educational Research, 62,* 129–169.

Kauchak, D. P. & Eggen, P. D. (1998). *Learning and teaching: Research-based methods.* Boston: Allyn and Bacon.

Kelly, G. A. (1955/1991). *The psychology of personal constructs.* New York: Routledge.

Lambert, R., Kirksey, M., Hill-Carlson, M. & Mccarthy, C. (1997). The repertory grid as a qualitative interviewing technique for use in survey development. Annual Meeting of the American Educational Research Association. Chicago, IL.

Lortie, D. C. (1975). *Schoolteacher: A sociological study.* Chicago: University of Chicago Press.

Mcqualter, J. W. (1985). Becoming a teacher: Preservice teacher education, using personal construct. *Journal of Education for Teaching, 11,* 177–186.

Mcqualter, J. W. (1986). Becoming a mathematics teacher: The use of personal construct theory. *Educational Studies in Mathematics, 17,* 1–14.

Munby, H. (1982). The place of teachers' beliefs in research on teacher thinking and decision making, and an alternative methodology. *Instructional Science, 11,* 201–225.

Munby, H. (1983). A qualitative study of teachers' beliefs and principles. Annual Meeting of the American Educational Research Association. Montreal, Canada.

Pajares, M. F. (1992). Teachers' beliefs and educational research: Cleaning up a messy construct. *Review of Educational Research*, *62*, 307–332.

Pope, M. & Denicolo, P. (2001). *Transformative education: Personal construct approaches to practice and research*. London/Philadelphia: Whurr Publishers.

Pope, M. L. & Denicolo, P. (1993). The art and science of constructivist research in teacher thinking. *Teaching and Teacher Education*, *9*, 529–544.

Reid, D. & Jones, L. (1997). Partnership in teacher training: Mentors' constructs of their role. *Educational Studies*, *23*, 263–276.

Richards, J. C. (1994). The sources of language teachers' instructional decisions. In J. E. Alatis (Ed.), *Georgetown University Round Table on Languages and Linguistics: Educational linguistics, crosscultural communication, and global interdependence*. Washington, D.C.: Georgetown University Press.

Roberts, J. (1999). Personal construct psychology as a framework for research into teacher and learner thinking. *Language Teaching Research*, *3*, 117–144.

Ryle, A. (1975). *Frames and cages: The repertory grid and approach to human understanding*. Sussex University Press.

Shaw, M. L. G. (1980). *On becoming a personal scientist: Interactive computer elicitation of personal models of the world*. London: Academic Press.

Solas, J. (1992). Investigating teacher and student thinking about the process of teaching and learning using autobiography and repertory grid. *Review of Educational Research*, *62*, 205–225.

Weinstein, C. S. (1990). Prospective elementary teachers' beliefs about teaching: Implications for teacher education. *Teaching and Teacher Education*, *6*, 279–290.

Woods, D. (1996). *Teacher cognition in language teaching: Beliefs, decision-making, and classroom practice*. Cambridge: Cambridge University.

Yaxley, B. G. (1991) *Developing teachers' theories of teaching: A touchstone approach*. London: Falmer Press.

Yeung, K. W. & Watkins, D. (2000). Hong Kong student teachers' personal construction of teaching efficacy. *Educational Psychology*, *20*, 213–235.

Zuber-Skerritt, O. (1988). Personal constructs of second language teaching: A case study. Babel: *Journal of the Australian Modern Language Teachers' Association*, *23*, 4–9.

22

Movement in Personal Change: The Practice of Dance Therapy

SABRINA CIPOLLETTA

STARTING QUESTIONS

"The person is a form of movement" as Kelly (1955) says. I'd like to play with this word: movement. Why should we only consider it in terms of high levels of consciousness? If we treat it in body terms some interesting things may happen: we may perhaps discover a new language through which our personal constructs are expressed.

My reflection on this point starts from an experience that many of us may have had: when I present my studies, especially in an academic context, people often tell me that Kelly emphasises the role of rationality or that, talking about emotions, he conceptualises them in terms of cognition. This argument in my opinion is particularly interesting if we think of the well-known James–Lange debate of whether emotions originate in the body and then are transposed in the mind or if cognition comes before and resulting physiological changes after. This way of treating the issue originates from the traditional dichotomy between mind and body. So we have to choose whether to localise in the former or the latter, but it actually seems to be a border land between these two worlds.

We may also consider further issues. First, the psychosomatic symptoms: how is it possible that psychological suffering is expressed through the body? And second, how is it, vice versa, that a physiological change, for instance,

---

Personal Construct Psychology: New Ideas. Edited by Peter Caputi, Heather Foster and Linda L. Viney. Copyright © 2006 John Wiley & Sons, Ltd.

produced by a drug, involves a psychological change? Third, changes in psychotherapy: often you may observe that a change in "mental" state also involves a change in the body for instance, in the weight of a person, the manner of dressing or sitting on the chair. I am thinking about one of my female clients who used to present herself as a man: she dressed, spoke and behaved as a man. During the therapy when she started to include in her perceptual field aspects of herself as a woman (dilation), she began to get engaged in such activities concerning the care of her self as putting make-up on, going to the hairdresser, or getting dressed. Her whole appearance changed completely. On the other hand, it can happen that a change in the body experience through dance-therapy corresponds to a change in the psychological state of the person. For example, the relaxation a person experiences in the therapy room allows him or her to face difficult relational situations in a similar way.

MIND-BODY PROBLEM

These problems are usually explained in terms of a psychological state that determines a physical state or a physiological state that determines a psychological state. For instance, if it is said that a person threw himself off a bridge because he was depressed and that depression came from a decrease of serotonin, it would be as if to say that it is serotonin that pushes a person off a bridge, as the causal relation between these two events suggests. This is quite difficult for me to imagine and then I ask myself how useful it is to talk of depression in order to understand the experience of that person.

So how can we consider these issues in terms of Personal Construct Psychology? Let us go back again to what Kelly says: he simply argues that a person is a form of movement without regarding it as a mental or physical movement; he simply goes beyond this distinction. There is no longer an *Ego thinking* on a *res extensa*, there is only an *ego moving*. As Merleau-Ponty (1945) says the "I think" is substituted by "I can". I'm what I'm doing in the world: in this sense cognition is action and life is cognition, as Maturana and Varela (1980, 1984) claim.

As a consequence it can no longer be said that there is an interaction between body and mind (dualism) because they are the same thing (monism). A phenomenon can simply be observed on one descriptive level or another, but it remains the same. The two levels are different "domains of knowledge" and one knows nothing of the other, just like the man who has always lived in a submarine does not know he has just avoided a rock, as an observer might say. He has simply followed a trajectory and pulled levers (Maturana & Varela, 1984).

Thus we consider the person as a whole and we can choose to "read" him or her in psychological terms or in physiological terms. Since we consider "being in the world" as "being in relation", we think it is more useful to adopt a psychological view, especially if our interest is directed towards personal change. That is, if we consider movement constitutive of a person, disorder as an interruption of this movement and therapy as a way to resume the movement.

KNOWLEDGE THROUGH BODY

We can now try to describe this experience in terms of movement itself, that is, in terms of dance because dance is "the action of the whole human body; or rather an action transposed in a sort of *space-time* that is no longer exactly the same as that in actual life" (Valery, 1957, pp. 67–94). It is just a way in which human beings express themselves, "the truth of what it is, but in the most immediate way, the truth of what lives" (Otto, 1962, pp. 95–101). This means that the dance experience deals primarily with those forms of action (constructs) that are at very low levels of consciousness, but that can be also nuclear dimensions for the existence of the person.

That is why it may be interesting to consider how certain fundamental psychological dimensions are implied in the central motion factors, identified by Laban (1960), but also by the authors of psychomotricity, Lapierre and Aucouturier (1974). Laban was a dancer who created a very rigorous movement notation system while Lapierre and Aucouturier share with Kelly the assumption of the bipolar nature of constructs: it is not by chance that they speak of "contrasts". All of them believe that existence cannot be distinguished between the mental and physical, but must be considered as a whole. Integrating these approaches allows us to describe and read in professional terms some personal experiences within a group of dance therapy.

Each dimension of movement will be considered from an experiential point of view and not as an "a priori" category. In fact, as Merleau-Ponty (1945) claims as regards space, there would not be any space if I had not a body because my body is not simply a fragment of space, but is what makes space exist.

SPACE

We may consider *inner space*, defined by the body boundaries, the extension of movement and body (small vs. big), lateralisation, the single parts or the whole body and the coordination between parts. All of these aspects are in different ways involved in any movement, and how they are involved tells us something about the person moving. For instance, if a person tends to make prevalently small movements we wonder what he or she would anticipate if he or she made bigger ones; if he or she prefers movements of the single parts rather than the whole body we see a well known way of construing reality, that is, in isolated islands unrelated to each other. Or we may find a person with a disorder involving one half of the body who chooses to use only one part of it, but this now generates suffering because he or she has proved that his or her experiments are no longer successful. Consider the following example: the case of a child who is lame in her left leg: in the same way she drags her leg, she uses all her strength to drag other people. I have had direct experience of this and I can attest that, even if she is very thin, she is very strong! But what kind of relation does she establish with other persons in this way? What are they for her if not objects who respond, or rather carry out what she wants? How can we help her to change this experience? One way could be to permit her to experience that it is also possible to touch without moulding the other and, maybe later, even to be touched. Maybe this will also change her relationship with *external space*: she sometimes goes running through the room, always far from the group and can only establish relations if the group rotates round her or the adult is looking after her. So we can use the modulation of *interpersonal space* and distance to permit her to experience new ways to enter in relation with others.

There are many of these aspects that can be experienced through dance: touching each other and touching oneself, massaging each other and massaging oneself to discover personal boundaries and interpersonal contact; being nearer or further from one another or the rest of the group to experience differentiation; changing width, direction, level of the movement to discover new possibilities to allow you to limit the amount of anxiety or threat.

TIME

Time is another fundamental dimension to describe an action: as in verbal behaviour the temporal component gives single letters a sequence (Hirsbrunner, Frey & Crawford, 1984), without time movement would be a mixture of frames without continuity, and *continuity* is one of the aspects that define a construct (Mills, 1996).

The main distinction in this dimension is between simultaneity and succession: we usually describe an action in terms of the first construct pole, that is in spatial terms. For instance we do not say that a dancer jumps from the past to the future (Arneheim, 1986) because this would mean to describe this action in terms of succession. It is probably more useful to describe other human experiences in this way.

In fact, time is a fundamental dimension to define our relation with others. It denotes agreement or disagreement: you can choose to keep time to the music or not, to answer the other's movements with the same rhythm or with another. You can chose different velocities of movements and even different velocities to pass from one movement to another (agility). Furthermore time, like space, gives different possibilities of approaching coordination.

We can imagine, for instance, a person with a hyperactive disorder: his or her way of being in the world is characterised by a form of impulsivity that prevents him or her from stopping and carefully considering a situation, he or she simply prefers to go further. Maybe it is also a way to draw in the outer boundaries of his or her perceptual field (constriction). Modulating time, especially in relation with others, also with contact (for instance, getting him or her to feel different times of movement through touch), may be an extraordinary experience for this sort of person.

FLOW

Fluidity is a very characteristic expression of movement: we can easily imagine the difference between sequences of interrupted movements – like those made by robots–and continuous, sinuous movements – like those made by snakes. But we must not identify the former with strength and the latter with weakness, which may be the case for a lot of people who prefer the former because the latter would mean a significant change in their construction of reality and of the self, if this construction is based on a preemptive dimension of strength. Movements can be fast and slashing, but also flowing as, for instance, in fencing.

Another important aspect of this dimension is that free flowing movements may foster loosening while defined sequences of precise movements foster tightening. So they can be used to resume the creativity cycle. If we think about the flow of consciousness we may understand how fundamental this dimension is for the definition of existence. To experience both poles of this dimension, to have the possibility to transform a broken movement into a continuous one, may be seen as an example of what we mean by standstill and resumption of movement in psychotherapy.

WEIGHT

Movement is not placed in a void, it always starts from something and above all leads to something. So if we want to jump we need not push and neither need we use our will-power, as the theories of push and pull maintain, we simply press the earth to go up. Now, we can just leave our weight or use it to start the movement, but we can also give weight with different intensities: from contact to complete release. Each of these experiences refers to different dimensions; one example may suffice for all: the question of trust. If I cannot trust my legs to support myself, but I trust another person to do it for me, maybe I'll put all my weight onto that person even if it may involve the demolition of that other person. This implies a particular kind of experience of relation, that is, in terms of *dependence*: the "other" is the only person who can satisfy all my needs and is just that, nothing else. This is the case of one of my clients, Ines. How many other people you know have experiences like that? How is it possible to help them to change their construction of others as support and only as support (preemptive and often impermeable construction)?

Perhaps one way is to experience diverse forms of support, there are different ways I can put my weight onto the other, so the other may be seen in different ways; maybe other things can be used as support, for instance the ground. And the ground is our privileged support: it can be very useful for a person with problems of equilibrium, like Ines. Later it is possible that this person will be able to relate to others even on the basis of other dimensions, for instance, the understanding of someone else's point of view and the consideration of the other as a person. In the case of Ines, I may help her to reach this goal starting from her intelligence and respect for others. You can help people to have such experiences, like others in therapy, through some simple experiments to create and validate alternatives.

LOOKING FOR A CONCLUSION

As in any constructivist psychotherapeutic approach, in dance therapy you just have to observe the person through these fundamental dimensions to arrive at a *transitive diagnosis* and use it for treatment. The specific aspect that using dance can offer is a setting that is felt by the person as less threatening because it is seen as being more playful and dance, like play, is an effective metaphor for life.

As Bateson (1972) points out, a game can take place only if the participants meta communicate each other the message "This is a game" and choose to play as if the game was a serious thing. In this way what happens within the game can be very effective to foster change in life: life itself is not external to our questioning and questioning ourselves, that is, it is not out of the game (Rovatti, 2000). We are inevitably plunged in the hermeneutic circle of our reciprocal understanding and this is the game. Then we can say that the game is not produced by the players but that each game is to be played because, as with dance, there are no aims outside the movement: the movement has neither will nor effort, it simply goes (Gadamer, 1960).

We may recognise in this interpretation of game Kelly's (1955) definition of a personal construct as a form of action. In this way we go back to our initial view of the person as a form of movement: if we consider that movement is action, we can understand why we can use a form of action like dance in therapy.

It could be particularly useful with people who prefer to express their constructs and, in particular, those dealing with their disorder, in non-verbal terms. Dance, therefore, is a form of action that does not necessarily pass through consciousness, and we also know that it is not necessary for change to pass through consciousness either.

REFERENCES

Arnheim, R. (1986). *New essays on the psychology of art.* California: The regent of the University.

Bateson, G. (1972). *Steps to an ecology of mind.* New York: Ballantine.

Kelly, G. (1955). *The psychology of personal constructs.* New York: Norton.

Gadamer, H. G. (1960). *Wahreit und methode.* Tubingen: J.C.B. Mohr.

Hisbrunner, H. P., Frey F. & Crawford R. (1984). Movement in human interaction: description, parameter formation and analysis. In: A. W. Siegman & S. Feldestein (Eds), *Nonverbal behaviour and communication.* Hillsdale: Lawrence Erlbaum.

Laban, R. (1960). *The mastery of movement.* London: McDonald & Evans.

Lapierre, A. & Aucouturier, B. (1974). *Les contrastes et la decouverte des notions ondamentales.* Paris: Doin Editeurs.

Maturana, H. & Varela F. (1980). *Autopoiesis and cognition: The realization of the living.* Boston: Reidel.

Maturana, H. & Varela, F. (1984). *The tree of knowledge: the biological roots of human understanding.* Boston: New Science Library.

Merleau-Ponty, M. (1945). *Phénoménologie de la perception.* Paris: Gallimard.

Mills, D. M. (1996). Dimensions of embodiment: toward a conversational science of human action. Brunel University, Uxbridge (UK): Doctoral dissertation.

Otto, W. F., Per la danza della scuola di Elisabeth Dunca, in: B. Elia (a cura di), Filosofia della danza, Il Melangolo, 1992, pp. 95–101.

Rovatti, P. A. (2000). *La follia, in poche parole.* Milano: Bompiani.

Valery, P., Filosofia della danza, in: B. Elia (a cura di), Filosofia della danza, Il Melangolo, 1992, pp. 67–94.

23

The Posture of Anticipation: Kelly and Alexander

DAVID M. MILLS

> The posture of anticipation . . . silently forms questions, and earnest questions
> erupt in actions.
>
> (Kelly, 1966, p. 31)

EARNEST QUESTIONS

Our actions, be they verbal, mental or physical, be they directed toward ourselves, other people or the physical world, pose "earnest questions" to our
world, and thus each action is taken in anticipation of a reply. Every action
a person takes, whether an action commonly thought of as thinking, perceiving, moving or even the act of constructing personal meaning, is an act
of that person as a whole and thus is expressive of the conditions of the coordination of the whole person. While methodologies such as, for example,
repertory grids, direct our attention to certain explicitly expressible aspects
of a person's construing, we know there are deeper dimensions to our conversation with the world. Construing has a wider sense which encompasses
the whole of a person's thoughts, feelings and actions in a single field,
one in which Kelly's phrase, "posture of anticipation", is not merely
metaphorical.

This chapter argues that a practical means of pursuing this wider sense of
construing can be found in the work of F. Matthias Alexander, and seeks to
provide a basis for considering Alexander's work from the perspective of

Personal Construct Psychology: New Ideas. Edited by Peter Caputi, Heather Foster and Linda L.
Viney. Copyright © 2006 John Wiley & Sons, Ltd.

Kelly's Personal Construct Theory (and vice versa) in order to produce an approach to a wider view of both. John Dewey has been enlisted to act as a bridge between the two.

The germ from which Personal Construct Theory grows, Kelly's Fundamental Postulate, states simply that "a person's processes are psychologically channelised by the ways in which he anticipates events" (Kelly, 1963, p. 46). The intent here is to open a fresh consideration of the particular significance of the words "processes" and "psychologically" in this postulate, and the way Kelly explains his use of them. He makes it quite clear that "processes" is intended to refer to the actions of the person as a whole "behaving organism". He goes so far as to say that, "For our purposes, the person is not an object which is temporarily in a moving state but is himself a form of motion" (Kelly, 1963, p. 48). Regarding the word "psychologically" Kelly means "that we are conceptualising processes in a psychological manner, not that the processes are psychological rather than something else" (Kelly, 1963, p. 48). The Postulate does *not* say that a person's psychological processes are channelised, but that the person's processes, in the sense of the whole of their actions, are channelised in ways which *may* be construed psychologically. It is important to keep in mind that what is being delimited is our way of attempting to construe a person's processes and not the processes themselves.

The whole notion of "Psychology" is based on the observation of "mental" or "psychological facts" which we find it convenient to construe "psychologically" as distinguished from facts which are "physical" or "physiological" and thus more conveniently construed within a system of "natural science" constructs. The ranges of convenience of these alternative construction systems are not, however, exclusive. As Kelly points out, "the events upon which facts are based hold no institutional loyalties" (Kelly, 1963, p. 10). A person's processes might be fruitfully construed physically, psychologically or both, but the processes themselves are, "something else". In Kelly's terms, the constructs and not necessarily the elements are psychological. Constructs, as the psychological dimensions of whole experience, are the ways in which we may anticipate that an element of experience will be like or not like other elements. The essential point is that we need not construe them as being psychological in order to construe them psychologically. In practice, however, it seems to be rather easy to miss this distinction and to treat personal processes as if they could be sorted into distinct "mental" and "physical" categories (standing, walking, making a tennis stroke, etc. being physical; thinking, perceiving, construing, etc., mental). Of course we may sort them thus, but there is always a price to be paid. It may be convenient to view events in the first set from the perspective of physics, biomechanics, etc., and the second set from a psychological perspective, but we encounter many events which fall in the borderlands between the two realms. Are drawing a landscape from memory, improvising at the piano or making a presentation at a conference or sitting at a computer, composing a doctoral dissertation, mental or physical acts? In regarding these borderland acts, and especially when I, as a living person regard my own acts, the issue becomes not only the value of recognising that I may construe events in either way, but that "mental-physical" is itself a very pervasive construct which may have become "inconvenient". Constructs are abstractions in that they are drawn from experience and are not prior to it. Yet this abstracting is a two way process. Elements of experience lead to abstract concepts which become a framework that structures experience. A preferred set of dimensions, that is, an habitual way of anticipating the consequences of my actions, amounts to a constructive "posture". This "posture of anticipation" is a stance taken up by a whole person in relation to their environment and is as much a matter of muscle as of metaphor. Every act, including the act of construing, of placing an interpretation on events, is an act of the whole person – in other words, meaning is embodied.

To anyone familiar with Kelly's perspective, this all may seem obvious. What is called for, however, is a practical way of taking the obvious into account in order to transcend it. Kelly himself asserts the essential scientific humility of his psychology of personal constructs by noting that "no one has yet proved wise enough to propound a universal system of constructs" (Kelly, 1963, p. 10). We must also be constantly careful in our application of what he calls our "miniature systems". What an individual person needs is not so much a personal version of a universal system of constructs but a means of continuing the "conversation" about their own meaning – both the "explicitly formulated" or verbally expressible and the "utterly inarticulate" meanings which are embodied in the organisation of their actions. This is no easy task. Emphasising that since "many of one's constructs have no symbols to be used as convenient word handles", it is difficult to bring them within the organisation of the "verbally labeled parts of the system" (Kelly, 1963, p. 110). Kelly notes that this makes it very difficult to be articulate about how one feels or to predict one's own future actions. For example:

> A person may say that he will not take a drink if he is offered one tomorrow. But when he says so he is aware only of what he can verbally label; he is not fully aware of what it will be like tomorrow when tomorrow's situation actually confronts him. The situation which he envisions is, to be sure, one in which he would not take the drink. But the situation which actually rolls around may loom up quite differently and he may do what he has promised himself and others he would not do. There may be a failure of his structure,

or, more particularly, that part of it which is verbally labeled, to subsume adequately certain aspects of the rest of the system. (Kelly, 1963, p. 110).

It is little wonder that we so often seem to others to be unwilling, and to ourselves, unable to reconstrue our situation – or to do very much to change matters. Often the only parts which we can conceive of reconstruing are those parts which we can explicitly become aware of having construed, and so long as the conversation is limited to the verbal or conceptual domain, too much of our construction lies hidden in the inarticulate. We cannot reflect on this unarticulated experience because we lack a language in which to converse about it. Kelly says that the reality of a concept "exists in its actual employment by its user" (Kelly, 1963, p. 106). But to employ a particular construction is to act out of a commitment to it, not merely to project it into some disembodied abstract space. Meaning, for me, is a relationship between myself and the situation in which I find myself and in which I must act. The construction of meaning has to do not only with the anticipation of events, but with anticipated action. Thus an action is not only a behavioral "experiment", but my engagement in conversation with my world, and an event in my experience is not only the result of an experiment, it is a response. To act out of commitment to a construction is to "live in anticipation" of that response. The task at hand is to find a means of bringing my part in the conversation to a more reflective level. We shall see that Alexander provides a means for meeting just that task.

BODY AND MIND

In my view John Dewey provides a natural bridge between Kelly and Alexander. Kelly says of Dewey that his "philosophy and psychology can be read between many of the lines of the psychology of personal constructs" (Kelly, 1963, p. 154). He finds Dewey's view "that we understand events through anticipating them" (Kelly, 1963, p. 157) beneath his own claim "that our lives are wholly oriented toward anticipation of events" (a claim with which Dewey would have agreed).

When John Dewey was asked to provide a biographical statement to be included in a book on his philosophy, he wrote:

My theories of mind-body, of the coordination of the active elements of the self and of the place of ideas of inhibition and control of overt activities required contact with the work of F.M. Alexander, and in later years his brother A.R., to transform them into realities. (Dewey, 1939, p. 44)

In a talk given to the New York Academy of Medicine in 1927, Dewey discussed what he considered the vital importance of the issue at hand. He began by lamenting the fact that the mind-body split is so pervasive in our experience that we seem to have no way of even expressing the underlying unity except by such hyphenations as "mind-body", which actually serve to perpetuate the split. Dewey proposed that the way out of the trap is to center our attention on "unity in action". And he felt it vitally important that we do find a way out. The talk was later published under the title, "Body and Mind". (Dewey, 1931, p. 299). He writes,

> Thus the question of integration of mind-body in action is the most practical of all questions we can ask of our civilization. . . . Until this integration is effected in the only place where it can be carried out, in action itself, we shall continue to live in a society in which a soulless and heartless materialism is compensated for by a soulful but futile idealism and spiritualism . . . for materialism is not a theory, but a condition of action . . . and spiritualism is not a theory but a state of action. (Dewey, 1931, p. 304)

It is precisely in the practical continuity of human action that Dewey finds the unity of mind and body. Indeed, he finds the degree of their unity that is evident in our actions to be a measure of humanity.

> The more human mankind becomes, the more civilized it is, the less is there some behavior which is purely physical and some other purely mental. So true is this statement that we may use the amount of distance which separates them in our society as a test of the lack of human development in that community. (Dewey, 1931, p. 304).

In order to find this unity, or rather this continuity, of mind and body in action, we must be able to distinguish other dimensions of meaning within our actions.

> We need to distinguish between action that is routine and action alive with purpose and desire; between that which is cold, and as we significantly say inhuman, and that which is warm and sympathetic; between that which marks a withdrawal from the conditions of the present and a retrogression to split off conditions of the past and that which faces actualities; between that which is expansive and developing because including what is new and varying and that which applies only to the uniform and repetitious; between that which is bestial and that which is godlike in its humanity; between that which is spasmodic and centrifugal, dispersive and dissipating, and that which is centered and con-secutive. . . . What most stands in the way of our achieving a working tech-nique for making such discriminations and applying them in the guidance of

the actions of those who stand in need of assistance is our habit of splitting up the qualities of action into two disjoint things. (Dewey, 1931, p. 305)

It is certainly possible to read Kelly's ideas between the lines here and say that Dewey is speaking for an alternative way of construing the quality of human action. But why do we then seem to be "unwilling to reconstrue" ourselves and our actions in this new way? Dewey points us in Alexander's direction in search of an answer when he refers to Alexander in pointing out that:

Until we have a procedure in actual practice which demonstrates this continuity [of mind and body], we shall continue to engage in some other specific thing, some other broken off affair, to restore connectedness and unity [and thus] increase the disease in the means used to cure it (Dewey, 1958, p. 296).

A NEW FIELD OF INQUIRY

The opening chapter of *The Use of the Self*, "Evolution of a Technique", (Alexander, 1932) is Alexander's own account of how he came to develop just such a procedure. In 1890 F. M. Alexander was a young Australian with a promising career before him as an actor and recitationist. He was, however, plagued by one serious, recurring difficulty – at some point during an evening on stage, his voice would become hoarse, sometimes so much so that he could scarcely speak by the end of the performance. His doctors could find nothing medically wrong and could advise no treatment beyond rest for his voice. After this happened at one particularly important engagement, young Alexander decided to find out for himself just what was causing his troubles and what he might do to prevent their return. He reasoned that as he only seemed to have his vocal difficulty while on stage, there must be something different about the way he used his vocal mechanism in the act of reciting that caused his trouble. His years of patient self-observation opened up what he saw as a "new field of enquiry" into the "psycho-physical" functioning of the human individual as a whole. His investigations produced a set of principles and an evolving method of putting those principles to practical use in daily activity. What Alexander discovered about himself was that his difficulties, and the means for addressing them, could not be separated into distinct categories of mental and physical. He found that every specific act was taken in the context of the functioning of the entirety of his "psycho-physical mechanisms" and thus that the quality of every act was determined by the conditions of the coordination of his whole self. This proved to be equally the case for the "mental" conception of the act to be performed, the "physical" movements made in carrying out that conception and the "sensory appreciation" by which he judged the fit between the two.

He found himself in the midst of a serious dilemma, however. Having become accustomed to performing the act of reciting in his familiar way, his sensory appreciation had become as habituated as had his muscular efforts. Thus even when he had demonstrated that he was not doing what he thought he was doing, it nevertheless "felt right". Worse still, he found that at the "critical moment" of actually initiating some movement – the moment, as he experienced it, of putting his intention to speak into practice – he relied on that very same faulty sensory appreciation to guide his action. These habitual patterns, both the specific patterns which defined acts such as "reciting" and the more general patterns which constituted what he called the "general manner of use" of himself, involved components which interfered with the very coordinating processes which otherwise would have brought about the result he desired. One could suppose that Alexander might have elicited a set of constructs underlying his conception of, for example, the act of reciting, a set of kinesthetic dimensions of how various ways of "using" himself in speaking differed from one another. From the perspective being developed here, however, his construction of any particular act to be performed would be inseparable from his construing of himself in the performance. This would include the interpretation provided by his sensory appreciation and thus would be in large part what might be termed a kinesthetic construction. To be capable of performing an act in a different way was also to conceive of the act itself differently – and thus to reconstrue himself in the doing. This he found himself unable to do. Indeed, he labeled as a "delusion which is almost universal" the assumption that because we find ourselves able to act at will in carrying out familiar habitual acts, we expect to be equally able to do so when the act we conceive is unfamiliar and counter to our habit. No matter how he might reconstrue the act at a verbal level by telling himself to do it differently, when the moment came and in spite of his best efforts, he carried it out in the familiar way. In fact, he discovered, the situation was worse; it was *because* of his effort that he found himself trapped in the familiar, and the greater the effort, the more he seemed dominated by his habit and the greater the amplification of the interference with his natural functioning. This is a phenomenon Alexander termed "end-gaining" and it proved to be the root cause of his original vocal problem.

Eventually Alexander came to realise that his original hypothesis had been only partially correct on two counts. It was not only his vocal apparatus that was involved, and not just in the act of reciting. It was his habitual use of his whole self in every act he performed. It was the malcoordination inherent in his everyday speaking habits, amplified by the effort of "reciting" as he construed it, which resulted in his loss of voice.

How are we to account for this inability to change? The situation is very similar to that in Kelly's example of taking a drink.[1] In effect, when a way of acting becomes habitual all of the constructs used to conceive it become subsumed under the single kinesthetic construct "feels normal–feels not normal" or to use a common alternate label, "feels right–feels wrong." As Alexander wrote, "The act and the particular feeling associated with it become one in our recognition" (Alexander, 1923, p. 132). We might also say that the associated feeling, as an element of experience, becomes a figure symbol for, and thus hides, the whole system of underlying constructs. The situation is self-perpetuating because continuing to act in commitment to that construction makes extremely unlikely just the sort of "unfamiliar sensory experience" which could provide the basis for significant reconstruction. Kelly refers to habit as "a convenient kind of stupidity which leaves a person free to act intelligently elsewhere". But he adds, "whether he takes advantage of the opportunity or not is another question" (Kelly, 1963, p. 169). In Alexander's view this failure to take advantage is not a matter of mere oversight. When what we hold fixed is just those aspects of our whole functioning which could coordinate our response to changing conditions and requirements, we hold ourselves in that unfortunate state in which our every effort to improve makes our situation worse:

> The truth is that so far man has failed to understand fully what is required for changing habit if the change is to be a fundamental one because he has not realised that the establishment of a particular habit in a person is associated in that person with a certain habitual manner of using the self, and that because the organism works as an integrated whole, change of a particular habit in the fundamental sense is impossible as long as this habitual manner of use persists (Alexander, 1941, p. 93).

It does not matter what sort of habit we are speaking of. Chronic muscular patterns, stereotyped reactive behaviors and rigid opinions or "fixed ideas" are all examples of the same phenomenon, and, as Alexander noted,

---

[1] There is a very similar illustration in chapter II of Dewey's *Human Nature and Conduct* (Dewey, 1957) where he writes of the man with a drinking problem, whose every effort to stop simply becomes another stimulus to drink. His drinking habit, Dewey says, is not merely a matter of failure "to drink water". It is an active predisposition to a certain course of positive action under certain conditions. Dewey's description, explicitly based on his view of Alexander's work, is a practical prescription for reconstruing our situation as a whole, not only the verbally labelable parts.

... the majority of people fall into a mechanical habit of thought as easily as
they fall into the mechanical habit of body which is its immediate consequence
(Alexander, 1910, p. 20).

Fixed construction, the inability to reconstrue one's situation, can also be
seen as habitual in Alexander's sense. That is, it is just the doing – in this
case, construing – in the old way which prevents a person from being able
to even fully conceive of, let alone carry out, doing in a new way. More precisely, in Alexander's view, it is the fact that the old way, however obviously
unsatisfactory we may know it to be, "feels right" to us. We know we are
performing a particular action "our way" by how it feels, and this feeling is
a sensory interpretation which we place on our own physical response to our
situation. It is itself constructed and constructive. When I am faced with a
stimulus from my environment, I respond, in ways channelised by how I
have construed the stimulus. What I "feel" is my sensations of my own
response; I perceive my own movement. But I also construe the meaning of
that feeling (sensory appreciation) and my awareness of "how I feel"
becomes itself a stimulus to further response. I had a student once who, after
working with me for several minutes, was able to release a good bit of habitual excess tension, particularly across the upper part of her chest. Her movements took on a freedom and quality of softness and grace that were
immediately recognisable by her and her friends who were watching. But
then she put her hand to her chest and said, "You know what this is". We
were all puzzled, wondering what "this" referred to. We were even more
puzzled when she continued, "This is defeat." This was a person who on
several occasions in her life had felt a need to be "strong" – and had done
so in part by means of a certain pattern of pushing and holding up her chest.
It had been, unnoticed by her, her way of embodying her concept of strength.
The only times when she was without the feeling which she associated with
this unconscious push had been on those occasions when her strength had
not been enough and someone or something had "defeated" her. Hence, when
in the context of an improved general coordination she was able to give up
her push, at first the only available interpretation she could find for the
absence of the associated feeling was a construal based on past kinesthetic
experience. What looked to us like power and freedom, and despite the fact
that she "knew" that it was, nevertheless to her "feelings" meant "defeat". I
have seen many other similar, if usually less dramatic, examples of this sort
of kinesthetic conception. The change in, for example, a person's way of
standing, is already the embodiment of a reconstrual, and the same context
of general coordination within which it was possible also permits a reinterpretation of the meaning of the feelings that the change elicits. My defeated

friend was able to recognise her felt interpretation as such. She was able to feel what she felt and at the same time to appreciate that the feeling (or more properly, the meaning she attributed to what she felt) was in essence an opinion she held and was itself open to change. It is often claimed that emotional memories are somehow "stored" in a person's body, and thus can be "released" when changes are made. What I have found in this and similar episodes is that rather than being stored in the tissue these states are embodied in dynamic patterns of movement. Thus to move differently is already to embody a reinterpretation.

This doubly constructive process is elaborative. In principle, it may be either expansive or constrictive depending on the stance taken. To be habitual is, in Kelly's terms, to expect the duplication of events rather than anticipating their replication.[2] It is to see, and respond to, every event as a repeated instance of something already known. Alexander saw it as a failure to recognise the psycho-physical unity of our self in action:

> . . . man's most tragic mistake has been his failure to acquire knowledge of himself as an individual functioning as a psycho-physical whole in his daily activities, for this has deprived him of the key to knowledge which could give him a new technique in living (Alexander, 1941, p. 218).

Whatever insights this discussion might provide into how we trap ourselves in this constrictive choice would be of only mild interest and indeed, would be, in Alexander's opinion, so much "useless philosophical speculation" unless it helped us come into possession of a means for doing something about it, a means for *demonstrating* the continuity of mind and body in practice. It was the possession of such a means that was Alexander's goal:

> . . . I was concerned with a technique for dealing with the working of the living human organism as a whole, which called for a knowledge of the so-called mental (psychological) and the physical (physiological and anatomical)

---

[2] There is a terminological difficulty which bears some mention here. The term, "habit", as used by Alexander, and somewhat by Kelly, tends to carry the common, narrow sense of a routine or robotic pattern of behavior. Even when Alexander speaks of one's "general manner of use of the self", the underlying construct could be alternately labeled as "habitual" vs. "non-habitual" or as "habitual" vs. "consciously directed". There is a wider sense of habit, however, which underlies much of Dewey's philosophy, habit as the basis for our inhabiting the world in which we act. From this wider perspective it is evident that when I escape from a particular dominant habitual pattern, however general, I do not become free of habit, but rather I come to a condition in which my present response to my world is the product of the interplay of *all* of my habitual dispositions taken together. Thus for Dewey being "consciously directed" is not the opposite of being habitual; it is simply being intelligently so. To move beyond habit in the narrow sense is not to be freed from habit but rather to become free to embrace its wider dimensions.

working of the human organism as an indivisible unity (Alexander, 1941, p. 135).

In essence, what Alexander developed was a coherent way of implementing the experimental method in the context of that indivisible unity, a comprehensive method for being a "personal scientist" regarding the "new field of inquiry" of the directing of our own actions, and thus a context within which certain kinds of reconstruing can take place. Among the conditions which Kelly discusses as "unfavorable to the formation of new constructs" is the unavailability of a laboratory, a space in which to "try them out" (Kelly, 1963, p. 169). But a laboratory situation implies that there is not only a space in which to experiment, but also a method of experimenting. If we recognise that when Kelly speaks of anticipating or construing he is not referring to "mental" acts, but to acts performed by the person as a whole in relation to their situation, and if we further take explicit note of the fact that such acts, like any others, involve just that "unity of mind-body in action" to which Dewey referred, then Alexander's work can be seen as providing just the sort of experimental method needed for the laboratory of new constructs. Such a method will prove equally vital whether the matters being reconstrued are those commonly thought of as physical, mental or otherwise.

ALL TOGETHER, ONE AFTER THE OTHER

It is easy to see how a rigid habitual stance also sustains Kelly's other two unfavorable conditions. We find it difficult to reconstrue in a context of "threat". In our ordinary habitual mode, where there has been a reduction to the "feels right vs. feels wrong" construct, any new, unfamiliar experience can only "feel wrong". Thus any unfamiliar new sensory experience is by construction, threatening. Also, if the primary kinesthetic criterion for evaluating the performance of any habitual action is that it feels essentially the same as it always has, we are kinesthetically always preoccupied with "old material". Construing is an abstractive process of interpreting experience in terms of similarity and difference. Habitual action, by focusing us on what feels the same, "marks a withdrawal from the conditions of the present" by attempting to escape their uniqueness. It is as if the dimensions of the familiar so dominate a person's experience that they have no access to the very fresh material in the present conditions which might lead them to a new construction.

A common, but nonetheless curious, illustration of this channeling of experience is seen, or rather heard, in the case of phonological differences between languages. In English the letters *l* and *r* represent distinct phonemes. Native Japanese speakers have notorious difficulty with the pronunciation of these sounds. The situation is more subtle than it at first appears, however. The "obvious" explanation for the Japanese speakers' difficulty is that their native language does not have a phoneme corresponding precisely with either the English *l* or *r*, and thus, if they have learned English later in life, they lack the requisite experience with producing those sounds and therefore often interchange them. Japanese does have a phoneme which does not precisely correspond with either *l* or *r*, but, from the English point of view, lies somewhere between them. The influence of their experience with this phoneme in their native language does lead to an imprecision in producing the English sounds. What is most curious, however, is the experience of the native English "listener". It is as though their auditory perception system incorporates a construct that could be labeled "sounds like *l* – sounds like *r*." Or rather, if for example hearing the word "around" and thus anticipating the sound of *r*, there is a simultaneous use of two constructs – the one above and another, "sounds like *r* – sounds not like *r*." The effect then is that any sound that is not quite the anticipated *r* sound is perceived as an *l*. Similarly, any imprecise pronunciation of *l* is perceived as an *r*. The hearer of course attributes the switching of the phonemes to the speaker. The same switching often occurs when native Spanish speakers pronounce the English *b* or *v* – and of course when native English speakers try to pronounce the corresponding Japanese or Spanish phonemes. What is strange is that any sound which is not quite right should consistently be perceived as the "wrong" sound. The kinesthetic counterpoint to this illustration is that any feeling we have in association with our action which does not quite "feel right" tends to feel "wrong" rather than "nearly right".

There are as well, some conditions which are favorable to the formation of new constructs: use of fresh elements, experimentation, and availability of validating data (Kelly, 1963, p. 161). Alexander's experimental technique meets each of these. The experimentation, by achieving a means of using aspects of one's physical experience normally frozen in habit as validating data, provides a context within which the fresh elements of unfamiliar sensory experience become possible. Indeed, this is precisely what Dewey found most significant about Alexander's work. He saw it as a method for generating new experience, and what is more, a new kind experience.

There is, I believe, one more significant parallel to be drawn between Kelly's insistence that it is only by engaging in the full cycle of experience that we begin to see the significance of a person's construing, and Alexander's insistence that it is only in relation to the use of the self as a psycho-physical whole that any specific act has meaning or utility. In Kelly's case it is not merely the whole of experience that matters, but the whole *cycle* of experience. To Alexander, an individual is not only "whole", but an *organised* whole, and it is attention to the organising principle of the functioning of the whole that is the key to his experimental "new technique in living". For both men there was a clear sense that a person's processes are both integral and sequential – in a phrase Alexander liked to use, "all together, one after the other". The implicit logical structure of these processes is what I refer to as "conductive", and from the present perspective a person's dynamic engagement with that logical structure is an engagement in "conductive reasoning".

It is in this interplay of thought and action – of the ways in which meaning is embodied and bodily action is meaningful – of the all together and the one after the other of our posture of anticipation – that a view which is both constructive in Kelly's sense and psycho-physical in Alexander's proves to be very fruitful. As a person reflects upon their own construing, the more dimensions of that process that can be brought explicitly into the conversation the better.

REFERENCES

Alexander, F. M. (1910). *Man's supreme inheritance.* London: Methuen.
Alexander, F. M. (1923). *Constructive conscious control of the individual.* New York: Dutton.
Alexander, F. M. (1932). *The use of the self.* New York: Dutton.
Alexander, F. M. (1941). *The universal constant in living.* New York: Dutton.
Dewey, J. (1931). *Philosophy and civilization.* New York: Minton, Balch and Co.
Dewey, J. (1939). "Biography of John Dewey" Ed. J. Dewey In *The Philosophy of John Dewey, The library of living philosophers*, Vol. 1, P. Schlip, ed., Evanston, IL: Northwestern University Press.
Dewey, J. (1957). *Human nature and conduct,* (reprint of 1922 edition). New York: The Modern Library.
Dewey, J. (1958). *Experience and nature,* (reprint of 2nd ed., 1930). New York: Dover.
Kelly, G. A. (1963). *A theory of personality: The psychology of personal constructs.* New York: Norton.
Kelly, G. A. (1966). "Ontological acceleration" In B. Maher (Ed.), *Clinical psychology and personality: Selected papers of George Kelly.* Huntington, NY: Krieger Pub.

24

The Art of Writing: Embodiment and Pre-verbal Construing

VIVIEN BURR

In this chapter I will elaborate on Kelly's notion of pre-verbal, or non-verbal, construing (Kelly, 1955). I will begin by presenting some personal experiences from the areas of the visual arts and from handwriting, which might not at first glance seem to have much in common, but I am going to argue that they do. I hope to show that construing is an embodied activity as much as something we do with our minds, and this is something that I and others have been keen to explore on previous occasions. I also want to explore how some aspects of our construing are not really available to symbolic representation in language. Finally, I shall briefly discuss what I think are the implications for what we mean by sociality.

A few years ago I began taking an art class. There were several of us in the group who had had little or no formal opportunity to develop whatever artistic talent we may have had. What struck me was the speed and consistency with which our artistic artefacts came to bear some kind of personal signature. One of our number, Jenny, began producing small sculptures in clay or plaster. With no intention to do so, she repeatedly produced spindly, matchstick-like but graceful figures having an ethereal, other-worldly appearance. The facial features too had a not-quite-human quality, an ascetic and fine-boned but somehow animal appearance that aroused powerful but indescribable feelings and were quite compelling. These sculptures "spoke" of something that I felt I recognised but it was hard to put into words. For

Personal Construct Psychology: New Ideas. Edited by Peter Caputi, Heather Foster and Linda L. Viney. Copyright © 2006 John Wiley & Sons, Ltd.

myself, my own life drawings quickly came to have a recognisable style, and one which I found, and still find, very difficult to depart from. I would begin a drawing with the desperate intention NOT to produce something that looked like a slight variation on my previous efforts, but usually in vain; it would come out looking just like the others, bearing the unmistakable features of what seemed to be emerging as my "style".

Of course we already think of artists in this way when we recognise their very idiosyncratic style; we can recognise a Turner or a Picasso in the same way that we can recognise a piece of music written by Beethoven or Mozart without ever having heard that particular piece before. And we already in some way accept that one's style of painting has a connection with the psychology of the painter. For example, we link the swirling, chaotic colours of Van Gogh with his anguished inner struggles.

The example from my own experience began to resonate for me with something I had been finding in my University teaching. I teach a module called "Gender", and I like to begin the teaching with a few class exercises that illustrate to students the many and varied ways that gender infiltrates our lives. One of these exercises involves briefly showing students some examples of handwriting and asking them to judge the sex of the writer. They can usually do this with some accuracy, and the results I was getting with my students were roughly similar to what has been reported in previous research. People are generally able to judge the sex of a writer with reasonable accuracy even with very little exposure (Baird, 1998; Eames & Loewenthal, 1990; Hamid & Loewenthal, 1996; Hartley, 1991; Hayes, 1996).

How do we recognise handwriting as masculine or feminine, and how should we understand the process whereby this everyday behaviour comes to bear the signs of our gender? I decided to conduct a small study of my own. Using a range of handwriting samples, I showed them for just four seconds to a sample of students and teachers. After asking them to judge the sex of the writer, I also asked them to tell me about the cues they were using to make their judgement. When a script was judged as female, this was typically because it was seen as neat, even or symmetrical, well-presented and "joined up", rounded and perhaps "fancy" or ornate with loops and curves, and sometimes lacking in confidence. Scripts judged as male were seen as scruffy or messy, hurried, inconsistent or uneven, spiky/sloping and sometimes as confident, assured or even arrogant.

It is not only adults who use such cues to judge handwriting. In one of the few previous studies that has looked at this (Hartley, 1991), the researcher asked 7–8-year-old children to write out a set passage in their usual hand, and then another group of children of the same age judged the sex of the writers. He found that they successfully judged the sex of the writer accord-

ing to neatness, size and apparent speed of execution. But then the experi-
menter introduced an intriguing addition to his experiment. He asked the
children to write out the passage again, but this time trying to imitate the
handwriting of the opposite sex – to "write it like a boy" or "write it like a
girl". He later asked the children what they had done to achieve this. The
girls said they made their writing larger and less tidy or scruffier. The boys
said they had made their writing smaller and neater. This suggests that their
usual handwriting style is not simply the product of physical or cognitive
abilities, as had sometimes been suggested, because it can be overcome by
the intention to do it differently. These children were, I believe, not just trying
to imitate and reproduce surface features of the writing of the opposite sex
(which they appeared to be able to do, with at least some success, without
practice) but to adopt something of the stance toward the world of a member
of the opposite sex, to in some way be like them, to step inside their identity in a small way.

If we look a little closer at the kinds of words that were used to describe
the handwriting samples, we can see that they are in fact of two different
kinds. There are those that relate to the form of the manuscript itself – whether
it is rounded, spiky, sloping, messy, consistent or irregular – and there are
others that relate more to the process of writing itself and to the attitude of
the writer – "careful", "hurried", and "confident". Without going too far down
the road into the territory of the graphologist, I think it is fair to say that our
handwriting says something about us, perhaps in the same way that our non-
verbal communication does. Non-verbal communication can be seen not as
a system of signs and symbols that "mean" particular things and signify particular emotions, but as one of the ways in which our psychology is embodied and our identity expressed. The way we carry ourselves, our gait, our
posture, our gestures, the way we sit and so on all say something about who
we are and who we take ourselves to be. We do not need scientific research to
tell us that women and men inhabit their bodies differently; the behaviour of
any drag queen hilariously reminds us of this. And these differences in
embodied life are not random or accidental. They speak volumes about mas-
culinity and femininity as it is lived and experienced by people. If we think
of handwriting as an embodied activity like this, we can begin to see it as
one of the ways in which the meaning of being a man or a woman in our
society is expressed. I have used this example of gender, but it is really only
one case of what can be thought of as a more general phenomenon of embodied, core construing. When I was a child, I remember spending hours practising my handwriting. I was not trying to bring it nearer to the standard of
perfection demonstrated by my class teacher, but to try out different styles
to see if they were "me" in the same way as I would try on different dresses

in a shop. I remember, when I became a psychology undergraduate, sensing that my previously somewhat rounded and artistic hand was now inappropriate for someone who aspired to the status of scientist, and my handwriting quickly assumed the less visually appealing form that it has today.

For me, these examples from handwriting and the visual arts first of all signal that construing is something in which our entire body, not just our cognitive processes, is involved. Kelly (1955) clearly endorses this when he says: "The overlapping functions of psychological and physiological systems in this regard help to make it clear that psychology and physiology ought not to try to draw pre-emptive boundaries between themselves" (p. 51) and "Construing is not to be confounded with verbal formulation" (p. 51). He argued that some constructs are never communicated in symbolic speech. When he introduces the notion of pre-verbal constructs, he talks about their range of convenience being things like physiological systems such as digestion and glandular secretions and so on. The reason we cannot give an answer to the question "how do you propose to digest your dinner?" is not because these things are beyond our control, beyond construing, but, he says, because we cannot anticipate them within the same system that we use for communication.

Later Kelly (1955) defines a pre-verbal construct as "one which continues to be used even though it has no consistent word symbol" (p. 459). But it later becomes clear that he used the concept of pre-verbal construing primarily in a developmental sense. He invoked the pre-verbal construct to help us understand the problem in therapy where the client has feelings he or she finds impossible to articulate and can only hint at them and continue to operationalise them in behaviour. From these clues the therapist must try to grasp the nature of the construing that is taking place. Kelly sees the pre-verbal construct as originating before language, in the experience of the infant, and this construing never becomes articulated in language. "The pre-verbal construct tends to be one which was originally formulated to deal with the elements of which a pre-verbal infant could be aware" (p. 463). For this reason, Kelly saw pre-verbal constructs as very likely to be about dependency. But whatever their origin, Kelly was clear that the client can only with great difficulty and to a very limited extent find words to label such constructs.

I think Kelly has identified something important here, when he writes of aspects of construing that can never be fully verbalised. Art is very often about the manner in which the body knows the world. It is about movement, textures, smells, viscosity, viscerality, depth, heaviness – things that often can only with difficulty be translated into language. So I see artistic artefacts as pre-verbal construing made visible. Such construing may initially be pre-verbal (in the sense of pre-dating the infant's acquisition of language) but such infantile construing then is not simply or even primarily about dependency issues. Such constructs are hardly social at all, and furthermore they continue to be used by us as embodied adults. If behaviour is our way of posing our questions in the world, then artistic activity is the way the artist poses certain questions, questions that are inadequately posed through language.

Artistic artefacts not only powerfully communicate through their content; as I mentioned earlier in this chapter, the style of the artist can be very expressive of his or her perspective on the world. Like artistic style, handwriting style shows rather than tells us (through language) something of the writer's stance to themselves and their world. So the process of writing cannot be separated from its visible artefact, the written words. The artefact is the expression and result of the writer's "attitude" to the page and the reader, the way the pen is held, and how it is moved across the paper. We can see the construing of the person in their handwriting and other visual artefacts they may produce by their own hand, such as paintings or sculpture, as we can see it in their gait and posture. Of course, such things as artistic style and handwriting, like gait and posture, are subject to many influences in addition to one's own personal construing, so I would not want to suggest that what we are seeing here is solely an expression of the person's construing. Nevertheless, these things cannot help but bear the mark of our engagement with the world and our construal of our place in it.

What artistic artefacts and handwriting share is that they are the visible face of our construing. These things deal with what we can show rather than say. And this, of course, has implications for how we might think about what it means to have an appreciation of another's worldview, to construe the constructions of the other. If we want to make a parallel with construing in language, it might look something like this:

Cognitive construing	**Pre-verbal construing**
we *tell* our story	we *show* experience
the other:	the other:
hears our words	sees our visible products
understands our view	recognises/takes on our view
has sociality	has sociality

In this sense, we may gain sociality when we, for example, try to "write it like a girl" or when we have literally "walked a mile" in someone's shoes, as our own bodies engage with the "trace" of experience left by and shown by theirs.

REFERENCES

Burr, V. (1995). *PCP and the body.* Paper delivered to the 11th International Congress on PCP, Barcelona, July.

Baird, J. (1998). What's in a name? Experiments with blind marking in A-level examinations. *Educational Research, 40,* 191–202.

Eames, K. & Loewenthal, K. (1990). Effects of handwriting and examiner's expertise on assessment of essays. *The Journal of Social Psychology, 130,* 831–833.

Hamid, S. & Loewenthal, K. (1996). Inferring gender from handwriting in Urdu and English. *The Journal of Social Psychology, 136,* 778–782.

Hartley, J. (1991). Sex differences in handwriting: a comment on Spear. *British Educational Research Journal, 17,* 141–145.

Hayes, W. (1996). Identifying sex from handwriting. *Perceptual and Motor Skills, 83,* 791–800.

Kelly, G. (1955). *The psychology of personal constructs Vol 1: A Theory of personality.* New York: W.W. Norton and Co. Ltd.

Index

Note: page numbers in *italics* refer to information contained within tables and diagrams.